VALLEY FORGE
CRUCIBLE
OF
VICTORY

By

John F. Reed

PHILIP FRENEAU PRESS

MONMOUTH BEACH, N. J.

1969

FOREWARD

Memory can never be dimmed of the quiet hours of a snowy evening at Valley Forge in December, 1957, as the man who had commanded the largest armies in history, General Omar N. Bradley, rose from his chair at my invitation to walk around the ancient kitchen of our 18th century home. In response to my question, he said: "Freedom is definable only as an extension of the heart and soul of a man. My personal definition is: 'Freedom—no word was ever spoken that has held out greater hope, demanded greater sacrifice, needed more to be nurtured, blessed more the giver, damned more its destroyer, or come closer to being God's will on earth. May Americans ever be its protector!' ". General Bradley and I had walked over the encampment of 1777-78 that afternoon, over the ground that eminent historian John F. Reed has written about so magnetically and accurately in his book, "Valley Forge Crucible of Victory."

Valley Forge has inspired great commitment and expression as it did in General Bradley. So long as the integrity of Valley Forge is maintained by the men and women of America, there shall be no ebbing of the American spirit.

"Valley Forge Crucible of Victory" by Mr. John F. Reed, respected and admired historian of Freedoms Foundation at Valley Forge, leads us to be individually deeply informed, stimulated in scholarship, and strengthened in will as patriotic Americans and citizens of a world determined to shed ourselves from the tyrannies of all times. I salute John F. Reed, believing that this generation and those ahead will be strengthened in personal commitment to the principles of faith, courage and hope. May Americans include "Valley Forge Crucible of Victory" in every school and home library. Its concepts stir the mind, touch the heart, so that the will for freedom shall be nourished.

Kenneth D. Wells, PH.D., *President, Freedoms Foundation*

PREFACE

The Pennsylvania Campaign of 1777 was over. Behind the army lay the recent defeats at Brandywine, Paoli, Germantown and the forts on the Delaware River, Billingsport, Mifflin and Mercer. The month was December and the sufferings for which Valley Forge has become so sadly famous, had already begun.

Valley Forge would make two great contributions to the fight for human freedom: the determination of an army to survive under the most trying conditions and the drilling of that army into an efficient fighting machine.

The author wishes to thank those organizations who, among others, have aided in the work involved in producing this book: The Historical Society of Pennsylvania, The Library of Congress, The National Archives, The Valley Forge Historical Society, The Valley Forge State Park Library, and The Washington Memorial Chapel Library at Valley Forge. Thanks are also due to the author's wife for the solace she brought to his labors, and especially to the memory of the men of the Revolution who kept such faith, and who were the inspiration of this work.

3

GENERAL GEORGE WASHINGTON. *Bust-length portrait of Washington painted at Valley Forge by Charles Willson Peale, at that time a captain in the Pennsylvania Militia. In 1841 the portrait was presented by artist John Nagle, to the Chester County (Pa.) Cabinet, a local society dedicated to literary, historical and scientific pursuits. On the dissolution of the Cabinet, its collections were transferred to the ownership of the West Chester State Teachers College now West Chester State College, West Chester, Pa., through whose courtesy the portrait is here reproduced. Miniatures of Washington were also painted during the period. John Laurens noted to his father, Henry Laurens, President of Congress, "Mrs. Washington has received the miniature, and wishes to know* whether Major Rogers [the artist, possibly Major John Rodgers, of the Pennsylvania Rifle Battalion] is still at York. The defects of this portrait I think are, that the visage is too long, and old age is too strongly marked in it. He is not altogether mistaken, with respect to the languor of the general's eye for altho' his countenance when affected either by joy or anger, is full of expression, yet when the muscles are in a state of repose, his eye certainly wants animation." This languor of eye also appears in Peale's portrait. John Laurens concluded, "There is a miniature painter in camp who has made two or three successful attempts to produce the general's likeness."* The locations of these miniatures are unknown. *J. Laurens to H. Laurens, Valley Forge, Mar. 9, Laurens 138-9.*

CHAPTER ONE

THE ARRIVAL

Selection of Camp-Site

"Marched to Valley Forge."[1] The date was Friday, December 19, 1778.

Out of a light mist of wind-driven snow the Continental Army appeared on the Old Gulph Road. The road led west from the army's previous encampment at The Gulph towards the Valley Forge where Isaac Potts and William Dewees had fashioned pig iron into farm and household implements prior to the burning of the forge by the British the previous September. Gradually the deserted road came alive with a shapeless movement that soon resolved into the forms of weary soldiers leaning for protection against the hard north wind. Up the road they came until they arrived on the wintry hills of Valley Forge that would prove a place of continued suffering.

Woodlands, broken by occasional stubbled fields of corn, wheat and rye, stretched before them. Buildings were few. Only the humble homes of Abijah Stephens, Wilsey Bodles, John Brown, John Brown, Jr., David Stephens and Zachary Davis, the latter a tenant of David Stephens, stood on the site of the prospective camp. To the east, and to the west and south in the mouth of the Chester Valley, stood a litter of equally small houses that would be useful for billeting officers. Beyond the northern extension of Mount Joy (so named by William Penn nearly a hundred years earlier)[2] lay the houses of ironmasters William Dewees and Isaac Potts, the latter of which would become General George Washington's Headquarters.

Across the road from the Potts house stood a grist mill. The British had failed to burn the mill when they had incinerated the forge during their encampment in the Chester Valley in September on their way to capture Philadelphia. The wreckage of the burned forge lay on Valley Creek between Mount Joy and its sister eminence, long called Mount Misery but now Valley Forge Mountain.

The expected arrival of the army was announced to the local inhabitants in the morning, shortly after the troops had begun their march from The Gulph at 10 a.m. An advance party rode to the campsite that had been chosen by Washington with the advice of the locally born and raised Brigadier Generals Anthony Wayne and Peter Muhlenberg. The first family aware of the impending arrival of the 11,000 odd troops was that of Abijah Stephens, who lived on the Old Gulph Road at the eastern fringe of the proposed encampment site.[3]

For eight long hours the relics of the army streamed into Valley Forge, though the distance to be covered from The Gulph was only six miles. The last troops straggled in as early evening fell. Private Joseph Martin noted in his diary that "there was no water to be found" because of the darkness. The snow had ceased and the thin covering it left on the ground was scarcely deep enough to wet parched throats. Martin "was perishing with thirst" though he had "searched for water till I was weary without finding any. Fatigue and thirst, joined with hunger, almost made me desperate." Fortunately, "two soldiers, whom I did not know, passed by. They had some water in their canteens which they told me they had found a good distance off, but could not direct me to the place as it was very dark. I tried to beg a draught of water from them but they were rigid"

in their refusal. "At length I persuaded them to sell me a drink for three pence, Pennsylvania currency, which was every cent of property I could then call my own."[4]

Gradually some order was brought out of the confusion created by the arrival of the troops. Grounds for the camps of the different brigades were pointed out and occupied. On the eastern perimeter of the camp, facing the British in Philadelphia eighteen miles away, lay a low ridge of hills rising from the Schuylkill River on the north and running west nearly to the precipitous foot of Mount Joy. This ridge, cleared of its trees, could serve as an outer line of defense. Mount Joy and its contiguous northern shoulder ran almost back to the river again, and would be splendid for a second, or inner, line of defense. With the river on the north, the area could be adequately defended, despite the comparatively easy access afforded by Fatlands Ford. Thus, the whole center of the camp could be enclosed by defensible positions.

While Washington would have preferred to remove his army further inland nearer its source of supply, the Pennsylvania Supreme Executive Council had insisted that it be stationed as near the enemy in Philadelphia as was practicable so as to protect the eastern part of the state and the government from the British. The Pennsylvania Council, governing body of the state, had been sitting at Lancaster since losing its previous home in Philadelphia to the enemy. The National Congress had retreated farther west, across the Susquehanna River to York, where it would sit for the next half year or so until the enemy evacuated the capital city.

Fortunately, tents had been brought with the army on its march from The Gulph, and by nightfall of December 19th most of the weary men were protected from the full blast of the north wind that had blown all day, and continued into the night. Washington himself was also tented, having promised his men he would not go into more comfortable quarters until they were reasonably well hutted. The other generals had made no such promises, and moved into the more permanent shelters which the army's scouts had found for them.[5]

Not so the soldiers; on the first night in camp many of the weary men were obliged "to set up all night by fires instead of taking comfortable rest in the natural and common way" because of the lack of blankets to keep them warm.[6] Luckily, before leaving The Gulph, Washington had ordered the sick sent to Reading so that the army could commence the winter encampment on a reasonably healthy footing.

Location of Brigades

The morning of December 20th found the brigades, except for a few stragglers, huddled in their tents in the positions ordered by the Commander-in-Chief. The northern flank of the front line, next to the Schuylkill River, was occupied by Major General Nathanael Greene's Division consisting, left to right, of Brigadier General Peter Muhlenberg's and Brigadier General George Weedon's Brigades. Next in line to the west lay Major General Baron Johan DeKalb's Division consisting

WASHINGTON'S MARQUEE. *This sleeping tent was used by the American Commander-in-Chief at Valley Forge December 19 through 25, 1777, prior to headquartering in the Isaac Potts House. Washington personally purchased his set of three tents, including this marquee, at Philadelphia early in the war, and used the tents until the close of hostilities in 1782. Photograph courtesy of the Valley Forge Historical Society, in whose museum the marquee is exhibited.*

of Brigadier General John Paterson's and Brigadier General Ebenezer Learned's Brigades. DeKalb was quartered with Weedon at Abijah Stephens' nearby house. General Learned was not with the army, having been furloughed home on sick leave, which ultimately resulted in his resignation from the army the following March.

Next in line was Brigadier General John Glover's Brigade, also without its commander. Glover had been ordered to Boston to assist Major General William Heath in supervising Lieutenant General John Burgoyne's army, captured at Saratoga the previous October. Both Glover's Brigade, and Brigadier General Enoch Poor's Brigade, which was next in line, were unattached to any division since there were too few major-generals to command all the brigades in divisional organizations. On Poor's right was Brigadier General Anthony Wayne's Division, consisting of the 1st and 2nd Pennsylvania Brigades. The lack of major-generals had forced Washington to place the Pennsylvanians in Wayne's care though Wayne was only a brigadier. Colonels James Chambers and Daniel Brodhead commanded Wayne's Brigades. The right, or western, flank of the front line was held by Brigadier General Charles Scott's Brigade of Major General Marquis de Lafayette's Division.

Separated from these last troops by ground that fell away from the west end of this line of hills was the right flank of the inner line of defense. This was manned by Brigadier General William Woodford's Brigade, also of Lafayette's Division, which occupied the southern base of Mount Joy. Some distance to the north Brigadier General Henry Knox's artillery would be stationed. Along the northern extension of Mount Joy were Major General Lord Stirling's (William Alexander) Division consisting of two brigades, those of Brigadier William Maxwell and the brigade, which by that time was denoted as "late Conway's." Thomas Conway was in York, having recently been promoted to the rank of major general and Inspector General of the army.

Brigadier General Jedediah Huntington's and Brigadier General Lachlan McIntosh's Brigades completed the inner line of defense to the Schuylkill River. McIntosh's Brigade, like those of Glover and Poor, was unattached to any division. Hunting-

ton's, together with Brigadier General James Varnum's Brigade, which occupied the bluffs overlooking the river and Fatlands Ford, belonged to Major General Alexander McDougall's Division. McDougall was also detached from the army, having been ordered to New York to assist Major General Israel Putnam in the defense of the Hudson River and the New York Highlands. Other units of the army present at Valley Forge were Brigadier General Casimir Count Pulaski's Light Dragoons, Colonel Daniel Morgan's Riflemen and elements of Brigadier General James Potter's Pennsylvania Militia. The senior command of the Militia was vested in Major General John Armstrong of French and Indian War fame.

Brigadier General William Smallwood's Brigade of Major General John Sullivan's Division was not with the army. The brigade, supported by Colonel Moses Hazen's 2nd Canadian Regiment, also of Sullivan's Division, had been ordered to Wilmington, Delaware. It had marched directly there, via Dilworthtown, from the army's previous encampment at The Gulph. Washington wrote George Read, Delaware Signer of the Declaration of Independence and President *pro tempore* of that state (President John McKinly having been captured by the enemy), "I have received information that the enemy mean to establish a post at Wilmington for the purpose of countenancing the disaffected in the Delaware State, and securing a post upon Delaware River during the winter" to protect the incoming supply ships that were so vital to British occupation of Philadelphia.

"As the advantages resulting to the enemy are most obvious, I have determined to send off General Smallwood with a respectable Continental force to take position at Wilmington." The Commander-in-Chief added, "If General Howe thinks the place of that importance to him he will probably attempt to dispossess us of it; and as the force which I can at present spare is not adequate to making it perfectly secure, I expect that you will call out as many [Delaware] Militia as you possibly can to rendezvous without loss of time at Wilmington, and put themselves under the command of General Smallwood."[7]

Washington was not only obliged to care for the wants of an army that was literally "barefoot and many hundreds without Blanketts" but he also had to watch over "the security of the Circumjacent [sic] country."[8] This country would undoubtedly be subject to enemy raids during the course of the winter. Although Delaware Bay and River were now open to enemy shipping, and some food for the populace could be brought into the city, such food consumed far less space in ship-bottoms than hay and other equine fodder. The English would undoubtedly discover it necessary to depend on the adjacent country for most of its horse forage.

It was also obvious that Washington must be constantly apprised of the enemy's plans. Already an efficient American spy system, based at Newtown Square in Chester County some twelve miles south of Valley Forge, was functioning smoothly under the supervision of Major John Clark, Jr. On the very day that the army reached Valley Forge, Clark wrote to Washington, "I dispatched several spies into the city . . . one of them this moment returned from Philadelphia."

As far as this spy could ascertain the British were busy strengthening their defensive works and there was "no talk at present of their moving" into the countryside, though "their light-horse were reconnoitering this morning on Marshall's Road" west of the Schuylkill River, and was "very inquisitive" concerning the state of the country beyond and American intentions. Otherwise, "nothing of any consequence was passing in the city . . . the inhabitants imagine the enemy mean to remain quiet in winter quarters." At present the British were only "cutting and hauling wood, from this side of the Schuylkill to the other without any annoyance . . . my spy says he thinks they might be easily caught."

Clark continued, noting a problem which would continue to plague the American commander. "I must again tell Your Excellency that the country people carry in provisions constantly [to Philadelphia]; a number went in today—one of them caught my spy by the coat, and called him a 'damn'd Rebel' before the enemy's advanced sentrys." Clark's man, "clapping spurs to his mare," left his Loyalist accuser "lying in the road . . . and one of our horsemen took him," upon which the captive "appealed to my spy if he did not know him to be well affected" to the patriot cause. Clark added, "I hope an example will be made" of the prisoner "to deter others" from dealing with the enemy.[9] Washington, though disliking severe measures, would eventually discover the necessity of implementing this advice, and would issue orders to check this commerce with the foe. This trade was not only encouraged by Loyalist feelings but also by a local craving for British gold.

British in Philadelphia

In Philadelphia, despite the increasing pleasure seeking disposition of the British and Hessian soldiers wintering in the city, some officers were none too pleased with the turn that affairs had taken in 1777. They were of the opinion that the captive city was worth far less to British interests than Burgoyne's recently captured army was worth to the Americans. Sir William Howe had risked Burgoyne's success against the capture of Philadelphia, capital of the incipient American nation. He hoped this would end hostilities and bring the Americans to reason.

Howe soon discovered his error. The American government had simply transferred to York, leaving in Howe's hands a half-emptied city of "20,000 souls" as estimated by Captain John Montrésor, the British engineer. Philadelphia had been second only to London as the largest city in the British Empire prior to the Declaration of Independence. The remaining inhabitants in the city were "mostly Women and Children," and, if adult, were suspected of being "connected with the rebels."[10]

These "20,000 souls" were becoming an increasing burden to the British Army and Navy since almost every civilian was dependent on the British for daily subsistence. The main British line of supply, via the Delaware Bay and River, was tenuous since threatened not only by American action but also by nature. A cold winter, frequent in this latitude, could easily freeze the river into a solid surface of ice. The British had been warned by local inhabitants that for "six weeks generally the Delaware is impracticable" for the navigation of vessels up to the city.[11]

The British, despite their nearly 20,000 soldiers, sailors and marines who occupied Philadelphia, could readily mourn. "The last campaign furnished sufficient proof that the stubborn and inexperienced rebels are too lucky." The British army, Hessian Major Carl Baurmeister noted, "active as it is, has got no further than Philadelphia, is master of only some parts of the banks of the Delaware and Schuylkill, and has no foothold whatsoever in Jersey." As for future prospects, Baurmeister continued, the Americans had been told by their political and military powers

"that their steadfastness and patience through one more campaign will secure their independence . . . Furthermore, they have more means of their own to keep up this war than was at first supposed." The Americans "are bold, unyielding and fearless. They have an abundance of that something which urges them on and cannot be stopped."[12]

Despite Major Baurmeister's pessimism, the British and Hessian officers in Philadelphia were prepared to make the best of Howe's decision to take the American capital. These officers commenced their winter's stay by seeking the best available quarters, a considerable undertaking in view of the antipathy of many inhabitants of the city to receiving guests, especially the non-paying kind. Under the press of British demands and in the interest of personal safety, most of the inhabitants were forced to yield. Even as late as December 19th, the day the American Army took up quarters at Valley Forge, and a full three months after the fall of the city to British arms, British and Hessian officers were seeking to better their living conditions in the expectancy that a cold winter was imminent.

Mrs. Elizabeth Drinker was the wife of one of the so-called Quaker Exiles. They had been sent by the Americans to Winchester, in Virginia's Shenandoah Valley, for fear that he and his fellow exiles' interests lay with the British cause. Elizabeth Drinker noted in her diary on December 19th, that "Major Crammond came in quest of better quarters for British officers. I told him that . . . I expected that we, who were at present lone women . . . would be excused" from quartering British or Hessian officers. Crammond had only replied that "he feared not," and warned, in an effort to insinuate British officers into the Drinker household without resorting to sterner measures, "as a great number of foreign Troops," meaning the Germans, "were to be quartered in this neighborhood, he believed they might be troublesome."

Mrs. Drinker had heard frequent stories regarding certain British as well as German officers. She had already noted in her diary such incidents. "Owen Jones' Family has been very ill-used indeed, by an officer who wanted to quarter himself, with many others, upon them. He drew his sword; used very abusive language, and had ye Front door split in pieces. Mary Eddy has some [officers] with her, who, they say, will not suffer her to use her own Front door, but oblige her and her Family to go up and down the alley. Molly Foulke has been affronted, and so have many others."

The distressed ladies appealed to Enoch Story, the Loyalist mayor of the city, for protection. Mayor Story was confident that in the case of Mrs. Drinker his influence could gain her the desired immunity, but he failed to reckon with the power that actually governed the city. The military, despite a pseudo-official civilian government erected by Howe, was in real control. Mrs. Drinker was forced to yield her privacy since the British officers had become "much chagrined at the difficulty they find in getting quarters, and ye reception they have met with" as a result of the bad reputations of some of their compatriots. Indeed, Mrs. Drinker remarked, "several young Noblemen," officers in His Majesty's army, "are at this time obliged to sleep at Taverns, on board Ship, or in ye Redoubts, for which, I think they may, in great measure thank themselves."[13]

DeKalb Assesses Valley Forge

At Valley Forge, the Continental Army gathered its courage and commenced preparations to face the winter in a far more primitive manner than the British in Philadelphia. If Major Baurmeister's assessment of the British situation was far from promising, that of Baron DeKalb, writing to the Count de Broglie in France, exhibited an even less assuring aspect for American hopes. DeKalb, who, though of German descent, had long served in the French army and had weathered many a bitter campaign, saw only a "wooded wilderness" around him at Valley Forge. It had little in common with the familiar scenes of civilized Europe; "certainly one of the poorest districts of Pennsylvania . . . almost uninhabited without forage and without provisions." Both armies had swept the country relatively bare during their passage through the district in the previous September.

"Here we go into winter quarters," the Baron continued, where the troops were expected "to lie in shanties . . . to enable the army it is said, to recover from its privations . . . while protecting the country against hostile inroads." The matter of a site at which to winter the army "has been the subject of long debates in the council of war . . . and good advice was not taken," in DeKalb's opinion, which was to winter to the westward in a less plundered and therefore more desirable district. "The idea of wintering in this desert can only have been put into the head of the commanding general by an interested speculator or a disaffected man . . . it is a pity that he is so weak, and has the worst advisers in the men who enjoy his confidence."

Although the Baron's feelings were clouded by bitterness, and he was correct in much of his assessment of the situation, he was wrong in one conclusion. Generals Wayne and Muhlenberg, who had suggested Valley Forge as a campsite, were neither speculators nor disaffected persons, but were doing the best they could to fill the Commander-in-Chief's specifications and at the same time satisfy the request of the Pennsylvania Executive Council.

DeKalb, proceeding with his written discussion, was fully "satisfied that our present position, if retained, will offer none of the advantages expected from it. On the contrary, the army," instead of recuperating from the recent campaign, "will be kept in continual alarms from being too near the enemy, and too feeble" to oppose any enemy activity, "for our whole effective force hardly amounts to six thousand men. To use them for the protection of the country, excludes every idea of rest. It might have been expected that a camp would have been formed in a secure position." DeKalb's military mind recognized certain defensive deficiencies in the post at Valley Forge and the need for a place "compact in its design, corresponding to the small number of the army; and that it would have been strongly intrenched so as to resist any attack."

At the time of DeKalb's writing (December 25th) no effort had as yet been made to construct defensive lines. Building huts and the unfortunate state of the troops precluded other less imperative labor. "Instead of this," the Baron continued, "the divisions are encamped so far assunder that we are practically split up into a number of petty detachments, isolated so as to be unable to support each other, and helplessly exposed to every assault. Who knows whether we shall not receive a severe blow" from the enemy "this winter?"

DeKalb then turned his sights on Congress. "Unless Congress will speedily throw off their present vacillation, and adopt energetic measures for completing the regiments and compelling the militia to serve three years . . . a time will come when the General will not be able to calculate upon

having twenty men to command next morning." The soldiers, the Baron complained, were only "drafted in classes," an inadequate number in each class, "and are only called upon to pledge themselves for service of two months" or so at a time. "This system of militia service will yet prove the destruction of the cause. The devil himself," DeKalb concluded, "could not have made a worse arrangement."

The army, DeKalb maintained, was indeed a pitiful caricature of a military force in European eyes. The Baron did "not know what is to be done in the clothing department; but it is certain that half the army are half naked, and almost the whole army go barefoot." Minor diseases likewise added to the scarecrow appearance of the troops. "Our men are infected with the itch . . . I have seen the poor fellows covered over and over with scab." DeKalb had ordered the victims in his division isolated from the rest of his troops in an effort to curb the disease. In addition, the army was "already suffering for want of everything" though the winter had only begun. "The men have had neither meat nor bread for four" of the preceding six days, "and our horses are often left for days without any fodder. What will be done," the Baron continued, "when the roads grow worse and the season more severe?"

The Quartermaster Department, DeKalb noted, was in a state of confusion. General Mifflin, the former Quartermaster-General, had resigned his office on November 7th. Although he had promised to continue in office until another officer was appointed to fill the position, Mifflin had failed to honor this promise, and had retired to his summer home "Angelica," near Reading. Congress was also to blame for the unhappy state of the Quartermaster Department, since that ultimate civil authority had failed to appoint a successor to Mifflin. Meanwhile assistant quartermasters attempted to run the department with little success. DeKalb criticized, "The very numerous assistant quartermasters are for the most part men of no military

THE ISAAC POTTS HOUSE, *now known as Washington's Headquarters. The house was built about 1760 by John Potts, the father of Isaac, and is said to be about 90% original. Isaac Potts was co-owner of the Valley (or Mount Joy) Forge with Col. William Dewees of the Pennsylvania Militia. Potts did not live in this house in 1777-8, but rented it to his former sister-in-law, the Widow Deborah Hewes, who rented the house to Washington.*

education whatever, in many cases ordinary hucksters, but always colonels," and he noted, "the army teems with colonels."

DeKalb had a personal complaint against the quartermasters, who provided "quarters for the Commander-in-Chief and for themselves, but for nobody else. The other generals, even some of the [field] officers, take their quarters where and as they please and can." Most of the generals and a number of other officers were quartered in houses outside the Valley Forge encampment proper and, DeKalb wrote, "plans of quarters are unknown." In fact every encampment, including that at Valley Forge, was a rather confused affair. "It is necessary to live a long time in every camp before you can find your way. All my remonstrances against this abuse were of no avail."

In disgust DeKalb had "abandoned the practice of suggesting improvements in the service and in organization." He could only be satisfied that "luckily we have an enemy to deal with as clumsy as ourselves." Otherwise, he concluded, "all things seem to contribute to the ruin of our cause. If it is sustained, it can only be by a special interposition of Providence."[14]

CHAPTER II

MISERERE

Setting Up Camp

The morning of December 20th dawned clearing, but the fairer weather had little effect on the unfortunate state of the army at Valley Forge. Certain members of the Pennsylvania Council at Lancaster had objected to Washington's decision to go into winter quarters. They had demanded an attack on the enemy in Philadelphia but Washington realized the futility of such a course. The troops could march no further, much less fight against a foe superior in numbers and training, and in health and equipment.

The major-generals of the American army "accompanied by the Engineers" were therefore directed immediately to "view the ground attentively and fix upon the proper spott and mode for hutting so as to render the camp as strong and inaccessible as possible. The Engineers after this are to mark the ground out, and direct the field Officers appointed to superintend the buildings for each brigade" and where they were to be placed. "The soldiers in cutting their firewood are to save such parts of each tree as will do for building, reserving sixteen and eighteen feet of the trunk for logs."[1]

Washington had already directed the design for the huts, and had ordered the field officers to divide their commands into separate "squads of 12, and see that each squad have their proportion of tools." He had promised "to reward the party in each regiment, which finishes their hut in the quickest and most workmanlike manner" with twelve dollars drawn from his own pocket. He also offered a hundred dollars reward "to any officer or soldier, who in the opinion of three Gentlemen he shall appoint as judges [Sullivan, Greene and Stirling] . . . shall substitute some other covering" for the huts "that may be cheaper and quicker made" than with boards, since boards would undoubtedly prove scarce even if time could be taken to seek or saw them.[2] Whether or not the latter reward was ever claimed is unrecorded, for the soldiers roofed their huts with whatever material came to hand, including staves, branches, leaves, sod and even with strips cut from the nearly irreplaceable tents.

The design for the huts as prescribed by Washington was: "dimensions viz: 14 by 16 [feet] each, sides, ends and roofs made of logs, and the roof make tight with split slabs . . . the sides made tight with clay, fire place made of wood and secured with clay on the inside 18 inches thick, this fire place to be in the rear of the hut; the door to be in the end next the street." Most of the huts were placed in rows, facing each other, with company streets between the rows, "the door to be made of split oak slabs, unless boards can be procured. Sidewalls to be 6-1/2 feet high. The officers' huts to form a line in rear" of those in which the non-commissioned officers and men were housed. Allotment of these quarters was to be made on the basis of "one hut . . . to the General Officers one to the Staff of each brigade, one to the field officers of each regiment, one to the Staff of each regiment, one for the commissioned officers of two companies, and one to every 12 men, non-commissioned officers and soldiers."[3]

While preparations for hutting commenced in earnest on the 21st, the Quartermaster-General was ordered "to delay no time, but use his utmost exertions, to procure large quantities of straw, either for covering the huts, if it should be found necessary, or for beds for the soldiers."[4] Knowing that bed-straw would soon become dirty and verminous, necessitating replacement, Washington issued a proclamation, hastily printed on broad sheets in both English and German (the latter for the Pennsylvania Germans who spoke little English). These broad sheets, which were distributed throughout the countryside, did "enjoin and require all Persons residing within seventy Miles of my Head Quarters to thresh one Half of their Grain by the 1st Day of February, and the other Half by the 1st Day of March next ensuing, on Pain, in Case of Failure of having all that shall remain in Sheaves seized . . . and paid for as Straw."[5]

Although new clothing was not to be had, Washington could at least acknowledge some hopefully cheering news he had received on the 19th. This was a report from General William Heath at Boston that a French ship, the *Flamand,* had reached Portsmouth, New Hampshire, with a cargo of assorted military supplies, including clothing, which had been sent from France through the agency of the fictitious *Rodrique Hortelez et Cie.* This dummy "company" had been organized by the famous French author, Caron de Beaumarchais, as a front to conceal the support being sent from France to the struggling Americans. The British were fully aware of the activities of this non-too-clandestine business; but since the business was unofficial, Britain could only make equally unofficial protests to the French Government.

In acknowledging Heath's news Washington was not overly optimistic about its immediate effect on the army. Portsmouth was far away. Snow clogged the New England roads, and the men at Valley Forge were already freezing. Furthermore, the Commander-in-Chief informed Heath, "the state of the Commissary's department has given me more concern of late, than anything else. Unless matters in that line are very speedily taken up and put in a better train, the most alarming consequences are to be apprehended."[6]

Congress on the same day was taking only semi-positive action in an effort to relieve the clothing situation. It recommended to the various states that they "enact laws, appointing suitable persons to seize and take, for the use of the continental army of the said states all woolen cloths, blankets, linens, shoes, stockings, hats and other necessary articles of cloathing," and also to cause clothing "to be made up."[7] However, such dilatory action could hardly be expected to meet the constantly imperative need.

During the first day at Valley Forge little observable progress was made towards establishing a permanent camp. By the evening of the 20th another night of unrelieved hardship was in prospect, since the cold continued intense and there was little food available. Private Joseph Martin recalled that he "lay here two nights and one day and had not a morsel of anything to eat all the time, save a small pumpkin," conceivably filched from a neighboring farm, "which I cooked by placing it upon a rock, the skin side uppermost, and making a fire upon it. By the time it was heat[ed] through I devoured it with an appetite as I should a pie."

American and British Foraging

As though near starvation was not a bleak enough prospect to face, Martin "was warned to be ready for a two days command," which order he received as having "never heard a summons to duty with so much disgust . . . How I could endure two days more fatigue without nourishment of some sort I could not tell."[8] With the arrival of morning on the 21st, Martin "was obliged to comply" with the order, and soon discovered that he and a "considerable number" of other soldiers were " to go into the country on a foraging expedition" which he considered "nothing more nor less than to procure provisions from the inhabitants . . . at the point of the bayonet." The men were able to set out with full stomachs, however, since "a beef creature was butchered for us" which furnished a meal and two days' allowance of beef plus some moldy bread.[9]

The enemy was also reported out foraging. A force sent to New Jersey consisted of "near one thousand" men accompanied by "six field pieces." Also a hundred Hessians with thirty wagons had drawn off from Darby, Pennsylvania, "hay and rye straw without interruption."[10] The Hessians had observed that much more fodder was available for the taking.

Washington, learning of the latter incursion into the country, immediately wrote to General Potter, of the Pennsylvania Militia based at Newtown Square, "I think it of the greatest consequence to have what Hay remains" in the general area of Darby "destroyed . . . as we cannot remove it" because of the lack of transportation. The Commander-in-Chief thought "it should be done as speedily as possible," as, by destroying the hay close to the city, "we shall probably oblige" the enemy "to come out into the Country to forage, which will perhaps give us an opportunity of cutting off a party." Potter, if necessary, was to draw support from Colonel Daniel Morgan and his riflemen stationed as scouts at nearby Radnor.[11]

The above orders to Potter were made doubly imperative by a report from American spies in Philadelphia "of the enemy's intentions to plunder" in the direction of "Darby, Marple and Springfield townships" during the next week, and of their having gathered some two hundred wagons with which to conduct the proposed business.[12] The spies also reported "a very plentiful market of beef" in the city, which circumstance was in sharp contrast to conditions at Valley Forge where there was "A general cry thro' the Camp this Evening among the Soldiers, No Meat! No Meat! the Distant vales Echo'd back the melancholy sound No Meat! No Meat! . . . What have we for Dinner Boys? Nothing but Fire Cake and Water, Sir . . . What is your Supper, Lads? Fire Cake and Water, Sir."[13]

In fact conditions in the camp were such that on the morning of the 23rd, Washington informed Henry Laurens, President of Congress, "that a dangerous mutiny begun the Night before, and [which] with difficulty was suppressed by the spirited exertion's of some officers was still much to be apprehended on acct. of their want" of provisions.[14]

Washington also informed Laurens that as of that afternoon he had been told "that the Enemy, in force," had left the city, "and were advancing towards Derby [Darby] with apparent design to forage, and draw Subsistence from that part of the Country." Washington noted that he had immediately "order'd the Troops to be in readiness" to march so that he "might give every opposition in my power" to the enemy force; "when behold! to my great mortification, I was not only informed, but convinced, that the Men were unable to stir on acct. of Provision . . . This brought forth the only Comy. [commissary] in the purchasing Line, in this Camp; [and] with him, this Melancholy and alarming truth, that he had not a single hoof of any kind to Slaughter, and not more than 25 Barls. of Flour!" From this circumstance, Washington invited Laurens to "form an opinion of our situation when I add that he [the commissary] could not tell me when to expect any" provisions for the army.[15]

Washington had ordered a column, consisting of the brigades of Huntington and Varnum under the command of Lord Stirling, and supported by a few dragoons, to proceed in the direction of Darby to oppose the British advance.[16] Huntington immediately informed the Commander-in-Chief that though his men thought "fighting will be far preferable to starving" in camp, the brigade could boast no provisions and could not be expected to move without supplies despite Huntington's strenuous efforts to start his men on the road. Huntington had "used every argument that my imagination can invent to make the soldiers easy, but I despair of being able to do it much longer," under the circumstances.[17]

Varnum's men were in no better state. They had existed

THE HOME OF ZACHARY DAVIS, *a tenant of David Stephens, was occupied by Gen. Huntington as his quarters. The original building, measuring only 21 x 18 feet is the small whitewashed wing of the larger structure. The latter is of early 19th century construction.*

precariously for two or three days with little subsistence, and "must be supplied or they cannot be commanded" to advance against the enemy. "The complaints are too urgent to pass unnoticed," Varnum added. "I know it will make Your Excellency unhappy, but if you expect the exertion of virtuous principles while your troops are deprived of the necessaries of life, your final disappointment will be great."[18]

The mixed detachment that was finally gathered under Stirling's command consisted of only about 300 men and a few dragoons. Two field pieces were also allotted to the detachment. No more could be sent since no other horses capable of the service could be discovered in camp. The column was far too small to do other than observe, and perhaps annoy the powerful enemy force that was rapidly penetrating the country in the direction of Darby.

The British commander, General Howe, finding his army supplied with only "a scanty supply of forage," had been compelled "to cross the Schuylkill on the 22nd with the larger part of the [British] army" in an effort to rectify this situation. Howe left only "Eight English battalions, the Queen's Rangers . . . Stirn's and Woellwarth's brigades" of Germans, and a few dragoons to guard the city, under the command of Hessian Lieutenant General Baron Wilhelm von Knyphausen.[19] Howe, in person, commanded the foragers, some 7,000 men in all.

The British and Hessian troops crossed the Schuylkill on the permanent pontoon bridge at the Middle Ferry (at the site of the present Market Street Bridge) and on a temporary floating bridge laid across the river at Grey's Ferry, a mile or so below the Middle Ferry. As night fell on the 22nd, the British column stretched its line of encampment from near Grey's Ferry southwestward along the road leading from that place to the vicinity of Darby.

The British commander was determined that there would be no enemy interruption to his foraging; hence the strength of his column, which was intended as an impregnable wall of defense to cover the foragers working between Darby and the Delaware River to the eastward. This was the very area in which Washington had recently ordered Potter and the Pennsylvania Militia to destroy the fodder. Potter's Militia, accompanied by Daniel Morgan's riflemen, too late to effect their original purpose, joined Stirling in the attempt to harass the enemy whenever opportunity offered.

Washington Blames Congress

At Valley Forge the American Commander-in-Chief, shocked by his inability to oppose the enemy foragers, began a discouraging report to Congress. "It is with infinite pain and concern," he wrote on December 22nd, that he must again dwell on "the State of the Commissary's department . . . I do not know from what cause this alarming deficiency or rather total failure of Supplies arises; But unless more Vigorous exertions and better regulations take place" in that Department, "and immediately, this Army must dissolve." He requested that the presently vacant offices of Quartermaster-General and Commissary-General should be filled "as soon as possible."[20]

On the following day, December 23rd, the Commander-in-Chief was even more explicit concerning the needs and condition of the army. He was "now convinced . . . that unless some great and capital change suddenly takes place" in the Commissary and Quartermaster Departments "this Army must inevitably be reduced to one or other of these three things . . .

Starve, dissolve, or disperse, in order to obtain subsistence in the best manner they can." Washington notified Congress that "this is not an exaggerated picture." Besides food, "Soap and Vinegar and other Articles . . . we see none of." As for soap, "indeed we have now little occasion of; few men having more than one shirt, many only the moiety of and some none at all."

THE HOME OF DAVID STEPHENS *was occupied by Gen. Varnum as his quarters. The building has been restored approximately to its original appearance, a full third story, now removed, having been added early in the 19th century.*

Many of the troops "were confined to Hospitals" and to local farmhouses for no other reason than a "want of Shoes" and other clothing. "By a field return this day made [December 23rd] no less than 2,898 Men [are] now in camp unfit for duty because they are bare foot and otherwise naked." The troops fit for duty, if any could really be denoted as such, "exclusive of the troops sent to Wilmington" with General Smallwood, had been reduced to the perilous number of "no more than 8,200," though more than 17,000 men were carried on the paper returns of the army.

The Commander-in-Chief took the occasion to reproach the Pennsylvania authorities who had suggested that the army should continue operations and attack the enemy. "I can assure those Gentlemen that it is a much easier and less distressing thing to draw remonstrances in a comfortable room by a good fire side than to occupy a cold, bleak hill, and sleep under frost and Snow without Cloaths or Blankets; however, although they seem to have little feeling for the naked and distressed Soldiers, I feel superabundantly for them, and from my Soul pity those miseries, wch. it is neither in my power to relieve or prevent.

"It adds not a little to my other difficulties and distress, to find that much more is expected of me than is possible to be performed, and that upon the ground of safety and policy, I am obliged to conceal the true State of the Army from Public view and thereby expose myself to detraction and calumny."

Washington then complained of the lack of proper officers to command the major units of the army, "Several Brigades having no brigadiers appointed . . . which means it follows that an additional weight is thrown upon the Shoulders of the

Commander in Chief to withdraw his attention from the great line of his duty." A committee from Congress that had visited the recent camp at Whitemarsh had promised to adjust the many matters that distressed the army, but no such adjustments appeared forthcoming. Washington, therefore, suggested that another committee from Congress, or "two or three Members of the Board of War," be appointed and sent to Valley Forge to "prepare and digest the most perfect plan that can be devised for correcting all abuses, [and] making new arrangements" in the constitution of the army.

He further suggested that the committee, after digesting matters, "submit the whole to the ultimate determination of Congress." If the suggestions were approved by Congress (Washington ever deferred to Congress as the chief military as well as civil authority in the nation), Washington "would earnestly advise the immediate execution" of the plans submitted and approved. Washington added, "every thing depends upon the preparation that is made in the several departments in the course of this Winter, and the success, or misfortunes of the next Campaign will more than probably originate with our activity or supineness this winter." He suggested that supply magazines should be immediately erected "in the Neighborhood of this Camp in order to secure Provision for us in case of bad weather." The Quartermaster Department "ought also to be busy . . . in short, there is as much to be done in preparing for a Campaign as in the active part of it."

In an effort to prevent complete starvation or the dissolution of the army, the best plan the Commander-in-Chief could initiate was to detach foraging parties "different ways" through the immediate countryside "to collect, if possible as much Provision as would satisfy the present pressing wants of the Soldiery. But will this answer?" he asked. Indeed no, for "three or four days bad weather would prove our destruction. What then is to become of the Army this Winter?"[21]

Under these difficult conditions, the defenses of the camp had to be planned and carried forward. The Commander-in-Chief observed that among other requirements, a drier and safer passage to the north shore of the Schuylkill River than that afforded by Fatlands Ford was an absolute necessity. The river was known to freeze over frequently during the winter, thereby making the ford impassable. The river must be prevented from becoming a barrier of unsafe ice should an attack come and a retreat north become necessary. Further, constant touch must be kept with the parties of Militia that Washington planned to station north of Philadelphia to protect that part of the country from British foraging parties and to watch enemy movements. Also, supplies, when available, might be brought to camp from across the river.

In view of these necessities, Washington directed that a bridge should be constructed across the river at the most feasible site in the vicinity of the camp. "Major General Sullivan, having obligingly undertaken the direction of a bridge to be built over the Schuylkill" was therefore "excused from the common duties of camp."[22] The bridge when completed would assume the name of its builder—Sullivan's Bridge.

Daily reports of the British foraging expedition to Darby were delivered to Washington in his sparsely furnished marquee.[23] The enemy enterprise had proved from the first "very successful" despite occasional American harassment.[24] General Stirling, unable to mount a major attack on the enemy forces, had separated his little column into smaller units in an effort to strike at detached parties of the enemy whenever possible.

The British viewed these attacks as no more than an expected annoyance, and felt there was little to apprehend unless General Smallwood, stationed at Wilmington, should abandon that post and attempt an attack on the British column. The British credited Smallwood's force with far more men than Washington had been able to detach to Wilmington. British reports had expanded Smallwood's force to some 4,000 men, nearly four times the actual count.

On Christmas Eve Colonels John Bull and Frederick Antes with a few Pennsylvania Militia, expecting the enemy troops left in Philadelphia to be preoccupied with the festive season, executed what was intended as no more than a diversion against the British lines north of the city. The Militia's attack commenced at "half past six in the evening" and ended in less than an hour.[25] The raiders proceeded down Fourth Street some little distance into the thinly populated outskirts of the city, halted in front of the British lines, and "alarmed the City by firing off some pieces of cannon" at no particular target, though "some of the balls fell about Christ Church," already a famous edifice, and within the confines of the Colonial barracks erected during the French and Indian War. The Militia then "made a good retreat . . . without the loss of one man."[26]

The enemy hastily reinforced their defenses and fired back at the empty night. On the eastern end of the lines the British thought they detected several American row gallies sneaking down the river under cover of darkness from the up-river ports to which the American fleet had retreated when the British had cleared the river of American defenses in the previous fall. A few cannon shots from a shore redoubt and the British frigate *Camilla* put the phantom row gallies to flight. With dawn the country in front of the British lines was again seen to be "so empty and desolate towards Germantown and beyond," that it became "almost useless to send patrols in that direction" in pursuit of the Americans.[27]

Christmas at Valley Forge

On Christmas Day snow began to fall and continued heavy into the night until there was an accumulation of four inches. The heavy fall of snow may have caused Surgeon Albigence Waldo at Valley Forge to complain, "We are still in Tents, when we ought to be in huts."[28] The snow so disrupted the business of directing the encampment and maintaining the army that Washington was forced to strike his marquee and its attendant tents and renege on his promise to the troops not to reside in snugger quarters until the men were at least reasonably well hutted. Headquarters was moved into the Isaac Potts residence, the stone building a few paces inland from the Schuylkill River near the mouth of Valley Creek. The move displaced Potts' former sister-in-law, the twice widowed Mrs. Deborah Hewes.

Christmas dinner at the new Headquarters, which was eaten in mid-afternoon as was the custom of the time, was a modest affair. Besides his immediate staff, Washington invited Lafayette and the officers of the day (Generals DeKalb and Paterson, Lt.-Colonels Thomas Paxton and Robert Ballard, and Brigade-Major Simon Learned.) Also present were Captain Caleb Gibbs and Lieutenant George Lewis of the Commander-in-Chief's Guard, which was stationed to the rear of Headquarters ready for immediate service to the Commander-in-Chief's person. Young Lewis was Washington's nephew, the son of his sister Betty.

The meal was Spartan-sparse, consisting only of small portions of veal, mutton, potatoes and cabbage served to each diner. Despite the Commander-in-Chief's fondness for Madeira, wine was conspicuously absent, and water was the only beverage. Washington's personal camp equipment had been left at Newtown, Bucks County, to facilitate his movements, so that there was even a shortage of tableware.

At the conclusion of dinner Washington wrote to Congressman Elbridge Gerry at York renewing his pressure on Congress to appoint a committee to study the physical needs of the army. "Our whole Military system might then be considered, and such alterations as should be found necessary and beneficial . . . be adopted." Washington also dwelt on the proposed half-pay pension plan for officers after the war was concluded, and recommended that, if Congress was serious in the matter, the plan should be announced as soon as possible since the Commander-in-Chief was sure "much good would result." The recent requests for the acceptance of their resignations sent to Headquarters by a considerable number of officers might, with a firm pension plan in view, be reconsidered, and future requests for such acceptances might be prevented.[29]

"A spirit of resigning their commissions," the Commander-in-Chief wrote to Governor Richard Caswell of North Carolina on the same day, "whether resulting from necessary causes or feigned ones . . . has been but too prevalent in the Army of late." The officers had become disgusted with Congress's apparent indifference to their present and future conditions. Washington had "discountenanced" these requests "as much as possible . . . [since] the practice is of a pernicious tendency and must have an unhappy influence on the service."[30]

Hunger was everywhere. Nightly, starving American soldiers took advantage of the cover of darkness to sneak from camp and engage in plundering local inhabitants, taking not only food but whatever else caught their fancy. So infectious did the practice become that Washington was obliged to denounce the evil in General Orders. "It is with inexpressible grief and indignation that the General has received information of the cruel outrages" perpetrated against the country folk, thereby alienating many American friends. The Commander-in-Chief ordered that any soldier "caught without the limits of the camp" lacking a pass and with no specific orders to be absent was to be "confined and severely punished."[31]

Christmas Day also found the British foraging column at and near Darby with most of the fodder and plunder in the area gathered and loaded in wagons before the Holiday storm broke. Despite the snow, the British commander reasoned that, as long as his column was out, he should extend his operations as far from the city as his men could safely proceed without severing communications with Philadelphia. He hoped thereby to acquire enough forage to end the need for further major foraging in the immediate future.

Howe therefore ordered a slight change of position towards Chester in an effort to disperse the light parties of Americans harassing his front, and to protect the wagons that were hauling "hay from Tinicum Island." American spies reported that in addition to the enemy acquiring hay, "near one hundred Hessians were driving in cattle"[32] toward the city, and that the country people, Loyalists and so-called neutrals alike, had taken the occasion of the British raid to carry their produce into the city both from a desire to acquire British guineas and "through fear of being plundered" as the British and Hessians returned from Darby.[33]

By December 27th the weather had moderated, permitting the completion of the British foraging. On the 28th, "about 8 in the morning" despite the fact that snow had again begun to fall, the British column "marched towards Philadelphia . . . The Light Infantry took post above the bridge at Grey's" Ferry until the temporary bridge of floating timbers at that place "was taken up, whilst the rest of the Army marched to Middle Ferry where they halted until the Light Infantry came up, when the whole crossed the Schuylkill and repaired to their several Encampments."[34] A party of American Militia attempted to strike at the British rear as it crossed the river but was decoyed into an ambush and taken.

Despite the acquisition of two hundred tons of hay and other fodder, plus considerable numbers of cattle and a number of American prisoners, the British raid was not as successful as Howe had hoped. En route to Philadelphia the wet weather had damaged a considerable quantity of hay. Nevertheless, the supply would suffice for a time. With the completion of this foraging operation, General Howe ordered his army into final winter quarters.

In remote England, Parliament had recessed for the Christmas season but not before it was known to its members that new and what the majority considered liberal terms of reconciliation were to be offered to the Americans. These terms would be a concession to most of the demands put forward by the Americans prior to the commencement of hostilities in 1775, though denying independence.

The British Ministry was fully aware that the American plenipotentiaries in France, Benjamin Franklin, Silas Deane and Arthur Lee, having long been officially ignored by the French Court, had not only been received in Court but were also engaged in serious talks with the French Government concerning a Franco-American alliance. Such a treaty would undoubtedly include French recognition of American independence. The British Ministry was considerably frightened at the prospect of such an alliance since it would almost inevitably lead to a war with France.

The American Medical Service

The days following Christmas brought no substantial relief to the American Army. Indeed conditions grew worse since, added to the previous miseries, smallpox was reported in camp. Dr. John Cochrane, Surgeon-General of the Middle Department, fearing that the disease would spread rapidly among those troops who had not yet been inoculated with cowpox, immediately ordered that a hospital for contagious diseases should be opened at Yellow Springs (now Chester Springs) some ten miles west of Valley Forge. Workers were dispatched at once to Yellow Springs to begin construction of the only building specifically designed as a military hospital during the entire length of the war.[35]

Until the new building could be readied, three local barns at the Springs were commandeered to house the first one hundred and fifty patients. Dr. Samuel Kennedy (who would die in the spring from a fever caught from his patients) was placed in charge of the installation. Dr. John Brown Cutting, Apothecary-General of the Middle Department, normally stationed at the principal pharmacy at Carlisle, was directed to bring to the new hospital at Yellow Springs whatever medicines and other hospital supplies he had on hand.

The hospital at Yellow Springs was only one of a chain of

hospitals established for the aid of the sick and wounded that flowed from Valley Forge. The chain when completed would extend to more distant places: to the Moravian Brethrens' House at Bethlehem, to Easton, Allentown, Lititz, Lancaster and elsewhere in Pennsylvania; to Trenton and Princeton and other points in New Jersey. Nevertheless, the sick list at Valley Forge continued to increase so rapidly that these hospitals soon became overcrowded. Washington presently found it necessary to requisition barns, churches and Quaker meeting houses, close to camp, to accommodate the overflow of patients. Besides the smallpox already noted, typhus, typhoid, pneumonia and half a dozen equally fatal diseases swept through the camp.

There was small wonder that virulent diseases became increasingly prevalent at Valley Forge. Despite Washington's orders to keep the camp and the men reasonably clean, weather conditions permitted few hygienic practices; and the rapidly debilitating condition of the troops as a result of starvation and the lack of clothing predisposed the men to all manner of sicknesses. Few conditions in camp were not contributing factors to sickness. One private soldier noted, "The warter we had to Drink and to mix our flower with was out of a brook that run along by the Camps, and so many dippin and washin [in] it which maid it very Dirty and muddy."[36] Despite the nearness of the Schuylkill River plus two considerable creeks and various springs, fresh water was ever in short supply.

Sanitary conditions in camp were an even greater source of sickness. Although "vaults" had been ordered built, the bad weather and lack of clothing and sickness induced many soldiers to ease themselves wherever they willed until Washington ordered the culprits flogged. Spoiled meat, too rotten even for starving men to stomach, was often cast unceremoniously among or even within the huts; and orders to police the camp of its garbage frequently had to be issued. Unburied dead horses were also a constant menace to health.

Sullivan Builds Bridge

Indeed, trouble seemed everywhere. The trouble that immediately faced John Sullivan as the year ended was the difficulty he was experiencing in commencing the construction of the bridge he had volunteered to build across the Schuylkill River. The extreme cold after a brief thaw on December 27th and snow on the 28th were not the only factors that delayed the work. "When I undertook to Compleat the Bridge in So Short a Space" of time as had been agreed on, Sullivan notified Washington, "I Expected every article" needed for the work "would be provided."

Sullivan was "unhappy to find that not one Single Article is provided in Season." He was aware that "the Safety and Convenience of the army Depends upon having it Compleated as Soon as possible." In the beginning he had been "well Convinced that Six Days would be amply Sufficient for Doing the whole provided that Every thing was in Preparation: for So soon as a proper Crew can Cut, hew and Frame one Pier So Soon might the whole be done . . . provided there were proper Tools for the Business and proper hands Employed."

He had discovered further, "the management [construction] of the present Bridge is really perplexing" because of unexpected impediments. "It Took my people the first Day to try their axes, [and] when they found" the cutting edges "Break . . . they had no Grindstone provided till the Second Day near five of clock," too late in the day to continue work.

Nor could work on the bridge itself commence immediately since "the men were that Day principally Employed in Building Hutts that they might" live close to their work and not have to waste time tramping from their original encampments.

"The next day," Sullivan continued, "some tools arrived but it was at Least a Days work for all my men to whet the Saws and Grind the Tools. I have been for two Days without Teams to hall the Timber to the place. Yesterday and this Day till two of Clock I have waited for waggons to hall Rocks" with which to anchor the piers, of which there would be some nine required. Sullivan had "applied to the Marquis Le Fayette" for thirty additional men "to load and unload" the wagons on the following day but had little prospect of acquiring them as Lafayette's men were in such poor condition. Sullivan therefore begged Washington to supply him with the ablest men in each brigade. With this assistance he was certain that his men could "Soon Compleat the Business if they are properly Supplyed." The recruits, however, must be better screened for their abilities than heretofore, for "Some of the Brigades who were to furnish me with Carpenters Sent me Taylors who had never used an ax in their Lives; [and] kept their good Carpenters at home to build hutts."

In closing his message Sullivan noted that he had thus written to the Commander-in-Chief "as a protest to Exculpate me from not Doing the Bridge" in the time expected. Sullivan likewise declared "that it will never be Done" at either the location he had selected a hundred yards below Fatlands Ford or elsewhere "unless affairs are placed on a Different Footing."[37]

Haste in building the contemplated bridge was not so imperative as Sullivan deemed. The supplies that the bridge was intended to carry across the river were not arriving at camp despite the fact that there were literally "hundreds of barrels of flour lying on the banks of the Susquehanna" some forty miles west that were "perishing for want of care in securing it from the weather." In fact the back country of Pennsylvania and its neighboring states was literally cluttered with supplies. There were "fifty wagon loads of cloths and ready made clothes for the soldiers in the Clothier General's store in Lancaster" which the Clothier-General, James Mease, was unable to move because of lack of transportation.[38] The near collapse of the Quartermaster Department prevented the delivery of food and clothing to Valley Forge.

The various states, Anthony Wayne noted to Thomas Wharton, Jr., President of the Pennsylvania Council, had each been requested by Congress to clothe their own troops. Wayne, whose troops were stationed in their home state and should have been at least semi-decently supplied, expressed his particular disgust with the Pennsylvania authorities for their failure to better clothe the Pennsylvania Line. He was bitter in "expressing both Surprise and Concern at the Council's directing the Clothing Collected in this State into the Hands of the Clothier-General" of the Continental Army for the use of the whole army, rather than directing the clothing to his own Pennsylvania troops.

Wayne complained that the Council's "following the Generous Course" was, in his opinion, "being generous out of time." Wayne observed to the Council that the Pennsylvania troops were clad only in rags. Some clothing had even arrived from New England for the use of the New England troops. As a result, Wayne wrote, the New Englanders were now comparatively "comfortable while ours are perishing."[39] In desperation Wayne, who as he informed Richard Peters, Secretary to the Board of War, would "provide for my poor fellows before I consult my own need,"[40] had already begun to by-pass the usual channels employed for clothing his troops. Wayne had reached an agreement in the previous fall with Paul Zantzinger, a Lancaster merchant who consented to act as a semi-private clothier for the Pennsylvania Line, including those Pennsylvanians in brigades other than Wayne's.

Washington, in a circular appeal to the governors of the various states in conjunction with the recent Congressional appeal, sent out an urgent plea for clothing, for, as he wrote ominously, if clothing and other supplies were not soon forthcoming "the Troops will never be in a situation to answer the public expectation and perform the duties required of them." He again took occasion to mention "how deficient, how exceedingly short" the regiments were "of the complement of Men" necessary for a strong and efficient army. "We may rest assured that Britain will strain every nerve to send from home and abroad, as early as possible, All the Troops it shall be in her power to raise or procure."

Washington had not been aware of the recruiting difficulties that Great Britain was already experiencing, now that war enthusiasm at home had waned; and he cautioned that Great Britain's "schemes for subjugating these States will be unceasing . . . Nor should we in my opinion turn our expectations to . . . the intervention of a Foreign War" between France and Britain. No news had arrived from the American plenipotentiaries in France, and American hopes of French intervention had "been disappointed hitherto, and I do not know that we have a right to promise ourselves from any intelligence that there is any certain prospect" of such an intervention. "Our reliance should be wholly on our own strength and exertions." Of course, if eventually "there should be aid derived from a War between the Enemy and any of the European powers, our situation will be so much the better," but if no such event should occur, "our efforts and exertions will have been the more necessary and indispensible."[41]

Desertions and Resignations

Desertions and officer resignations were constantly depleting the army. "Upwards of fifty Officers in Genl. Greene's Division resigned their Commissions" in a single day. The uncertainty of Congressional provision for the officers' future, the cost of maintaining themselves, and the reports from home of the "Officers' Families being so much neglected at home" on account of a constant lack of provisions and other necessaries were the principal sources of the officers' discontent. The officers' "Wages will not by considerable, purchase a few trifling Comfortables here in Camp and maintain their families at home, while such extravagant prices are demanded for the common necessaries of Life." Not only were prices inflated but the Continental currency had descended abysmally low in its purchasing power. Actually, comparatively little of this debased currency fell into the hands of the troops since payment of the wages of officers and men alike was constantly in arrears.

In a measure, the officers had more source for complaint than the men. The officers were expected to pay for their own clothing. "The present Circumstances of the Soldier is better by far than the Officers" in the matter of contentment at home, "for the family of the Soldier is provided for at the public expence if the Articles they want are above the common price . . . When the Officer has been fatiguing thro' wet and cold

and returns to his tent where he finds a letter directed to him from his Wife, fill'd with the most heart aching tender Complaints . . . what man is there—who has the least regard for his family—whose soul will not shrink within him?"[42]

So desperate had the situation concerning resignations become that Washington was forced to refuse further applications for furloughs even when well deserved. The Commander-in-Chief even rejected the applications of Generals Knox and Wayne, though the latter complained of illness and lived almost within sight of camp, and could have returned to the army practically at a moment's notice. No officer, Washington notified the numerous disappointed applicants, could be spared.

As for desertions, that plague had commenced to infect the army on an increasing scale even before the troops had arrived at Valley Forge. Numerous soldiers who were stationed within even a long walking distance from home slipped out of camp by night and proceeded to cheerier firesides. Other soldiers, particularly those who were foreign born and had no immediate ties with the American soil and people, took the easy road to Philadelphia and the enemy lines.

The desertions along this route were not all one way. Even in the bitter cold of December 30th eleven deserters, "some Hessians and some English," appeared on the fringe of the camp at Valley Forge from the direction of Philadelphia. The Hessians were sick of service in a foreign land against a people with whom they had no personal quarrel. The English deserters were embittered for other reasons, such as the harsh punishments for minor infractions of military regulations. One of the Hessians, an American soldier-diarist noted, on reaching the bank of the Schuylkill opposite Valley Forge "took an Ax in his hand and cut away the Ice of the Schuylkill which was 1-1/2 inches thick and 40 Rod wide and waded through to our camp" after having been "1/2 an hour in the Water."[43]

These British and Hessian prisoners were temporarily locked in the Provost-Marshal's pen that had been erected in the rear of Wilsey Bodle's house on the north side of the encampment. Here the captives joined "great numbers of [American] prisoners," principally re-captured deserters, all of whom were "suffering extremely from the severity of the season," which continued bitterly cold.[44]

The British and Hessians would be shipped, when weather permitted, to join their fellow countrymen imprisoned at Reading. At present, the cold was too "amazing" for such a transfer, and the roads were still drifted with snow. The Schuylkill River was frozen solid as far east as Philadelphia, and the Delaware River was "full of floating ice," which the British engineer Captain John Montrésor, recorded, "forced a brig and a schooner" bringing supplies to the British Army "on shore . . . at Gloucester," on the New Jersey side of the river, "where the rebels took possession of them."[45]

The enemy to the American cause was not limited to men in uniform. Major John Clark, Jr., informed the Commander-in-Chief "that there are a set of gentry that infest the public roads" in Philadelphia, Chester and Bucks Counties who "call themselves 'volunteers'" in the American service, but who in reality were "under no authority, and pay no respect to persons having [American] passes or not, and indeed are no better than so many highway robbers, and unless they are speedily removed will make many enemies of those who are now our friends . . . These people rob, steal, and plunder persons without distinction and lay it on the army, and 'tis believed" by many of the victims that "They've orders for doing so."

The brigands even threatened "the lives of the inhabitants if they go to complain."[46]

The pseudo-American "volunteers" were not the only desperadoes who infested the neighborhood. Counterpart British "volunteers" made the country equally precarious. The infamous Doane Gang of Bucks County attacked friend and foe alike; and in Chester County the famous Robin Hood, "Captain Fitz" Fitzpatrick, rode his thieving way. "Captain Fitz" would eventually tighten a length of American rope, but the Doanes were not finally broken up until after the war ended.

By the 29th, although considerable progress was evident in the hutting at Valley Forge, Washington discovered it necessary to exhort "the officers of every rank to use their utmost exertions to have their huts" and those of the men "completed as soon as possible."[47] Some nine hundred huts were under construction, set around the perimeter of the camp so as to be near the lines of defense when time and the strength of the men would permit construction of entrenchments.

Although a considerable number of the huts were finished, some of the builders had made little progress, particularly those troops who had been obliged to leave their work to observe the enemy raid to Darby. Work was also retarded somewhat by the scarcity of tools, though the soldiers for the most part had been "like a family of beavers, every one busy; Some carrying logs, others mud, and the rest plastering them together." Most huts were raised "in a few days, and it is a curious collection of buildings, in the true rustic order."[48]

Truly, "the following Contrast" could be readily drawn, "The British had comfortable Quarters in the City of Philadelphia, good houses to secure them from the approaching Winter," where they could play and laugh and sing despite their "prescribed Situation" in the city; "the Americans [had] such Quarters as Industry cou'd procure" in a bleak and forbidding countryside.[49] Though it was true that the patriot army was indeed undisciplined, dirty and ragged, still, as Surgeon Waldo commented, "All Hell couldn't prevail against us, If Heaven continues no more than its former blessings—and if we keep up the Credit of our Money."[50] Thus ended 1777.

CHAPTER III

EBB TIDE

New Year at Valley Forge

"The new year opens favourably upon us," an anonymous patriot proclaimed in the *New Jersey Gazette,* "but what its future complexion will be, depends upon the manner in which we employ the present winter. Our successes" which had culminated in Burgoyne's defeat and capture "encourage the most sanguine hopes. Our losses forbid the least presumption . . . The period is therefore arrived when, by arming our beloved General with the united force of the States, we shall enable him to take the field with a superiority of strength."[1]

At Valley Forge, human courage was of more immediate importance to America than literary clichés, inspirational and wise as those clichés might prove. In an effort to bolster morale and to instill a little holiday spirit into New Year's Day, Washington ordered "a gill of spirits be Served to each non-commission'd officer and soldier."[2] The commissioned officers were required to provide and pay for their own holiday entertainment.

Congress, in one of its occasional sympathetic moods, attempted to recompense the heroes who so staunchly interposed themselves between American aspirations and ruin, and had resolved on the next to last day of the old year that the Commander-in-Chief be "directed to inform the brave officers and soldiers" at Valley Forge "that, as the situation of the enemy" had forced the American troops to take up undesirable winter quarters, "Congress, approving of their soldierly patience, fidelity and zeal, in the cause of their country, have directed one month's extraordinary pay to be given to each" man who stood firm at his post.[3]

Congress further exhibited some desire to reorganize the army in concurrence with the Commander-in-Chief's recent requests. The beginnings were small, but at least instilled hope for an eventual equitable arrangement which might please all ranks of the army. Congress recommended to the states that they forthwith cease appointing officers to replace the constantly recurring vacancies caused by resignations, since "the number of officers" who remained with the army was still "out of all proportion to that of privates" and that they should wait before issuing new commissions "until they hear further from Congress," which was on the verge of appointing a committee of its own members to study the needs of the army first-hand at Valley Forge.[4]

Congress, in addition, re-affirmed the extraordinary powers with which it had vested Washington the previous fall. These powers permitted the Commander-in-Chief to suspend or replace officers below the rank of brigadier without consulting Congress, arbitrarily seize provisions within seventy miles of camp when necessity warranted, remove goods "serviceable to the enemy" from enemy reach, and summarily court-martial any persons found dealing with the enemy or otherwise acting in a subversive manner.[5]

Washington had received a personal gratification on the final day of 1777 that somewhat eased the depressing prospects of the coming year. Lafayette, in his Gallic enthusiasm for the American cause, had permitted himself to be blinded to the machinations of Thomas Conway, Horatio Gates and other persons, notably members of Congress, against the Commander-in-Chief. The clique sought to replace Washington with Gates. From the time of his arrival with the army Lafayette, unaware of the recent Conway Cabal, had been friendly with Conway, since the latter had likewise served in the French Army. For some time, Lafayette continued a frequent and friendly correspondence with Conway. Since Lafayette had made no conscious attempt to keep the correspondence secret, Washington was fully aware of its existence, but said nothing.

On discovering Conway's design against Washington, Lafayette immediately wrote an intra-camp explanatory letter to Washington, denying any intimacy with Conway to the detriment of Lafayette's amicable feelings for the Commander-in-Chief. On December 31st Lafayette received a reply from Washington in which the Commander-in-Chief assured Lafayette of his pleasure at receiving a "fresh proof of that friendship and attachment" that Lafayette had exhibited ever since joining the army in August. The Commander-in-Chief was certain that Lafayette had "a Mind too exalted to condescend to dirty Arts and low intrigues" in order "to acquire a reputation." Washington also privately took the occasion of his letter to castigate Gates for overweening ambition, and noted the dissatisfaction of many officers, including himself, with Conway's unwarranted promotion to the Inspector-Generalship

despite Washington's efforts to prevent the promotion.[6]

On receipt of Washington's letter, Lafayette at once replied from his quarters on the opposite side of camp expressing relief that friendly relations between himself and the Commander-in-Chief had not been impaired by Lafayette's ignorance of the true state of affairs. "Every assurance and proof of your affection," Lafayette wrote, "fills my heart with joy."[7] Because of this incident, so earnest did Lafayette become in rooting out opposition to the best interests of the Commander-in-Chief that he was presently writing to Henry Laurens, President of Congress, "You [the Americans] are surrounded by secret enemies, you have thousand among you, some perhaps in Congress itself. If Howe should know in this moment our present circumstances," political as well as military, "I dare not say what my mind foresees."

Lafayette then warned Laurens of Horatio Gates' ambitions founded on the victory at Saratoga where, Lafayette noted, because of the vastly superior American numbers "it was almost impossible to him to not conquer." Lafayette praised Washington as a man "born for the salvation of his country and the admiration of the universe."[8] Laurens needed no such warning against Gates and his cronies, nor praise for the Commander-in-Chief, as he was likewise Washington's unswerving friend and confidant. His son, John Laurens, one of Washington's personal aides, had helped make certain of that.

Officer Discontent

Thomas Conway's arrival in camp from York on December 29th on a tour of inspection had induced the general officers to draw up a memorial to Congress protesting against the irregularities in the promotion of officers. Although Conway was not named, the memorial left no doubt that his recent promotion to major general and Inspector General was the basis for the present protest. Lafayette's case was different. The army had been fully apprised of the political importance of his sudden elevation to a major-generalcy, and had acquiesced to his commission with scarcely a murmur.

"We are exceeding sorry to say," the memorial read, "that in this Army no regular Line of Promotion has been observed. Promotions without any apparent Reason have taken place, which reflect Disgrace and Dishonor upon us, and the same Irregularities have taken Place among Officers of inferior Rank . . . The Grievance has become intolerable both to them and us. Unprecedented and surprising Promotions are frequently taking Place in favor of Persons who have never distinguished themselves as Soldiers, And who have . . . trumpited their own Praise to Congress, [and] have ventured to cross the Atlantic to seek that Bread in America."

This was true not only of Conway but of numerous foreign officers of every rank, which rank "they failed to obtain in their own Country . . . We ever wish to see Congress vested with the Power of rewarding Merit; But as this . . . is liable to be misapplied, we must consider it our Duty as Free men to take the Liberty of complaining when such Misapplications take place."

As a result of these "misapplications" many officers, the memorial noted, had become disgusted with the service, especially when foreigners were unconscionably promoted over the heads of Americans, and officers were "daily retiring from the Service," as Congress well knew, "and leaving their Places to be filled by Persons whose inexperience promises but little" for the American cause.

The memorial continued, "Our Duty as Soldiers and Citizens obliges us to inform Congress that we See Signs of the Dissolution of this Army," a peril in great measure due to a lack of sufficient competent officers, since many of this class of officers had already resigned. "We therefore . . . request Congress to appoint some Persons to inquire into the Grievances complained of; who may have the power to regulate the Rank of the Army; Call in Commissions which have been prematurely granted, to fix the Rank of the Officers upon a proper Footing; and to settle a regular Line of Promotion, not to be departed from, but in Cases of extraordinary merit, or upon great political principles."[9]

New Year's Day was scarcely a day of rest either for the army or the Commander-in-Chief. Time was too precious. Washington again urged Congress to appoint a successor to Mifflin in the "important office" of Quartermaster-General, and recommended Colonel Udny Hay, an experienced officer, for the post, a recommendation on which Congress declined to act. Nor had Alexander Scammell's appointment to the Adjutant-Generalcy received its final Congressional sanction. Without these appointments the army would continue in ferment.[10]

Turning from Congressional to field problems, on New Year's Day Washington found it necessary to strengthen the defense of the roads leading north from Philadelphia in order to keep the enemy as tightly bottled in the city as American means would permit. He requested Thomas Wharton, Jr., President of Pennsylvania, to make every possible effort to provide a constant body of at least 1,000 Militia, the men to be rotated with the others so that no man would be too long assigned to the duty. The Militia, if supported by this number, would be able to give "check to small parties" of enemy raiders, "and answer all the purposes of preventing an Intercourse between the City and Country." On General Armstrong's recommendation Washington thought "it will be absolutely necessary" to furnish the Militia with light horse in order that the

Militia might proceed with its duties more efficiently.[11]

Because of the deficiency of forage in camp and the small prospect of rectifying this lack, Washington ordered General Pulaski to remove his Light Horse from Valley Forge to Trenton, New Jersey, for the remainder of the winter. Pulaski was cautioned to beware of enemy surprises aimed at his new position, as the enemy, Washington noted, would undoubtedly soon be informed by Loyalist spies of Pulaski's change of position. Pulaski also was to prevent, if possible, British raids across the Delaware into New Jersey; and was directed to provide "safeguard to the Shipping laid up at Borden Town," to which place the major remnant of the Pennsylvania and Continental Navies had retreated to hoped-for safety.[12]

Huts Are Built

In camp as the new year opened, the hutting went on "briskly, and our Camp begins to appear like a spacious City," despite the crudeness of the huts.[13] "The North Carolinians" stationed on the bluff overlooking the Schuylkill River above Headquarters "are the most backward in their buildings, and for want of sufficient energy to exert themselves . . . will be exposed to lasting evils" unless they hurried their work.[14] Regretably also, the North Carolina troops, being unfamiliar with a northern climate, constructed their huts entirely above ground. The New England and Middle-Atlantic troops were more experienced. They pitted their huts below the level of the ground, thereby giving additional protection against the wind and cold.

Huts were sparsely furnished. The blank walls to the left and right of the entrances (there were no windows) were double-decked with crude bunks, six to a side, on which straw was thinly piled for some measure of comfort. Blankets, most of them ragged and too few for the number of men in each hut, were traded from man to man as they slept in rotation.

Each hut contained a plank table roughly split from logs. Often a single dish of wood or pewter had to suffice for each mess of a dozen men. Horn spoons and tumblers were in such short supply that they had to be loaned from mess to mess. Each soldier carried his own knife, which he used for carving what little meat was available, as well as for other purposes. Except for potatoes, vegetables failed to grace their tables and, no meat was available for the first two days of 1778. Occasionally salt herring was issued, though the fish were often in such a putrid state that the individual fish could not be handled from the barrels, but were shoveled out in a glutinous mass.[15]

Bread was frequently as scarce as meat despite the unremitting efforts of Christopher Ludwig, the German-born Baker-General, who constructed ovens in the basement of the Dewees house near Headquarters. Later, brigade ovens, crudely built on the ground, would supplement the efforts of the harassed Baker-General.[16]

Notwithstanding all the hardships, Washington attempted to retain a semblance of genteel hospitality by continuing his established custom of dining with the officers of the day. The Commander-in-Chief, however, soon discovered that this practice interfered with the duties of these officers and he therefore altered his custom to that of inviting to dinner the duty officers of the previous day. The meals were frugal. A piece of meat, some hard bread and perhaps a few potatoes provided the regular fare, washed down with a little toddy unless a bottle of Madeira had come to hand as a gift or purchase. Dessert, if any was served, usually consisted only of a plate of hickory nuts passed around the table.

Outdoors, the bitter weather continued unrelenting. Men on picket duty were observed standing on their hats to insulate their feet from the snow and cold underfoot. Many of the men's feet and hands became black with frostbite, and amputations were frequent. While on duty, men often fell asleep from exhaustion and hunger, never to awaken. Also "that delectable disease, the itch," scabies, made its rounds. Private Martin recalled that he contracted the disease "to such a degree that . . . I could scarcely lift my hands to my head," so scabrous were his arms. Fortunately, some relief could be had. His fellows "had acquaintances in the artillery and by their means we procured sulphur." The men then mixed "a sufficient quantity of brimstone [sulphur] and tallow, which was the only grease we could get, at the same time not forgetting to mix a plenty of hot whiskey toddy, making up a hot blazing fire and laying down an oxhide upon the hearth. Thus prepared . . . we began the operation by plying each other's outside with brimstone and tallow and the inside with hot whiskey sling." Happily the patients "obtained a complete victory, though it had like to have cost some of us our lives." Two of the men "were so overcome" by their exertions coupled with the effects of the warmth and whiskey "that they lay all night naked" despite the dwindling fire and creeping cold.[17] Few of the men at Valley Forge could find the ingredients for so drastic a cure, and the "itch" continued to plague many of the troops until the Medical Department could take positive measures to eradicate it.

So bad were conditions in camp that it was a pleasure by contrast for soldiers to be sent on foraging expeditions. As they progressed through the local country the foragers met with little resistance from the inhabitants, and could "take what we would from their barns, mills, corncribs or stalls, but when we came to their stables, then look out for the women." When the foragers would attempt to take their horses, the women would claim "they had no other to ride to church." The ladies pleaded that the foragers certainly would not deprive them of their only remaining conveyance to their devotions. Even when the foragers got possession of a horse, the women were known to "slip the bridle from the horse's head and then we might catch him again if we could." The women "would take no more notice of a charged bayonet than a blind horse would of a cocked pistol . . . they knew as well as we did that we would not put our threats in execution." They would only "laugh at us, and then generally ask us into their houses and treat us with as much kindness as though nothing had happened."[18]

The foragers were usually treated well by the country folk, especially the Friends or Quakers, despite the latter's antipathy to military pursuits. These country Quakers, as distinguished from Philadelphia Quakers, were usually neutral in their politics. Quakers residing nearer the city were inclined to take sides in the quarrel, and the side they generally chose was British. They preferred the *status quo* of Colonial times and were loyal to their Mother Country even though they were shocked by the actions of some of the British Army.

No real effort was made by the British high command to veil the fact that the British troops, contrary to Howe's orders, were "permitted every pleasurable indulgence." Among the extensive gambling crowd one officer "kept a pharo bank and accumulated a considerable fortune by preying on the British youth, many of whom were ruined, and obliged to sell their commissions."[19] A Hessian captain in Philadelphia boasted, "we are well supplied with all that is necessary and superfluous. Assemblies, concerts, comedies, clubs and the like make us forget that there is any war, save that it is a capital joke."[20] In contrast, at Valley Forge Washington forbade cards and dice even for simple pleasure for fear that indulgence in these games of chance might lead to gambling, quarrels and ruin for his troops.[21]

A Fortunate Capture

On January 1st an unexpected prospect of at least partially alleviating the sufferings of the American Army was reported to Washington. General Smallwood at Wilmington "upon hearing of an armed brig," the *Symetry*, belonging to the enemy, "being aground" in the Delaware River "five miles above this post, detached a strong party with two field pieces to take her. The Captain of the brig upon the first summons refused to surrender, thinking the party" of Americans "was armed only with musquetry, and prepared for defending himself; but being undeceived by two or three cannon shot, he struck" his colors.

The prisoners taken from the *Symetry*, exclusive of the crew, were "a British captain of foot, 67 privates, and about 40 women" who were wives of British officers.[22] The cargo of the vessel was of far greater consequence than the personnel since it was "the greatest prize ever taken" from the enemy; consisting of "cloth sufficient to Cloath all the Officers of the [American] Army, and Hats, Shirts, Stockings, Shoes, Boots, Spurs" and other military equipment. Among the luxuries captured were General Howe's personal silver service and "many chests" of enemy officers' private baggage.[23]

Washington, in a gentlemanly gesture, would order the release of Sir William's silver and the officers' wives and baggage, but the acquisition of the military stores was an incomparable windfall to replace dwindling American supplies. Unfortunately it caused some unexpected disturbance among the American officers and troops. Smallwood's men claimed that, as the captors, the goods or their value should accrue directly to them. Washington ruled that the goods should be transferred to Valley Forge and the clothing distributed equally among those officers of the entire army who had need of them. Smallwood's troops, considering themselves "much Injured" by the Commander-in-Chief's decision, sent a strong remonstrance to Headquarters. Nevertheless, they finally acquiesced, though grudgingly, to his decision.[24]

Differences of opinion concerning the distribution of the clothing did not cease with this acquiescence. Quarrels developed among the officers at Valley Forge as to which officers should have precedence in purchasing the captured clothing, and several discontented officers, thinking themselves slighted in the matter, threatened to resign if an equitable distribution of the clothing was not instituted.

General Duportail, the French engineer who had been entrusted with the Engineering Department, since no American officer could be found who was sufficiently versed in that aspect of military science, had commenced his plans for the defenses of Valley Forge. During the first week in January, Duportail could be seen riding about the perimeter of the camp sketching a map which he balanced on the pommel of his saddle while he surveyed the topography.

Washington frequently accompanied the French officer, the two generals consulting together by means of the interpreta-

tions of John Laurens, the Commander-in-Chief's aide, since the French engineer spoke English rather poorly, especially when technical military terms were employed. Duportail, having completed his sketches, directed the French engineers of his staff to make fair copies of his map.

The defenses would encompass the eastern perimeter of the camp (that side nearest to the enemy in Philadelphia) with a line of entrenchments flanked on the north, near the Schuylkill River, by three redoubts designed for riflemen, one unnamed in history, the others designated as Forts John and Mordecai Moore after the brothers who owned the lands whereon the forts were to be constructed. This line of entrenchments would boast an abatis of brushwood and stumps in front and a reasonably distant field of fire when the front was denuded of trees.

The right, or western flank of this gently curving line would be covered by the fortifications on Mount Joy. These would consist of an infantry redoubt named Fort Washington, cannon redans near the foot of the declivity, and rifle pits and entrenchments higher up the slopes. These entrenchments would be extended around the eastern face of Mount Joy and along the northern ridge as far as the bluffs overlooking the river a mile west of the front-line defenses, thereby forming a second, or inner line of defense.

On the east-west bluff above Sullivan's Bridge would be dug the Star Redoubt, so-called from its star-like configuration, as a defense for the bridge approaches. The river acted as the main line of defense on the north side of the camp. Unlike the Star Redoubt, the contours of the other forts would be square or rectangular. All the forts would consist of dirt walls some ten or twelve feet high, with ports for entry in the rear.

The entrenchments were to be constructed by digging a continuous zig-zag pit that followed the contour of the ground to be defended. The excavated dirt was to be thrown to the rear of the pit, away from the direction of attack, and the dirt kept in place by a series of stakes, thereby forming a parapet some four feet high behind which the troops could kneel and

FORT WASHINGTON, *on the lower southeast slope of Mount Joy, helped anchor the right flank of the inner line of defenses. Of all the forts at Valley Forge, Fort Washington is the only one nearly in its pristine state.*

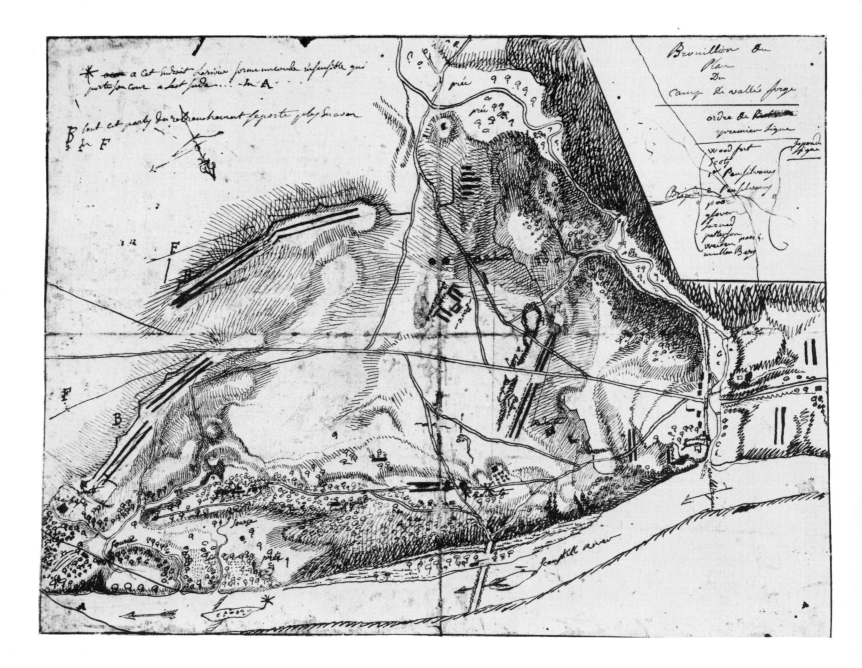

DUPORTAIL MAP OF VALLEY FORGE. *This map made by Brigadier General Louis Lebeque Duportail, French Chief of Engineers of the Continental Army. Most subsequent maps are based on Duportail's rough sketch. The original map is in the Historical Society of Pennsylvania, and reportedly was discovered in the present century in the attic of Duportail's quarters at Valley Forge.*

fire, with a dry moat in front some six feet wide and three to four feet deep.

In order to strengthen the rear line of defense where it was weakest (*i.e.,* in front of the low ridge extending north from Mount Joy) a line of abatis consisting of sharpened timbers was to be angled into the ground in the direction of an enemy attack. A few cannon would be spotted at intervals along the defenses, but the main artillery park would be centered near the middle of the encampment so that the cannon could be rushed to any threatened point.

Although the defenses of Valley Forge were never totally completed, the camp, because of the natural strength of the ground, was made reasonably secure. Only a gap in the front line, where the ground swept low, offered a possibly easy point of assault; but this low ground could be covered by entrenchments echeloned to the left and right, and any attacking

force would have received a flanking cross-fire.

On the hills immediately west of the main encampment, between the Welsh Hills and the Schuylkill River, the artificers' camp was established. Shops were built along Valley Creek opposite Headquarters. Here muskets, wagons and other implements of war were repaired. Since this ground was rugged, and faced away from the enemy in Philadelphia, there appeared scant necessity of defending that side of the camp, and no fortifications were dug. Near the artificers, and within easy communication distance of Headquarters, was the Adjutant-General's quarters. Further to the rear, on the grounds of the present Freedoms Foundation, the Commissary Department eventually set up a provision store at the residence of Frederic Geerhardt.[25] In the spring a horse yard would be instituted a few miles west of the camp, at the present Corner Stores, for the accommodation of draft horses.

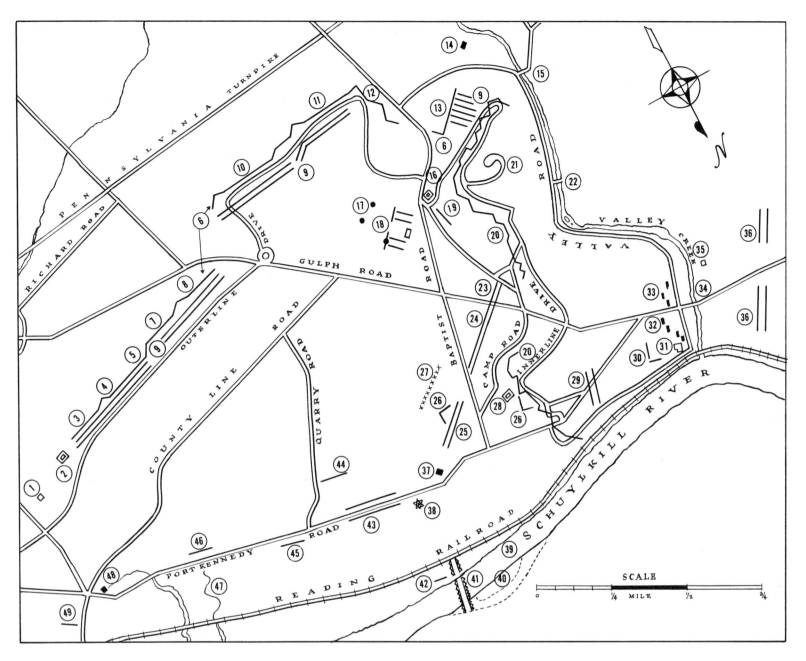

INTERPRETATION OF DUPORTAIL MAP OF VALLEY FORGE

All elements shown on the Duportail map are placed in relation to present day road system and other points of current reference. The Brigades are listed by Divisions in the order of their arrival at Valley Forge. 1. Fort John Moore, now called Fort Greene (reconstructed). 2. Fort Mordecai Moore, now called Fort Muhlenberg (reconstructed). 3. Muhlenberg's Brigade (Greene's Division). 4. Weedon's Brigade (Greene's Division). 5. Paterson's Brigade (DeKalb's Division). 6. Outer line of entrenchments. 7. Learned's Brigade (DeKalb's Division). 8. Glover's Brigade (unattached). 9. Double and multiple parallel lines represent rows of huts. 10. Poor's Brigade (unattached). 11. 1st and 2nd Pennsylvania Brigades (Wayne's Division). 12. Scott's Brigade (Lafayette's Division). 13. Woodford's Brigade (Lafayette's Division). 14. John Brown, Sr. (Gen. Knox's Quarters). 15. Ford. 16. Fort Washington. 17. Circular dots unidentified; they may have represented some of Knox's artillery. 18. Gen. Knox's Artillery Park, entrenchments, huts and fort. 19. Unidentified (possibly a rifle pit). 20. Inner line of entrenchments. 21. Mount Joy. 22. Site of the Valley (or Mount Joy) Forge burned by
British, Sept. 18, 1777. 23. Maxwell's Brigade (Stirling's Division). 24. "Late Conway's Brigade" (Stirling's Division). 25. Huntington's Brigade (recently of Gen. McDougall's Division). 26. Redan (small fortification). 27. Abatis (spiked stakes). 28. Fort Huntington. 29. McIntosh's North Carolina Brigade (unattached). 30. Commander-in-Chief's Guard, Capt. Caleb Gibbs commanding. 31. Isaac Potts (Washington's Headquarters), carriage house and miscellaneous buildings. 32. William Dewees (Bake House). 33. Tenant houses (no longer extant). 34. Ford. 35. Joseph Mann (Gen. McIntosh's Quarters; no longer extant). 36. Artificers' camp and shops, Lord Stirling commanding. 37. David Stephens (Gen. Varnum's Quarters). 38. Star Redoubt. 39. Site of Fatlands Ford. 40. Fatlands Island (no longer extant as an island). 41. Sullivan's Bridge. 42. Guard house. 43. Varnum's Brigade (recently of Gen. McDougall's Division). 44. Unidentified (possibly picket guarding Gen. Huntington's Quarters). 45. Picket post. 46. Wilsey Bodles (Provost Guard and stockade). 47. Spring. 48. Small Commissary Quarters and spring. 49. Unidentified (probably picket post).

On January 2nd, a thaw, accompanied by rain in the evening, set in permitting a few wagon loads of provisions to arrive in camp, but both the thaw and the food were only temporary alleviations. The thaw was brief and the food was soon consumed, leaving the army in no better condition than before. Bleak times continued; and dissolution of the army was again threatened even though Washington was hopefully promising the Board of War, "I shall use every exertion . . . for subsisting the Army and keeping it together."[26]

Conway Complains

General Conway still lingered in camp but made little pretense of working at his new office of Inspector-General. He consumed much of his time complaining to Congress, and to anyone who would listen, of the cool reception he had received from the Commander-in-Chief; and in composing his apologies for his recent advancement to his fellow officers. Conway's complaint to Congress brought a query from that body to the Commander-in-Chief concerning his grievances.

Washington replied, "If General Conway means by cool receptions . . . that I did not receive him in the language of a warm and cordial Friend, I readily confess the charge. I did not, nor shall I ever, receive him with warmth till I am capable of the arts of dissimulation. These I despise, and my feelings will not permit me to make professions of friendship to the man I deem an Enemy . . . At the same . . . time he was received and treated with proper respect to his Official character, and he has no cause to justify the assertion" made by him "that he could not expect any support for fulfilling the duties of his Appointment" to the Inspector-Generalcy.[27]

Conway also complained to his friends in Congress regarding the recent memorial sent to that body by the general officers. He "did not think" that he "should be the only person singled out" for the generals' resentment and criticism "without any notice being taken of other foreigners."[28] This statement was undoubtedly an oblique slap at Lafayette. Such an anathema had Conway become among the officers that Lafayette "and all other French gentlemen," (in a sense Conway's compatriots despite his Irish ancestry since he had long served in the French Army) would "hardly speak to him."[29] Nor were American-born officers inclined to be of a more social disposition towards the new Inspector-General.

As January advanced, the shadows in camp grew deeper as mortality rose. Surgeon Albigence Waldo in his diary that he was "call'd to relieve a Soldier tho't to be dying, [but] he expir'd before I reach'd the Hutt. He was an Indian . . . His memory ought to be respected . . . There the poor fellow lies not Superior now to a clod of earth—his mouth wide open —his Eyes staring."[30] How many patriots died in camp is unrecorded. The toll of deaths at or as a result of Valley Forge eventually ran to three thousand or more. Most of these dead, though stricken with disease and malnutrition at Valley Forge, actually died in the hospitals near and far. The hospitals, Dr. Benjamin Rush wrote, "robbed the United States of more citizens than the sword."[31]

Rush's description of the health conditions of the army are still poignant. "Young men," he pointed out, "under 20 years of age were subject to the greatest number of camp diseases. The Southern troops were more sickly than the northern or eastern" troops. The principal disease was typhus. "Men who came into the hospitals with pleurisies and rheumatisms soon lost the types of their original diseases, and suffered, or died" by catching the deadly typhus from their fellow patients. "Many causes combined to produce and increase this fever: such as the want of cleanliness, excessive fatigue, the ignorance or negligence" of poorly-trained hospital staffs, improper diet, the absence of sterilization of the bed-clothes used by the sick, "and the crowding of too many patients together in one hospital . . . Soldiers which were billeted in private houses generally escaped the hospital fever, and recovered sooner from all diseases."[32]

Dr. James Tilton recorded, "It would be shocking to humanity to relate the history of the general hospitals in the years 1777 and 1778." The hospitals "swallowed up at least half our army, owing to a fatal tendency in the system to throw all the sick of the army" together, no matter what their diseases. As a result "infection and consequent mortality too affecting to mention" resulted.[33]

The monotony and misery of the camp at Valley Forge were occasionally broken by little excitements. An officer of General Greene's Division, found guilty of theft, was "mounted on a horse, back foremost, without a Saddle, his Coat turn'd wrong side out, his hands tied behind him," and was summarily "drummed out of the army . . . by all the drums of the division" to which he had belonged.[34] To set an impressive example, a Virginia soldier was sentenced to be publicly hanged for desertion. The gallows that would serve throughout the winter and spring for such offenses were constructed on the low hill overlooking the Grand Parade from the south, in full view of most of the army.

"Battle of the Kegs"

On January 5th the enemy in Philadelphia discovered their own brief excitement, the so-called "Battle of the Kegs." Several civilian youths, observing a number of rather strange-looking kegs floating down the Delaware River above the city, rowed out to make a closer inspection of the peculiar contraptions. The youths soon regretted their hasty action since one of the kegs, on being physically examined, exploded, sinking their boat and injuring the youths. The explosion alerted the British and, as the kegs drifted down to the vicinity of the city, rumor spread fast that each keg contained an American soldier fully armed to attack the city. The shipping and waterfront batteries commenced playing their guns on the mysterious contrivances, which exploded when hit.

The kegs proved to be an invention of Asa Bushnell, who in 1776 had invented an unsuccessful submarine device designed to blow up the enemy shipping in New York Harbor, and who intended in this instance to damage or sink the British vessels in the Delaware. Many of the explosive devices had been manufactured in the cooper shop of the patriot, Joseph Borden, at Bordentown. The kegs had been set afloat on the first day of the year, but the ice in the river and the changing tides had prevented the deadly inventions from arriving at Philadelphia for four days.

Although the keg attack proved unsuccessful, the attempt afforded Americans considerable merriment at British expense. Francis Hopkinson, a Signer of the Declaration of Independence and a son-in-law of Joseph Borden, composed a famous satirical poem in which he dubbed the action by its forever-after title, "The Battle of the Kegs."

The *New Jersey Gazette* sneered, "The city [Philadelphia]

has lately been entertained with a most astonishing instance of the activity, bravery and military skill of the royal navy of Great-Britain . . . The shipping in the harbour, and all the wharves of the city were fully manned — The battle begun, and it was surprising to behold the incessant blaze that was kept up against the enemy, the kegs . . . From the *Roebuck* and other ships of war, whole broadsides were poured into the Delaware. In short, not a wandering chip, stick or drift log but felt the vigour of British arms. The action began about sun-rise, and would have been compleated with great success by noon, had not an old market woman [this part of the tale was wholly fictitious] coming down the river with provisions, unfortunately let a small keg of butter fall over-board, which, as it was then ebb, floated down to the scene of action and at sight of this unexpected reinforcement of the enemy, the battle was renewed with fresh fury—the firing was incessant till evening closed the affair. The kegs were either totally demolished or obliged to fly . . . It is said that His Excellency, Lord Howe, has dispatched a swift sailing packet with an account of this victory to the Court of London."[35]

Had the tale of the admiral's dispatching a packet to London been true, it is doubtful that the British Court, much as it grasped hungrily at good news, would have exhibited much gratification. With the January re-opening of Parliament that body as well as the Court and Ministry were engrossed in the distasteful task of discussing the conciliatory terms that Britain might offer the Americans in an effort to prevent a possible Franco-American alliance.

Also on the agenda of the Parliamentary discussions was the unilateral action to which the Ministry had taken arbitrary recourse during the Parliamentary recess for the Christmas and New Year Holidays in an effort to bolster the British military forces in the event that a compromise with the Colonies proved unsuccessful. The loss of numerous trained troops at Saratoga in the previous fall had proved costly.

In an effort to replace these troops, since the American Congress appeared disinclined to return them to England as stipulated in the Saratoga Convention, and since voluntary enlistments had almost ceased, the Ministry resorted to public subscriptions for bounty money to induce enlistments. The Ministry's appeal for money had proved reasonably successful in Scotland despite the general poverty in that country. On the contrary, utter refusal had come from Ireland and varying results, mostly disappointing, were experienced in England despite ministerial pleas that a war with France might soon be imminent.

The Whig opposition in Parliament, led by Fox, Burke, Barré and others, when informed of the Ministry's action, condemned the procedure as unconstitutional. Parliament, not the Ministry, the Opposition asserted, had the sole right to raise and finance troops. The Ministry's presumption, therefore, was an infringement on the rights of Parliament and the British people, whom Parliament legally represented. A similar ministerial presumption, the Opposition noted, had caused the present rebellion in America and threatened the loss of the American Colonies. Despite Whig condemnation, the ministerial action was sanctioned by the Tory majority in Parliament.

Britain, like America, was experiencing both military and political troubles. Most of Britain's professional army was stationed overseas and the prospect of reinforcements for these troops was slim. Few trained troops were in England to defend the nation if France allied herself with America.

CHAPTER IV

MID-WINTER REQUIEM

Deplorable Camp Conditions

By the middle of January most of the huts at Valley Forge were finished, or as finished as they ever would be. The improvisations resulting from the diversity of building materials were undoubtedly startling to behold. Even the Potts-Dewees forge, though burned by the British in September, was raided for whatever remnants of the buildings might prove of use. Colonel Dewees, viewing the stripped state of the forge, complained to Headquarters "that the remains of his buildings are likely to be destroy'd by this Army."

Washington, therefore, positively forbade "the least Injury to be done to the walls & chimnies of Colo. Dewees' buildings, and as divers Iron plates" used to protect the forge flooring from damage by sparks "have been taken from them, the Commanding Officers" of regiments were to investigate every regimental hut and report the whereabouts of the plates that they might "be restored when demanded."[1] The plates made excellent doorsteps for huts. This inspection was also ordered as setting a precedent for the officers to see that the camp was kept clean by burying or burning all offal and other putrescent matter "once a week."[2]

Daily, the need for clothing became more evident. The clergy of every denomination in Pennsylvania, except the known pro-British members of the Church of England, were asked to urge their congregations to surrender to the army all the "woollens and linens" that could be spared. These were especially needed "for the sick soldiers in the hospitals."[3] Many

POTTS-DEWEES FORGE. *The long-lost Valley (originally Mount Joy) Forge. Due to the silting of Valley Creek, the site of the forge had been lost for more than a century. Having been re-discovered in 1929, it was dug out from under 11 feet of silt. This was the forge belonging to Isaac Potts and William Dewees that was burned by the British, September 18, 1777. The forge stood between Mount Joy and Valley Forge Mountain. The photograph shows the north wall during excavation. The building was constructed of stone without mortar binder.*

of the clergy immediately set about the business; but few parishioners had clothing to spare.

In contrast, a number of persons in the vicinity of Philadelphia inclined to the patriot cause but apparently embittered by the enemy capture of the city and the present inactivity of the American Army, were reported to be murmuring "against the weak conduct of General Washington." They asserted that "his slackness and remissness in the army are so conspicuous that general languor" was bound to ensue.[4] These critics obviously knew little how far the American Commander-in-Chief was "from having so considerable an army as all Europe and a great part of America believe he has."

If the facts were more widely known, Baron DeKalb acknowledged to Henry Laurens, the picture would undoubtedly have a debilitating effect on public morale, but maintained that Washington "does more every day than could be expected from any general in the world, in the same circumstances." DeKalb thought Washington "the only proper person," because of Washington's "natural and acquired capacity, his bravery, good sense, uprightness and honesty to keep up the spirits of the army and people."[5]

Despite his "natural and acquired capacity," Washington's most unremitting efforts might come to nothing without an adequate army. Fortunately Congress had at last acceded to the Commander-in-Chief's frequent requests that a committee from Congress or the Board of War proceed to camp to discuss the re-organization of the army. Initially Congress appointed to the Committee on Conference, as the committee came to be called, three members from each of the above-mentioned bodies, but two of the three Board of War appointees begged to be excused because of the press of regular business. From its own body, Congress appointed Francis Dana as Chairman, Joseph Reed and Nathaniel Folsom. Folsom was also a member of the Board of War, and was the only member to accede to his appointment.

Congress ordered the truncated Committee "to repair to General Washington's headquarters as soon as may be, and, in concert with him, to form and execute a plan for reducing the number of battalions" or regiments in the army in order to increase the strength of the individual regiments, "reporting to Congress the names and ranks of such officers of merit" who would be dispossessed of their commands so that these officers might be provided with other assignments or honorably discharged from service. The Committee was also directed "to recommend to Congress the necessary appointments of general officers" in order that Congress might satisfy Washington's recent complaint that the army was in dire need of more officers of that rank.

The Committee was empowered "to remove officers in the civil departments of the army for misconduct, negligence, or incompetency, and to appoint others in their room, till the pleasure of Congress can be known; to remove all just causes of complaint relative to rank" and seniority among the officers; "to determine and report . . . to Congress their opinion of the necessary reinforcements for the army and the best mode of obtaining them; to report such alterations as they shall deem expedient in the regulations of the several departments of the army, and, in general, to adopt such other measures as they shall judge necessary for introducing economy and promoting discipline and good morals in the army."[6] Washington must have received the news of the appointment of the Committee and Congress' directive with relief; and, while awaiting the arrival of the Committee, began a written memorial for the Committee's guidance.

In a further effort to expedite the reorganization of the army, Washington directed General Knox to proceed to Boston. Knox had long solicited this assignment not only for military considerations but also to be reunited, during the break in field operations, with his wife, Lucy, and his new-born child. Militarily, Knox's principal duty in Massachusetts would be to resurrect the Artillery Department in preparation for the expected spring campaign.

Knox's orders read, "As the short inlistment of the Artificers have been, and still may be, productive of bad consequences you are to inlist for the War, or during the pleasure of Congress, all the different Artillery Artificers necessary to carry on the different branches of work" in the manufacturing and repairing of equipment at Carlisle, Pennsylvania, and Springfield, Massachusetts, the two principal artillery arsenals. Knox was also "authorized to procure and collect such Ordnance Stores as shall be wanted for the next Campaign, and to form Magazines of fixed Ammunition, at such places as shall be pointed out to you."[7]

General Muhlenberg, as he too had long requested, was permitted to leave the army on temporary furlough, but for personal reasons only. Although a Pennsylvanian born (his parents still lived at Trappe, a few miles north of Valley Forge), Muhlenberg had long resided at Woodstock in Virginia's Shenandoah Valley, to which place he proceeded in order to attend to his long neglected private concerns.

Sickness and Death

Not only the army but also the hospitals were in need of considerable reorganization. A swift expansion of the facilities of this department was one of the army's principal concerns, since there was never adequate space to care for the constantly increasing number of patients. All winter long the hospitals, near and far, were taxed beyond their limits.

THE HOME OF JOHN BROWN, SR., *was occupied by Gen. Knox as his quarters. Except for the two additions to the right, the house remains much in its original state.*

24

COLONIAL SCHOOLHOUSE, *measuring only 32 x 21 feet. This building was used as a hospital by the Continental Army. The interior has been restored as an early schoolhouse.*

established, there were also established little cemeteries, the sites mostly unmarked if cemeteries were not already extant.

In camp, temporary log hospitals were erected to shelter the sick until the patients could be transferred to better facilities. The officers commanding brigades were ordered "to fix on some suitable place" to the rear of each brigade "where hospitals may be erected, one for the sick of each Brigade."[11] These hospitals were only slightly more pretentious than the huts in which the army was housed. Washington directed that their dimensions should be "15 feet wide & 25 long, in the clear and the Story at least nine feet high; to be covered with boards or shingles only, without any dirt."

Unlike the soldiers' huts, a window was to be made "on each side" so that air could be admitted when weather permitted, and so that natural light could aid the surgeon's work. A single fireplace and chimney "at one end" would serve to heat the premises. The men were falling sick so rapidly that four days after issuing the initial order for the construction of these hospitals, Washington found it necessary to direct "two such hospitals are to be made for each brigade," rather than one only, and placed "as near the center" of each brigade "as may be," and, against the spread of infection to the healthy troops, "not more than three nor less than one hundred yards" from the brigade.[12]

Steuben Reaches America

On January 8th, Washington received a letter from Portsmouth, New Hampshire, announcing the arrival in America of Baron Friedrich Wilhelm Augustus Henry Ferdinand von Steuben, a German officer who had formerly served under Frederick the Great of Prussia. The announcement was accompanied by a letter from Steuben himself. Washington immediately replied: "I yesterday received the Honor of yours . . . inclosing the Copy of a Letter from Messrs. Franklin and Deane," two of the three plenipotentiaries in France, who had recommended Steuben's services to the American cause.

After inviting Steuben to proceed to Valley Forge "as soon as it is convenient" Washington notified the Prussian officer, "as it will lay solely with Congress to make a suitable provision for you in the American Army, you will be under the necessity of prolonging your Journey" by going to Congress at York "in order to lay before them . . . the testimonials which you bear of your former Service" in Europe. "I return you my thanks for the polite manner in which you express your desire of serving under me."[13]

Congress had also received notice of Steuben's arrival, but was not so prompt in acknowledging the information. In doing so, Congress resolved "that the president, present the thanks of Congress, in behalf of these United States, to the Baron Steuben . . . and inform him, that Congress cheerfully accept of his service as a volunteer . . . and wish him to repair to General Washington's quarters as soon as convenient."[14]

The expected arrival in camp of the Committee on Conference, as well as that of Baron von Steuben, bode well for the future of the army, but more immediate measures were needed for the sustenance of the unpaid and ill-supplied troops. Congress, having witnessed the effects of issuing quantities of paper currency, sought other means to avoid a financial debacle. They resolved "That ten millions of dollars be borrowed" from the patriot citizens "on the credit of the United States at an annual interest of six percent and that loan office certificates . . . be

On one occasion seven hundred patients were crowded into the House of the Single Brethren of the Bethlehem Moravians, a building that could at its comfortable best hold no more than four hundred. Even though this hospital was probably the best of the lot, and the medical staff and the Brethren exerted every effort to alleviate and cure the suffering patients, deaths occurred constantly. The Strangers' (Non-Moravians) Row in the little Moravian Cemetery was rapidly filled with the bodies of patients and doctors alike. "Of the eleven junior surgeons and mates ten took the infection," from which three died and another narrowly escaped death.[8]

Dr. James Tilton, on visiting the hospital at Bethlehem, took the occasion to "propose a competition" between the various hospitals "not whose hospital had done the most good but whose hospital had done the most mischief."[9]

Constant complaints reached the Commander-in-Chief of the excessive number of patients sent to the hospitals; and he was informed that no more men could be accommodated. Washington was also notified that the distance the weaker patients had to travel in jolting wagons had a bad effect on their recovery. In an effort to solve this problem temporarily, Washington ordered the requisition of every available barn, church and meeting house within the vicinity of camp for the accommodation of the surplus sick. The Lutheran Zion and German Reformed Churches beyond French Creek to the west, as well as other churches belonging to these and similar sects, were relinquished to the army by their congregations.

The requisition of some of the Quaker Meeting Houses met with opposition. The Uwchlan Meeting House in Chester County was an example of Quaker reluctance to surrender their places of worship. "The key of the Meeting House was demanded by some of the physicians of the Continental Army in order to convert the same into a hospital for their sick soldiers. The Friend who had the care of the house refusing to deliver it up, forcible entry was made into the house and stable."[10]

The Red Lion Tavern at the same location also became a hospital. At each place where these local hospitals were forthwith" issued for that purpose.[15] Few citizens were willing to risk what little cash they possessed and the Congressional solicitation of funds proved rather futile. As a result, Congress was forced to resume issuing bills of credit, thereby further depreciating the authorized currency.

Although Congress had brought a printing press from Philadelphia to York which could be used for printing the loan certificates and other official publications, type was in short supply. On orders from Congress, General Armstrong and the Pennsylvania Militia had removed the type from Philadelphia together with the official Journals of Congress, and had hidden them in the country to prevent their capture. Congress now found it necessary to have the type and Journals brought to York since Congressional business was hampered without them. At its request, Washington attempted to recover both the type and the Journals, and on January 9th reported that he had "dispatched a Gentleman well acquainted with the ground and Inhabitants in the vicinity where the Journals of Congress" and perhaps the type "were said to be deposited, in order to make inquiry concerning them."

The Commander-in-Chief's agent happily found the Journals "without difficulty, and they will be sent forward to York under the Escort of Colo. Hartley's Regiment" of Pennsylvanians, who would remain at York as a Congressional guard. "The search for the Types," Washington informed Congress, "was not attended with equal Success; all that could be discover'd respecting them was, that the person who had possession" of the Journals "said he suspected the Types were concealed in some interior part of the Country."[16]

Congress, therefore, was dependent for printing on the private presses of Hall and Sellers, who printed the money as well as other necessary items including the displaced *Pennsylvania Gazette,* and of John Dunlap who, having fled from Philadelphia with his press, resumed operations in York. Dunlap did extensive printing for both Congress and the Pennsylvania authorities, which business he sandwiched between continued publication of his patriotic newspaper, *The Pennsylvania Packet.* Dunlap made certain that his newspaper continued before the public, thus counteracting the releases of the Loyalist *Pennsylvania Ledger* which had commenced supporting the enemy cause in Philadelphia shortly after the fall of the city.

Committee on Conference

The Committee on Conference arrived at Valley Forge from York the second week in January and took up residence at Moore Hall some three miles west of Headquarters on the road to Pottsgrove. Congressman John Harvie had been added to the little group of Francis Dana, Joseph Reed and Nathaniel Folsom. With only four members initially present, the Committee would prove short-handed for the amount of business to be transacted, and Charles Carroll of Maryland and Gouverneur Morris of New York would soon be added to its membership. Carroll, however, would be called home to the bedside of his ailing wife prior to proceeding to Valley Forge, and would never attend any Committee meetings.

The presence of the Committee at Valley Forge, plus the extended absence of Carroll, further denuded Congress of its working members. Rarely during this fateful period of the war was Congress able to assemble a quorum. Nor was Congress the vibrant body of men it had been in 1776 at the time of the Declaration of Independence. The Congress at York

was often pervaded by inertia, debilitated by absenteeism, and torn by petty factions. Congressman Philip Livingston, noting the general rot that seemed to pervade Congress and the various national departments, civil and military, was "so discouraged by our public mismanagement, and the additional load of business thrown upon me by the villainy of those" persons who were pursuing personal and factional interests "that I almost sink under it."[17]

Not only was Congress too weak to supervise adequately the course of events, but the military and civil departments, especially the Commissary, were in many instances in the hands of sharpers and swindlers who cheated the army and government, and concentrated on making their private fortunes.

The fall of a foot of snow on January 11th prevented Washington from personally consulting with the Committee on Conference. Nevertheless, he sent the Committee a preliminary report on the present state of the army. On the credit side, more clothing for the New England troops was now on its way to camp. Washington had ordered the clothing convoy routed across the Delaware River through Easton to prevent its possible capture by enemy raiders from Philadelphia. Loyalist spies constantly kept Howe informed of American efforts to supply the troops at Valley Forge. In case the convoy had already crossed the Delaware south of Easton, Washington ordered it to "strike up into the country, and take a circuitous route to camp."[18]

With the exception of the New Englanders and Virginians, Washington informed the Committee, the troops would continue ragged unless some drastic measures were instituted. Food supplies also remained in a critical state despite the foragers who constantly scoured the countryside. The "camp itch" continued to plague the army, despite the fact that the Commander-in-Chief had ordered the "collecting of all dirty tallow . . . for the purpose of making soft soap" with which the troops could cleanse themselves, thereby keeping the disease under some control until the Medical Department could institute measures to rid the army of the disease entirely.[19] Unfortunately the Medical Department continued in a rather disrupted state, causing Washington to suggest to Dr. Benjamin Rush, the Physician-General, that "no time ought to be lost in amending" the whole department.[20]

On the whole, Washington noted to the Committee, matters could be little worse than they were without causing an instant dissolution of the army — what army indeed remained. Although the Muster Rolls at the beginning of the year had listed some 20,000 men, both sick and well, scarcely 5,000 at Valley Forge remained fit enough for duty to answer the morning and evening roll calls. In view of this situation, John Laurens, Washington's aide, had suggested to his father, the President of Congress, that a corps of Negro slaves should be freed and recruited into American service.[21]

Now that the huts were mostly finished, the small numbers of the army made it more imperative than ever to press the construction of the defenses against a possible enemy attack. "The works marked out by the Engineers for the defence of the camp," General Orders of January 15th read, "are to be executed with all possible dispatch." Generals Greene, Stirling and Lafayette were directed "to consult with Genl. [Du] Portail on the proper means and number of men necessary to execute the works."[22]

The principal outposts facing the enemy, those at The Gulph and Radnor, were augmented to regimental size. A system of "sentry trees" was also put into effect. For miles between Valley Forge and the approaches to the enemy-occupied city, the cresting branches of overtopping trees were lopped off and platforms built from which the American sentries could watch almost as far as Philadelphia for any enemy march, and signal from tree to tree all the way back to the parent sentry station atop Mount Joy in the midst of the camp.

Completion of Bridge

Before the end of January, despite the constant delays, General Sullivan had completed his bridge across the Schuylkill. Sullivan invited the Commander-in-Chief and other officers to christen the bridge by being the first persons to walk across it officially. Washington and his officers beheld a series of nine stone-filled rectangular log coffers or piers between which rough log stringers had been laid. The flooring, made of split saplings, had been pegged at right angles to the stringers with wooden dowels in lieu of unobtainable spikes. The rounded sides of the saplings were turned upwards, thereby affording a bumpy but effective roadway. Railings hedged the sides of the bridge against possible accidents. On each railing post the soldiers had carved the name of a general officer of the army, the center posts being honored with that of General Washington.

Actually the bridge was a double structure: the principal bridge, 228 paces long, spanned the river proper, while a secondary structure carried the road across a small neck of swampland that separated the south shore of the river from the mainland. A local citizen, noting that the underside of the bridge was only six feet above low water-level, warned Sullivan that the bridge would probably be endangered by the spring ice-floods. Sullivan scoffed profanely at the prognostication.[23] Fortunately the predicted catastrophe did not result from the spring thaws of 1778, but the following year the bridge was mostly carried away.[24]

Although completion of the bridge presented a rapid access to the north side of the Schuylkill by which supplies could be brought into camp, and better communication could be established with the Pennsylvania Militia, under Brig. Gen. John Lacey who had succeeded the furloughed Brig. Gen. Potter, the opening of the bridge posed a new problem to the defense of Valley Forge. The Ridge Road and the Germantown Pike to the north could easily be traversed by any sudden enemy thrust. These highways and the connecting by-roads led directly to the bridge and the American camp. The Star Redoubt was planned and constructed by Duportail to guard the southern approach to the bridge. On the north side of the river a system of road barricades was erected to cover the river approaches from that direction. Pawling's Ford and Egypt Roads were both heavily barricaded, and barricades manned.

The completion of the bridge scarcely eased the sufferings in camp. The lack of transportation for supplies made the bridge at first rather useless as a route for supplying the troops. The few wagons that had started from up-country for camp had mostly either broken down because of the physical difficulties encountered on the roads, or had been simply abandoned by the teamsters who had refused to struggle further through snow-drifted and rutted roads.

The routine of camp life was only slightly disturbed on January 18th by a report from the Sugartown Road, some miles south of Valley Forge, that an enemy raiding party of about one hundred and thirty dragoons under the command of Banastre Tarleton had attacked a small outpost commanded by Captain Henry, "Lighthorse Harry," Lee of the American Light Dragoons. By "the assistance of a guide" of Loyalist inclination "who conducted them through bye roads," by which precaution the enemy "avoided the videts" (videttes or mounted sentinels stationed in advance of the pickets) "surrounded the house where Capt. Lee lay so suddenly that he had scarcely time to bolt the doors."

Lee's small force consisted only of the visiting Major John Jameson, also of the 1st Continental Dragoons, "who lodged with him that night, Lieutenant [William] Lindsay and five private troopers." The remainder of Lee's outpost force was quartered "in a neighboring house," and too distant to be of aid. The enemy immediately began a smart firing, and the American defenders "returned the fire from the windows with spirit, and, by showing themselves at different places, made as great an appearance of numbers as possible."[25]

"Capt. Delancy, who commanded the enemy's advance guard, led it on bravely 'till he arrived under cover of the eaves, while the main body" of British attackers "kept up a constant fire from a distance." Tarleton himself reportedly joined in the "repeated efforts" the British "made to enter the house," and was the target of a pistol aimed at close range that refused to fire.

Lee and his companions, though both Major Jameson and Lieutenant Lindsay were slightly wounded, finally repulsed the assault, whereupon the enemy dragoons "made an attempt to seize the horses which were in the stable." They were again driven off by the "well directed constant fire" of the defenders.[26] With great presence of mind Lee had disheartened the attackers by loudly calling out to the enemy to surrender and feigning "that Morgan's infantry was coming up," and would surely "cut them to pieces." The sharp-shooting reputation of Morgan's frontiersmen was well known to the British, and Lee undoubtedly calculated that Morgan's supposed presence would shake enemy hearts.

With their attack a failure, and fearing that the sound of the firing would summon other American troops to the scene, Tarleton's force soon "turned tail & made for Philadelphia."[27] The attack had lasted some twenty-five minutes from start to finish. "The loss of the enemy" the Americans estimated at "one commissioned officer and three or four privates" at least wounded.[28] No enemy dead were found. The American losses, besides the wounding of Jameson and Lindsay, were reported as five videttes missing and probably captured.

By this action Captain Lee, the *New Jersey Gazette* proclaimed, had "added another cubit to his fame."[29] On the day following the fight, Washington, in General Orders, commended Lee and his men and Major Jameson for their stubborn defense and extended his "warmest thanks" to the participants "for the Victory" they had achieved over almost insurmountable odds.[30] Washington also posted a private letter to Lee in the same vein.

The British repulse had been little in keeping with the celebration of the queen's birthday on the same day in Philadelphia, where there had been a considerable "firing of Guns from ye shipping, and the colors flying" in honor of Queen Charlotte, wife of George III.[31] Nor could the comedy *No One's Enemy But His Own* or the farce *The Deuce Is In Him,* both played at the Fourth Street Theater to conclude the day-long celebration, nor the memory of the parades and pomp of the day erase British consciousness that Tarleton's repulse was only another evidence that the American Army was still in existence. The circumscribed British position in Philadelphia was not exactly to be envied, a fact that was made doubly evident by the report that scurvy resulting from a lack of fresh foodstuffs had been discovered among the Hessian troops.[32]

In the same General Orders which commended Henry Lee and his men, Washington directed that "the General Officers commanding Brigades are desir'd to meet at General Sullivan's Quarters" on the following day "in order to consider the expediency of opening a publick Market" in or near the camp in an effort to induce the local farmers to market their produce to the troops, thereby eliminating forceful requisitions.

The officers were to take into consideration "the proper Places & days of holding markets, the regulations and proper guards necessary to preserve good order, [and] the prices proper to be offered upon each article in the Settlement of which they Should endeavor to consult Some of the most intelligent Country men."[33] Originally the market was small. Nevertheless, since the local farmers were wary of having their products requisitioned for the army and paid for with certificates that might in the end prove utterly worthless, there was a gradual acceptance of the market idea.

Proposed Attack on Canada

Toward the end of January, rumor reached Headquarters at Valley Forge that the Board of War was planning an attack against Canada similar to the expedition of 1775-6. The Board, it was said, hoped that a renewed attack on Britain's dominions north of the United States might produce happier results than the ill-fated earlier campaign. The Board privately assured Lafayette that the command of the expedition would be his, an offer that had a double attraction, since Lafayette's desire for action would be satisfied, and a Frenchman in command of the expedition might favorably influence the sympathies of the French-Canadians. Lafayette also might be weened from his close allegiance to Washington. The latter consideration was most important as far as the Gates-Mifflin-Conway clique was concerned. Gates was still being proposed by certain highly placed persons as a replacement for Washington.

Despite Lafayette's publicly expressed aversion to Conway, the Board of War, with Gates at its head, nominated Conway as second in command of the expedition, from which post Conway would be in a position to keep his friends on the Board well informed of Lafayette's actions. In an effort to insure Lafayette's acceptance of the appointment, the Board proposed that the force given to him should be largely officered by Frenchmen, including those French officers who were presently petitioning Congress for commissions. Lafayette, the Board was aware, was extremely interested that these officers, having crossed the ocean at their own expense with expectations of rank and glory, should receive the blessings of Congress.

Lafayette notified Washington of the proffered command, but expressed some disinclination toward leaving Valley Forge not only because he suspected that the Board had, as an ulterior motive, his segregation from Washington, but also because of the method of his appointment. Lafayette's official orders to proceed to Albany, New York, immediately, which place would be the assembly point for the expedition, though directed to Headquarters, bore the Frenchman's, not Washington's name, an obvious breach of military rule and courtesy. Washington handed the packet to Lafayette. Upon opening the orders,

Lafayette discussed with Washington whether he should accept the command. The Commander-in-Chief expressed no opinion, thereby leaving the decision to Lafayette.

At Lafayette's request, a meeting was held with the Committee on Conference; and it was agreed that Lafayette should proceed to York in order to confer with Congress and "find out the extent of their views in sending forces into Canada." The Board of War had informed Lafayette that his explicit orders would await him at Albany in the hands of Conway, but Lafayette had no desire that "the secret of" the Board's "intentions" should be kept from him until he had committed himself to an acceptance of the command.[34]

Lafayette arrived at York on January 30th only to find that Conway had already left for Albany. Having been told of Lafayette's impending visit to York, Conway had left Lafayette's written instructions in the hands of the Board of War. On his arrival at York, Lafayette conferred privately with the President of Congress, Laurens, who fully agreed with Lafayette that Conway was not the best man to act as second in command since Conway represented a factional interest opposed to the Commander-in-Chief.

On the following day Lafayette addressed an official letter to Congress in which he emphasized his desire that, contrary to the apparent wishes of the Board of War, the proposed expedition should not be considered as an entirely separate command but simply as a detachment acting under the direct supervision of General Washington. Further, Lafayette took the occasion to criticize the procedure by which he had received his orders directly from the Board of War rather than through the hands of the Commander-in-Chief.

Lafayette's letter requested that as many French officers as possible should be attached to the expedition, thereby satisfying their demands for employment. More importantly, the presence of these officers might "be of some weight" in influencing France to throw in her lot with the Americans. So as to allay any prejudices Americans might feel towards an all-too-French aspect to the expedition, Lafayette expressed his feeling that an American-born officer rather than Conway should be appointed as second in command. Lafayette had in mind Alexander McDougall, who already commanded the American forces on the Hudson; but discovering that McDougall was physically indisposed and that there was very little American objection to foreign officers commanding the expedition, he requested that his long-time friend DeKalb be substituted for Conway. In closing his letter, Lafayette informed Congress that he was prepared to refuse the proposed command unless the conditions he set were met.

That evening Lafayette was interviewed by the Board of War and was promised every assistance. Lafayette reiterated the demands he had sent to Congress, and threatened, if they were ignored, not only to decline the appointment but to return to France. Such a desertion of the American cause would be a distinct blow to American hopes of French help.

Lafayette probably had little intention of implementing the latter part of his threat, but the mere threat would undoubtedly have the effect of bringing the Board around to his point of view. The Board begged for time to consider its decision. Only one night's consideration was necessary. The members agreed to recommend McDougall, if he was physically able, or DeKalb as second in command; but altered Lafayette's original instructions from that of a full-scale invasion of Canada to a "mere incursion or ravage."

Lafayette returned to Valley Forge where Washington advised him to accept the command. He left immediately for Albany with Washington's assurance that since McDougall's "late severe illness and present feeble state," would not permit him "to proceed on the intended incursion into Canada, Baron DeKalb will follow" agreeable to Lafayette's expressed "wish and the direction of Congress."[35] Conway was totally excluded from the expedition.

On January 28th the Committee on Conference held its first official meeting with Washington at Moore Hall. The Commander-in-Chief gave a description of the conditions and needs of the army. He informed the Committee that there were at present only ninety head of beef cattle in camp for the entire army, and that there was scant prospect at present of acquiring more. The Committee had already seen for itself the pitiful state of the troops. The Commander-in-Chief notified the Committee that he was in the process of putting the finishing touches to a definitive memorandum concerning the much-needed reorganization of the army. Although the memorial was intended for Congress as a whole, Washington promised to present the paper for the Committee's appraisal on the following day. On its part the Committee promised to plead with Congress to engage in more concrete efforts to bring relief to the army.

On the credit side Washington was able to notify the Committee that there was every prospect that Matthew Clarkson would accept his recent appointment as Auditor-General of the army. In fact, though it was as yet unknown to the Commander-in-Chief, Clarkson had accepted the appointment on that very day.[36]

Proposals for Army's Reorganization

On January 29th Washington submitted his memorandum on the reorganization of the army for the Committee's perusal. "The numerous defects in our present military establishment," the memorial commenced, "rendering many reformations and many new arrangements absolutely necessary . . . I shall begin with a few reflections," a somewhat inaccurate preamble since Washington immediately plunged into a long and definitive dissertation that consumed numerous pages.

Concerning "a half pay and pensionary establishment" for the officers, Washington was "earnest in recommending this measure, because I know it is the general wish and expectation" of the officers, and "many Officers whom . . . we should wish to retain in the service are only waiting to see whether something of this kind will or will not take place to be determined in their resolutions either of staying in, or quitting it immediately." The Commander-in-Chief was aware that the expense "will be a capital objection to it, but to this I oppose the necessity. The Officers are now discontented with their situation."

As for "completing the regiments and altering their establishment" by reducing their number, Washington noted "the necessity of the first is too self evident to need illustration or proof, and I shall therefore only . . . offer some reflections on the mode. Voluntary inlistments seem to be totally out of the question; all the allurements of the most exorbitant bounties and every other inducement that could be thought of, have been tried in vain." As to drafting for the whole period of the war, or for a term of years, this would probably meet only with general bitterness. "I would propose an annual draft of men, without officers," the latter of whom there was perhaps a satisfactory number, "to serve 'till the first day of January in each year;

that on or before the first day of October preceeding" the former date "these drafted Men should be called upon to reinlist for the succeeding year; and as an incitement to doing it . . . a bounty of twenty-five dollars should be offered."

The men who failed to re-enlist would be replaced by new draftees called to the colors on the following January 1st. While on the subject of increasing the number of troops to their full complement, Washington suggested the need of increasing the cavalry corps, an arm of the service in which the Americans had always been numerically deficient.

Concerning the size of the army, including the troops on the Hudson River, Washington reported that there were at present ninety-seven battalions, or regiments in the field, but that all were considerably undermanned. For instance at Valley Forge only 572 men out of 1,072 in the nine North Carolina regiments had been returned fit for duty as of December 31st, and the situation of these regiments had become even more debilitated as January progressed. The North Carolina regiments therefore should certainly be reduced in number in order that each regiment might be increased to its full regimental strength.

Washington hoped that Virginia, rather than reducing the number of her battalions, would fill her present regiments with a proper number of men by means of a state draft. Although the present Maryland contingents could be termed numerically satisfactory in both regiments and numbers of men, the Commander-in-Chief hoped that Delaware, whose troops were integrated with the Marylanders, might furnish an extra regiment. Washington was not certain that Pennsylvania could complete her 13 regiments because of "intestine divisions" within the state as a double result of internal political quarrels and the prevalence of Loyalists and unwarlike Quakers in the eastern part of the state. As for New Jersey, New York, Connecticut, Rhode Island, Massachusetts and New Hampshire, Washington had "reason to hope their exertions" in producing recruits and draftees "will keep pace with their abilities."

By spring, or at least by summer, the Commander-in-Chief hoped to have 80 full regiments, properly officered and equipped, to replace the 97 ragged battalions now on hand, and that "the total amount of them if complete" would number "40,320 rank and file" a hope that would never be realized. "Upon this number of battalions" he expected to be able to base his "arrangements" for the new army. Whether or not the army was revised on a regimental scale, Washington's brigade and divisional plans demanded an increase in general officers of both major-general and brigadier ranks.

This last assertion directed the Commander-in-Chief's attention to the subject of army rank. "No error can be more pernicious," he cautioned, "than that of distribution of rank . . . with too prodigal a hand . . . It lessens the value and splendor" of commissions and "breeds jealousies and animosities" among the officers. Congress, the Commander-in-Chief could hope, would take this caution to heart thereafter.

On the subject of promotions, which subject was intimately bound to that of rank, Washington noted that "irregular promotions have also been a pregnant source of uneasiness, discord and perplexity in this army. They have been the cause of numerous bickerings and resignations among the officers . . . This shows how indispensibly necessary it is to have some settled rule of promotion." While supreme merit might warrant unusual promotions, and might serve to arouse a spirit of emulation among the officers, such unusual promotions were "a matter, that ought to be handled with the utmost caution and delicacy. Nothing is more alarming and prejudicial" to the service "than an injudicious inflation of rank. It discourages merit and foments discontent and disorder. No departure from the established maxims of preferment is warrantable which is not founded upon the most apparent and unequivocal reasons."

Assessment of Departments

Washington then turned his thoughts to the subject of clothing the army. "The mode of providing" clothing and related necessaries "hitherto in practice" had indeed proved "by no means adequate." The individual states should be less depended on to clothe their own regiments, as in most cases it had proved unsatisfactory, and a new system of clothing the troops on a national basis should be instituted, thereby preventing inequities throughout the army. The subject of clothing led naturally to an appraisal of the Quartermaster and Commissary Departments. Both departments, Washington accentuated, had proved very defective, and should be revised from top to bottom beginning with the appointments of talented officers to fill, as the Commander-in-Chief had often requested, the still vacant posts of Quartermaster-General and Commissary-General.

Washington then briefly surveyed the "imperfections" in the Medical Department. "One powerful reason" for these imperfections was "the extreme scarcity of proper supplies." Another pernicious influence was "the continual altercations" between and within the various medical staffs. "They seem always to be at variance and recriminating the sufferings of the sick upon each other."

The Commander-in-Chief was reasonably satisfied with the Paymaster Department under the supervision of Colonel William Palfrey, but could not refrain from remarking that "the want of money" to pay the troops and purchase even the most essential supplies from local inhabitants, "which too frequently happens, is extremely injurious to our affairs." Paying for these supplies "with punctuality . . . is perhaps more essential in our army, than in any other, because our Men are worse supplied and more necessitous;" and the suppliers who had any dealings with the army, if not paid promptly, "grow dissatisfied and clamorous." Thereby "the credit of the army . . . is impaired," the acquisition of further supplies impeded "and the price of every article . . . raised." This situation only added to the constantly creeping inflation that vexed the nation.

In contrast to the majority of the departments, Washington noted that both the Commissary of Musters and Commissary of Prisoners Departments were in capable hands and had been admirably handled. He anticipated a change for the better in the Auditors of Accounts Department with the appointment of Matthew Clarkson and his assistants. "The sooner the gentlemen appointed enter upon the execution of their office, the better . . . The public has sustained a loss of many thousands" of dollars "which might have been prevented" if adequate supervision of the army's accounts had been instituted earlier. These losses had resulted from "the negligence, dishonesty and death of numberless officers" who had been permitted to handle the army's funds without a strict accounting of their financial transactions.

As for the Artillery, Washington and Knox had already formulated plans for its reorganization into four complete battalions, and the department, therefore, could soon be expected to be "a very respectable establishment." Washington had nothing but praise for General Duportail and the Engi-

neering Department; but noted that Duportail had need of more trained assistants than his small corps of Frenchmen afforded. Americans should be trained in the work.

Washington then briefly discussed a number of lesser matters. He requested Congress to decide on the disposition of the foreign officers who were clamoring for commissions, but warned Congress to avoid displacing American officers. He further suggested that a corps should be enlisted which consisted entirely of foreigners, officers and men alike. There were numbers of foreign-born rank-and-file already commingled in the American ranks who might be exceedingly pleased to be transferred to the proposed corps; and there certainly was no shortage of foreign officers demanding employment.

In addition Washington suggested the employment of two or three hundred Indians as scouts. The Indians might "strike no small terror into the British and foreign troops" in British service. Congress too should obviate the complaints of exchanged prisoners by restoring them to their proper ranks and seniority on their return to the army.

In conclusion the Commander-in-Chief criticized the present military regulations governing the various crimes committed by American soldiers. In Washington's opinion there was no "proper gradation of punishments: the interval between a hundred lashes and death is too great and requires to be filled by some intermediate stages. Capital crimes in the army are frequent, particularly in the instance of desertion, [and] to inflict capital punishment upon every deserter or other heinous offender would incur the imputation of cruelty."

Often, principally in the cases of deserters, there were mitigating circumstances that warranted less drastic punishment than death. Under the present regulations the courts-martial had no alternative other than to inflict the ultimate penalty. Crimes are "so various in their complexions," the Commander-in-Chief continued, "that there ought to be a gradual scale of punishments" well publicized for the information and government of the troops. "Whipping should be extended to any number" of lashes at the discretion of the courts.

"Upon the whole," the Commander-in-Chief did not doubt that Congress would be fully impressed "with the defects of our present military system, and the necessity of speedy and decisive measures, to put it upon a satisfactory footing. The disagreeable picture, I have given you . . . is a just representation of evils . . . and unless effectual remedies be applied without loss of time, the most alarming and ruinous consequences are to be apprehended."[37]

Thomas Paine

The already famous pamphleteer, Thomas Paine, had recently visited the army at Valley Forge and was inspired by the fortitude of the soldiers, to write his *Crisis No. 5*. Paine's new opus, as had his previous essays, employed the double purpose of denigrating enemy capabilities and inspiring American spirits. It commenced with a bitter attack on Sir William Howe, on whose person, Paine observed, "America is anxious to bestow her funeral favors." Happily for the Americans, Paine continued, Howe's "military exploits have been without plan, object or decision." Again and again the British commander's dilatory tactics had saved the American Army from ruin.

"If the principal events of the three campaigns" of the three previous years "be attended to," Paine remarked for Sir William's benefit, "the balance will appear against you at the close of each . . . The long doubtful winter of war" that the Americans had experienced was already "changing to the sweeter prospects of victory and joy . . . Go home, sir," Paine advised, "and endeavour to save the remains of your ruined country, by a just representation" to the British government and people "of the madness of her measures."

Paine then appealed "to the inhabitants of America" to stand firm. The writer was willing, and so advised patriots, to "confess myself one of those who believe the loss of Philadelphia to be attended with more advantages" to the American cause "than injuries . . . The enemy imagined Philadelphia to be of more importance to us than it really was . . . [since] the enemy believed . . . that the soul of all America was centered there, and would be conquered there . . . [but] their possession of it, by not answering the end proposed, must break up the plans they had so foolishly gone upon." The Americans never had, Paine staunchly averred, "so fair an opportunity of final success as *now*."

Paine then seconded Washington's constant call for recruits. "The only way to finish a war," Paine counselled, was "to collect an army" of a size "against the power of which the enemy shall have no chance. By not doing this, we prolong the war, and double both the calamities and expenses of it. Vigor and determination," Paine concluded, "will do any thing and every thing. We began the war with this kind of spirit, why not end it with the same?"[38]

CHAPTER V

FAR AWAY DAWN

February Arrives

January slid into February without any appreciable change at Valley Forge except that spring was a little nearer. Early in February a brief thaw permitted a few provisions to be flatboated down the Schuylkill River from Reading; but well before the middle of the month, winter returned in earnest. The river froze, and drifting snow made travel difficult.

For four days, no meat could be issued in camp and a near famine again threatened the army. Even when food was available, rations were scant. Often the men could be allowed only a few ounces of meat and three pounds of wormy flour for several days' nourishment. Yet, by all reports extensive quantities of provisions and other supplies lay at no great distance.

"The quantity of provision," Washington noted, "Flour especially," stored in eastern Pennsylvania that was "carried into Philadelphia" for enemy stomachs by local farmers "is by all accounts so great that the British Army is well supplied with almost every Article" despite the Pennsylvania Militia's efforts to prevent the traffic. General Lacey, the Militia commander, was never able to assemble enough men to patrol adequately the country given into his care.

Washington, impelled both by his own desire and that of the Committee on Conference "that this pernicious intercourse" between the farmers and the enemy "be cut off," notified the Militia that he knew of "no other way to prevent the supply of Flour" from reaching the enemy than "disabling the Mills." The Militia, therefore, was ordered on February 1st to "disable all the mills upon Pennepack, Frankford and Wissahickon Creeks" by removing "the spindles and saw[ing] off the spikes of the water wheels as soon as possible."[1] In pursuing this business the Militia was to observe the utmost secrecy lest the enemy become aware of the measure and send a preventative column from Philadelphia.

February also brought renewed quarrels in the Medical Department. Dr. Benjamin Rush, Surgeon-General of the Middle Medical Department, quit his post after a severe quarrel with Dr. William Shippen, the Surgeon-General of the Army. Rush accused Shippen of misusing departmental funds, and the contagion of this quarrel rapidly spread through the whole Middle Medical Department. Some of the physicians sided with Rush, others with Shippen, though it was stated by neutral observers that "much was said on both sides" that was born of frustration, and that both parties "were wrong at least in some degree."

Actually the basic quarrel stemmed from intramural jealousies. Richard Peters, Secretary to the Board of War, noted to Robert Morris, "if the Jealousies which seem to exist" in the Medical Department "continue to rage much longer, I don't see how any Man of Feeling or Sentiment can continue in a public Department where every measure is looked upon with a jaundiced Eye" by colleagues, and where "all Mistakes are magnified into Sins political or moral." Rush was a member of the political faction that opposed Washington; Shippen was Washington's firm friend.

"Unless great Alterations take place" in the department, Peters pursued, "the first and most capital of which is the Restoration of personal Harmony" among the members of the medical profession, the department would surely collapse. Peters observed, if the political undertones that were secretly sabotaging every department of the army were not soon rectified "the Enemy will prevail more by our Animosities than they have yet been able to do by their arms . . . It is hard upon us to be overcome by ourselves when our affairs with Regard to the Enemy afford the most flattering Prospect, and Nothing is wanting but Union and Exertion to drive the Miscreants from our Country."[2]

Washington's aide, Lieutenant Colonel Tench Tilghman, noted that though the Commander-in-Chief was doing everything in his power to effect a plan of re-organization, politics might yet reduce his efforts to nothing. Tilghman observed, also to Robert Morris, "Our Enemies have already heard of and exult at" the continuing "appearance of division and faction among ourselves, and the Officers of the Army who have been all of them at one time or another under" Washington's command "are exasperated to the highest degree, at the thought" of the often rumored proposal "of displacing him" through political chicanery. The principal political quarrel, as noted, was aimed at the downfall of the Commander-in-Chief. Most other quarrels stemmed from this source.

Tilghman continued, "I have never seen any stroke of ill fortune affect the General in the manner that this dirty underhand dealing has done. It hurts him the more because he cannot take notice of it without publishing to the World that the spirit of faction begins to work among us. It therefore behoves his Friends to support him against the malicious attacks of those who can have no reason to wish his removal but a desire to fill his place" with their own candidate, Gates. "If the General's conduct" was in any provable way "reprehensible let those who think so" unmask their secret plotting and "make the charge, and call him to account publickly before that body [Congress] to whom he is amenable. But this rascally method of calumniating" the Commander-in-Chief "behind the Curtain ought to be held in detestation by all good Men."[3]

While these internal troubles continued, a hopeful turn took place in far away France. By February 6th the final negotiations between the American plenipotentiaries and the French Government concerning a "Treaty of Amity and Commerce," and a "Treaty of Alliance, Eventual and Defensive," as the treaties were titled, had been consummated in Paris. On the same date the two treaties were officially signed by the three American representatives and by Conrad Alexandre Gérard for France.

The text of the Treaty of Amity and Commerce commenced, "There shall be a firm, inviolable and universal Peace, and a true and sincere Friendship" between the signatories of the pact. The treaty then erased most of the trade restrictions between the two countries and guaranteed that France would protect American vessels on the high seas even if such protection led to a French clash with Britain. France assured the Americans that France would make no attempt to repossess Canada should hostilities arise between Britain and France; a stipulation intended to suppress the expected objections of many American patriots to an alliance with an old enemy. Many patriots still remembered the long struggle between Britain and France for the mastery of Colonial North America.

The Treaty of Alliance, though stipulated as "defensive," could well be construed by Britain as otherwise. If ratified by the signatories, the Treaty virtually assured an eventual declaration of war between Britain and France. Indeed, the first article of the "Treaty of Alliance" provided for such an eventuality. If war should break out between France and Great Britain, during the continuance of the present war between the united States and England, His Majesty," Louis XVI of France, "and the said united States, shall make it a common cause, and aid each other mutually."

The second Article of the Treaty was an even greater incitement to a severance of French-British relations and was the crux of the whole alliance. The Article stated, "The essential and direct End of the present defensive alliance is to maintain effectually the liberty, Sovereignty, and independence absolute and unlimited of the said united States." Most of the remainder of the Treaty spelled out the various lesser agreements between the signatories. Canada and Bermuda, if conquered by the United States or, in the event of French-British hostilities, by the Franco-American allies, would accrue to the Americans. Any successful conquests achieved by either party or achieved mutually in the West Indies would accrue to France.

In an effort to perpetuate the Alliance, "Neither of the two Parties" signatory to the Treaties would be permitted to "conclude either Truce or Peace with Great Britain, without the formal consent of the other first obtain'd; and they mutually engage not to lay down their arms, until the Independence of the united States Shall have been formally or tacitly assured by the Treaty or Treaties that shall terminate the War." In order to eliminate any American suspicion of the treaties, and to obviate expected British propaganda that the treaties favored France, the Treaty of Alliance guaranteed that "there shall be no after claim of compensation on one side or the other whatever may be the event of the War."

Other European powers were invited to join the alliance. On accepting such an invitation, they need not necessarily be bound by all or any of the stipulations of the present treaties. (As a result of this stipulation Spain, when she ultimately joined the hostilities against Britain, did so only as an ally of France and not of the United States.) In conclusion, the two treaties were required to be ratified by the governments of both signatories within the ensuing six months or become automatically void.[4]

Accompanying the Treaty of Alliance was a special Act Secret and Separate which merely refined the Article in the Treaty of Alliance which would permit Spain to be admitted under whatever conditions might prove desirable to the Spanish Court.[5] This Act was kept secret not so much to hide its existence from prying British agents as to refrain from risking Spanish ire that Spain had been mentioned in the negotiations without her express consent or knowledge.

Britain, through the agency of her ambassador to France, Lord Stormont, had been told of an imminent Franco-American agreement. The Ministry immediately warned her officers and friends in America of the prospect of such an event so that American Loyalists might employ every possible means to counteract American inclination to accede to a treaty with Britain's ancient foe.

The sole measure that the Loyalist press could devise, however, was a resort to fabrication. The press assured the American public "that the Court of France is positively, and has in earnest determined, that they will show no countenance whatever to the rebellion in America, [and] have given the most satisfactory assurances that they will not assist the Americans in any manner, or suffer" any American "vessels to trade at their ports."[6] That this assertion was a fabrication was known to many Americans, Loyalists and patriots alike, who were fully aware that military supplies to aid the rebellion were already reaching America from France in rather sizeable quantities.

CHAPTER VI

CAMP, FORAGING AND POLITICS

Life in Camp

As the middle of February arrived, snow again piled against the huts, and life in camp seemingly cut off from the world both by the weather and by Washington's recent order restricting visitors, became more monotonous than ever. The restrictive order resulted from "the most pernicious consequences having arisen from suffering persons, women in particular," Washington noted, "to pass and repass from Philadelphia" and the city's vicinity "to camp under Pretence of coming out to visit their Friends" and relatives. Some of these visits proved to be "with an intent to entice soldiers to desert." General Orders issued to prevent this practice specified that such persons "when found in camp" were to be summarily expelled or, if acting suspiciously, arrested and tried.[1]

Also about the middle of February, Washington decided to proceed with an expansion of the Engineer Corps provided at least a few American officers could be induced to transfer from their present assignments for training in that service. With the expected re-organization of the army and the consequent reduction of the number of regiments, transfers to the engineering service would provide posts for officers who would otherwise be forced to retire from service. "Officers who are desirous of taking Commissions in the company of sappers under the Command of Brigadier DuPortail," the officer corps was notified, and who "possess the necessary qualifications, such as the

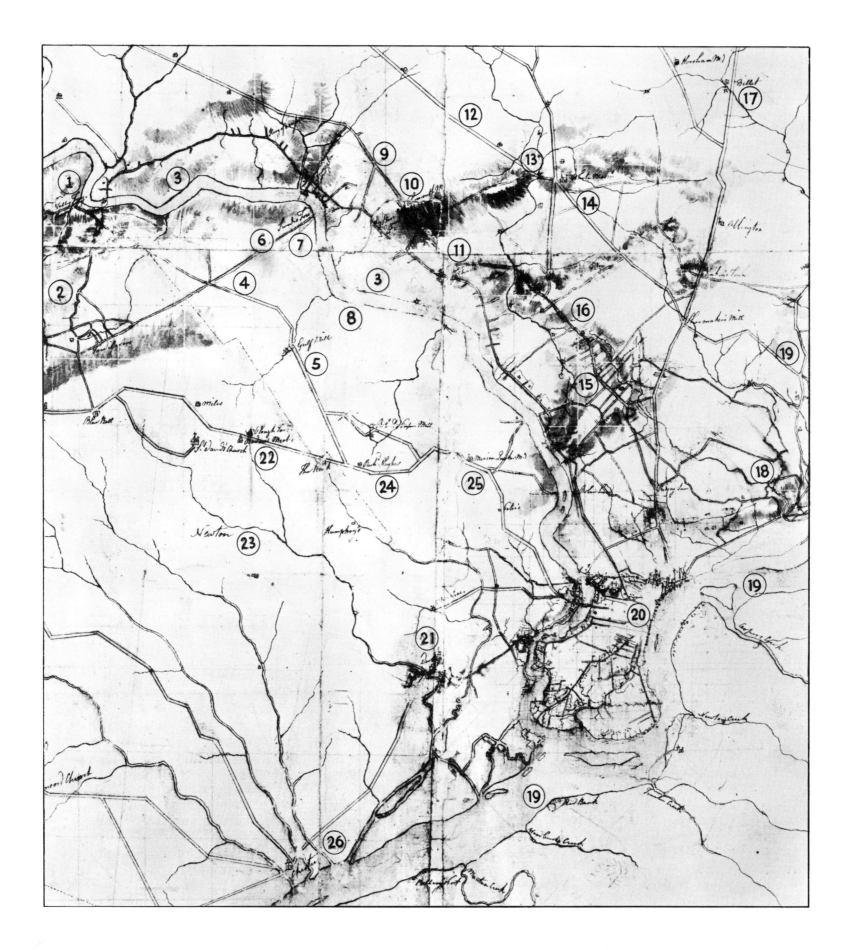

AREA FROM VALLEY FORGE TO PHILADELPHIA. *Section of a map in the Clinton Papers, William L. Clements Library, Ann Arbor, Michigan; Clinton Map 257; Brun Guide 556. The numerals are additions to the map. 1. Valley Forge 2. Valley Creek 3. Schuylkill River 4. Gulph Rd. (Nutt Rd. west of Valley Forge) 5. The Gulph, or Gulph Mills 6. Swedesford Road 7. Swede's Ford 8. Matson's Ford 9. Ridge Pike 10.* Plymouth Meeting *11. Barren Hill 12. Skippack Pike 13. Broad Axe 14. Whitemarsh 15. Germantown 16. Germantown Pike 17. The Crooked Billet 18. Frankford 19. Delaware River 20. Philadelphia 21. Darby 22. Radnor Meeting 23. Newtown Square 24. Lancaster Road 25. Merion Meeting 26. Middle Ferry 27. Chester. A finished partly colored topographical map, author unknown.*

knowledge of practical Geometry and drawing," were requested to "give in their Names to the Adj. General's office. Three Captains, three first Lieutenants, and three second Lieutenants" were the officers initially needed.[2]

Now that the first difficult days of camp had passed, Washington put into effect stricter military regulations. Reveille was to "beat at day break." The call to camp duty was to be "at 8 in the morning, the retreat at sun set, taptoo at nine o'clock in the evening." The drummers' call to these duties was to commence "at the right of the front line and answered throughout that line; then the second [line] and Corps of Artillery beginning at the left; The reserve to follow the second line." Immediately on the completion of this call, "three rolls" of the drums were "to begin and run through in the like manner as the call, then all the drums of the Army at the head of their respective Corps should go thro' the regular beat," the drumming finally "ceasing upon the right which will be the signal for the whole to cease."[3] With all this sound, no soldier could offer an excuse that he had failed to hear the notification to duty or rest.

The institution of the market on the far side of Sullivan's Bridge, which was open on "Tuesday and Friday," having proved exceedingly successful, a second market, already previously proposed for the Stone Chimney Picket on the opposite side of the camp, was opened and "the Army was desired to take notice of the same. Markets will be held at the same place every monday, and on thirsday." As for the Sullivan's Bridge market which had previously been held on the north side of the river, Washington no longer had any compunction against the vendors crossing the bridge, since they had shown an inclination to trade in an honest and orderly manner.

The popularity of these markets, and the distance that the troops in the rear of the camp of necessity had to travel to market, induced the Commander-in-Chief to order the opening of a third market which was allowed to do business "every Wednesday and Saturday" in the vicinity of the Adjutant-General's Office.[4] Eventually the two earlier markets would be permitted to operate on Wednesdays and Saturdays also. Hand bills were printed stipulating the regulations and prices governing the trade and were distributed to soldiers and vendors alike, to prevent any haggling and quarreling among the buyers and sellers.

At Moore Hall the Committee on Conference continued its daily sessions, dissecting bit by bit the recent recommendations that Washington had submitted in writing for its consideration. The Committee occasionally consulted with the Commander-in-Chief, and frequently interviewed officers of the various departments of the army in an effort to arrive at a first-hand picture of the condition of each department.

Of great importance in February, was the fact that Congress acted on the Commander-in-Chief's many requests for an investigation of the operations of the Commissary Department. They ordered "That the Board of War be directed forthwith to enquire into the causes of the deficiencies in the department of the purchasing commissaries and report to Congress" at the earliest possible time.[5]

Prisoner Exchange

Early in February, General Howe had notified General Washington that he was ready, "to give his consent to a general exchange of prisoners upon the terms formerly offered by Genl. Washington," i. e., officer for officer of equal rank or several inferior officers for one of superior rank, and soldier for soldier, the surplus prisoners held by either side to be freed on parole until exchanged. Although the British commander alleged "his desire to relieve the men and officers from the misery which unavoidably accompanies captivity, as his only motive," actually the care and support of the numerous American prisoners in British hands had become a burden to the British Commissary Department.

This burden resulted despite a previous agreement that each side would furnish its prisoners in enemy hands with requisite necessities, or with money with which to purchase them. When American money arrived in Philadelphia for the prisoners' benefit, not only did it fail to relieve the British Commissary, but it was paid in the only money the Americans could offer, depreciated paper currency. The British paid for their prisoners' support in specie. This one-sided arrangement was a further inducement to Howe to expedite an early exchange.

Washington had frequently complained to Howe of "the cruel treatment and confinement of our officers."[6] Sir William took the occasion of his letter to Washington on prisoner exchange to "disavow the cruel treatment" of American prisoners in British hands.[7]

Washington replied to Howe's letter that he was glad to avail himself "of the reasonable Terms, you are at this time willing to adopt for the mutual relief of the Prisoners," but requested a clarification of Sir William's proposal that the officer prisoners be immediately traded prior to any agreement on a formal exchange. Were these officers to be considered on parole until the exchange was formally consummated, or were they free to return immediately to their former military duties? Otherwise Howe's proposals were clear; and Washington agreed with the British commander that in order to facilitate the proposed exchange and eliminate lengthy points of discussion "two Commissioners from me shall meet a like Number from you, on the 10th day of March in German Town at the King of Prussia Tavern . . . to adjust upon equitable Terms" the exchange "and such other matters, as they may be severally empowered to determine."[8]

On the same day that Washington was replying to Howe, he was exhibiting increasing anxiety concerning a personal matter. Mrs. Washington, as was her custom when military conditions permitted, had been expected at Valley Forge for several days. On February 10th the Commander-in-Chief's worry ceased when he was notified that Mrs. Washington's coach had been observed approaching. Upon her arrival, the troops welcomed her enthusiastically, since they knew from experience that Martha Washington was always "pleasant and kind," and could be expected "to visit the hospitals" without the least fear of the prevalent diseases, and that she had always shown a "motherly care" for the soldiers, both sick and well.[9]

Soon after stepping from her carriage and entering Headquarters, "Lady Washington," as the troops called her, noted that "the General's apartments are very small." Through the rear windows she could see that he had had "a log cabbin built to dine in" as a temporary addition to the principal building.[10] This primitive annex would frequently witness dinners at which her husband and his guests would observe Lady Washington's "mild dignified countenance, grave yet cheerful." Peter Duponceau later remembered that "her presence inspired fortitude," and that "those who came to her with almost desponding hearts retired full of hope and confidence."[11]

Lady Washington's arrival indeed proved helpful. She frequently visited the soldiers' huts to aid the sick; and, with the wives of other officers, including Lady Stirling and the Stirlings' daughter Lady "Kitty" Alexander, Mrs. Nathanael Green, (also "Kitty") and others, knitted, sewed, patched and darned for the troops. Local women often joined in the work.

Mrs. Nathaniel Greene, "a handsome, elegant and accomplished woman," always in the forefront of social activities, at first contented herself in her husband's humble quarters at the Isaac Walker house. Upon Greene's appointment to the Quartermaster-Generalcy in March, the Greenes moved to Moore Hall, which became "the resort of foreign officers" as well as Americans. Mrs. Greene was a particular favorite of the French "because she understood and spoke the French language" with quaint facility, "and was well versed in French literature."[12] A number of officers' wives came to live at camp. "They often met at each other's quarters, and sometimes at General Washington's, where the evening was spent in conversation, over a dish of tea or coffee; [but] there were no *levees* or formal *soirees;* no dancing, card-playing, or amusement of any kind except singing. Every gentleman or lady who could sing, was called upon in turn for a song."[13]

Washington's Birthday

Lady Washington had arrived just in time for the celebration of her husband's forty-sixth birthday which was commemorated on February 11th. (The Commander-in-Chief reckoned his age by the old-style Julian calendar that had gone out of general use in the middle of the eighteenth century). In deference to the times, the celebration at Headquarters was simple. Despite the lowering clouds and persistent rain, a band of music from Colonel Thomas Proctor's 4th Continental Artillery attended at Headquarters and serenaded the General. Happily for Lady Washington, the band consisted mostly of fifes and drums. She could therefore listen with pleasure to instruments, which she preferred "to any music that was ever heard."[14] The appreciative Commander-in-Chief dug into his own pocket and paid the band five shillings in specie (a rare treat in the paper-money-infested army) for the compliment the band had paid him. The ceremonies concluded with a birthday dinner.

The principal intended business of the day would have proceeded despite the festivities had not the weather prevented His Excellency from attending a meeting with the Committee on Conference at Moore Hall. Instead, the Committee sent Washington a letter discussing the proposed exchange of prisoners. Washington on his part informed the Committee that some brigades had been four days without meat, and that even the common soldiers had been at his quarters to make known their wants. The few horses that remained alive in camp were in equal misery, many of them dying. In the event of an enemy attack, the artillery pieces would have to be abandoned to the enemy for want of horses to move them. Smallpox was spreading despite Washington's desperate efforts to have the troops inoculated. The list of sick and dead was increasing by a third week by week.

Since recent intelligence from Philadelphia seemed to indicate a possible large scale enemy foraging raid; Washington notified Nathanael Greene that it was "of the utmost Consequence that the Horses, Cattle, Sheep and Provender within Fifteen or Twenty miles west of the River Delaware between the Schuylkill and Brandywine be immediately removed, to pre-

vent the Enemy from receiving any benefit therefrom, as well as to supply the present Emergencies of the American Army. I do therefore Authorize impower and Command you" to forage that part of the country, giving certificates promising future payment to the local farmers in lieu of cash, which at present was painfully absent. "All the Provender on the Islands" skirting the west shore of the Delaware River "between Philadelphia and Chester," which had not fallen into enemy hands in December, was to be destroyed if possible, since it was too near the enemy garrison and ships to be removed safely.[15]

As ordered, Greene commenced foraging as soon as sufficient reasonably healthy troops from his division could be assembled, though the district to which he had been directed had already been mostly swept clean of stock and produce in the preceding months by the contending armies. Meanwhile Washington pleaded with President Wharton to strengthen the Pennsylvania Militia, which had all but "dwindled away to nothing" instead of the "1,000" men the Pennsylvania authorities had promised.[16] It would be somewhat useless for Greene to attempt to deny supplies to the enemy from the lower side of the Schuylkill if the well-stocked farms of Philadelphia and Bucks Counties, which the Militia was supposed to protect, remained undefended from enemy depredations.

Wayne Forages in New Jersey

In a further effort to withhold supplies from the enemy and at the same time supply the American Army, Washington detached Wayne to New Jersey with 550 men picked for their physical condition and the comparative excellence of their equipment and clothing. Wayne left Valley Forge on February 13th for Wilmington, where he hoped to cross the Delaware River. On reaching Wilmington, Wayne found that both the absence of ice in the river and the lack of enemy cruisers in the area would permit a safe passage to Salem County, New Jersey. Wayne, with the assistance of Captain John Barry's row gallies, transported his force over the river, though not without attracting enemy attention.

General Howe received a report of Wayne's maneuver and immediately ordered an expedition to counter the American column. Wayne, however, had time to linger unmolested in Salem County for several days during which time he was able to collect a significant herd of cattle and other forage, which he attempted to transport across the Delaware to New Castle, Delaware. Failing in this attempt because of the arrival of enemy cruisers, Wayne determined to proceed northward through New Jersey in a wide sweep east of the river, with the intention of recrossing the Delaware at a safe distance above Philadelphia. His troops would act as a shield to cover the cattle and forage wagons, which would swing in an arc further east, thereby preventing enemy interception.

Meanwhile, Wayne directed Barry to sail his small fleet of row gallies up the Delaware, to make landings on the Jersey shore, and burn whatever hay he discovered on the farms.[17] During the progress of this naval expedition, Barry was fortunate to intercept the British sloop *Alert* of ten guns and her convoy of supply ships, the *Kitty* and *Mermaid.* Barry immediately attacked the *Alert* with all his force though she was a considerably larger ship than any of his own vessels. Numbers, however, counted, and Barry and his men soon successfully boarded the enemy sloop and the two unarmed vessels she was escorting to Philadelphia.

35

Barry at once ended his hay burning operations and sailed his valuable prizes to a hopefully safe haven in the creek-indented west shore of the Delaware, and immediately set his crews to work unloading the cargoes. Enemy cruisers, alerted by the sound of firing on the river, appeared shortly; and Barry was forced to set fire to the vessels to prevent their recapture, although he was able to rescue most of the precious cargo.

Wayne, as planned, marched north toward Haddonfield, and en route requested Colonel Ellis of the New Jersey Militia to gather whatever Militia was available and meet him there. Wayne further requested that Ellis scout an enemy force reportedly landing at Billingsport in an effort to strike at Wayne's column. Actually some 1,500 enemy troops at that very moment were on the march from Billingsport to Salem, and missed intercepting Wayne by only a slight margin. Another enemy force was landing at Cooper's Ferry, opposite Philadelphia. The latter force was in a position to cut across Wayne's intended line of march. Wayne, informed of this situation, but receiving scant intelligence concerning the enemy's further movements, requested Count Casimir Pulaski, stationed at Trenton with his legion of Light Horse, to assist in scouting the enemy force in the vicinity of Cooper's Ferry. The Polish officer immediately descended to Burlington, where on February 28th he joined Wayne, who had successfully avoided the enemy force attempting to intercept him at Haddonfield.

Pulaski's scouts reported that the enemy, having failed to entrap Wayne, had dispersed into small foraging parties. Wayne, reinforced by Pulaski's fifty horsemen and Colonel Ellis's New Jersey Militia, determined to attempt to take advantage of the enemy's scattered situation, and marched back toward Haddonfield. The enemy's scattered units, learning of Wayne's reinforcements, withdrew to Cooper's Ferry where they concentrated their forces under the protection of cruisers hastily summoned to the scene. The British force, thus protected, appeared too strong for Wayne to attempt an attack with much hope of success.

Wayne, thereupon, withdrew to Bordentown, where he learned that his drove of cattle and the forage wagons were well on their way to Coryell's Ferry, now Lambertville-New Hope, far up the river and safe from enemy capture. Wayne paused briefly at Bordentown until receiving confirmation that the enemy's force at Cooper's Ferry was crossing the Delaware to Philadelphia, then crossed over at Bristol, and rejoined the army at Valley Forge. The British column at Salem also withdrew from New Jersey at the prospect of being severed from its line of communication by the New Jersey Militia.[18]

While waiting for Wayne to complete his long distance foraging mission, Washington had directed Captain Henry Lee to proceed with his Light Horse to Delaware and drive "towards Camp" any cattle that might be available in that state "as fast as" Lee's men could round them up. If any of the cattle appeared too lean for immediate consumption, Lee was to drive them into Lancaster and Berks Counties in Pennsylvania for fattening.[19]

As a supplement to foraging, a herd of some 130 fat beef cattle was reported on its way from New England, and could be expected to arrive in camp soon. The report of this herd unfortunately had reached the enemy, but the British permitted the herd to proceed. When well within Pennsylvania, a troop of British dragoons disguised as country folk then made a night march from Philadelphia to the Skippack Pike, some twenty miles northwest of the city, and intercepted the herd. The loss

of this beef was severely felt at Valley Forge, and Washington, when told that no guards had accompanied the herd, reprimanded General Lacey and the Pennsylvania Militia for this failure, although he could scarcely quarrel with Lacey's explanation that he had no troops for the duty.

The Virginia Generals

The middle of February brought to a head the long contentions of the Virginia generals, Woodford, Weedon, Scott and Muhlenberg, concerning their seniority in rank. Muhlenberg, who was notified that the matter was soon due for final adjudication, concluded his Virginia furlough and hastened back to camp. The quarrel had actually commenced as early as 1776 when Adam Stephen had been appointed a brigadier despite the recognized seniority of the then Colonel Woodford. Woodford had huffily resigned in protest, but presently returned to service and resumed his rank of colonel. Soon thereafter Woodford, Muhlenberg and Weedon were advanced to the rank of brigadier. Woodford, despite his brief resignation, had demanded unequivocal recognition that his commission was senior to those of Muhlenberg and Weedon.

With the dismissal of Adam Stephen in December, 1777, as a result of his drunkenness at the Battle of Germantown, Woodford actively commenced to press his claim to seniority in the hope of receiving the appointment to the vacant major-generalcy, which rank Stephen had held. The ensuing disruption among the Virginia generals, including a protest by General Scott that he too was senior to Woodford as a result of Woodford's resignation, induced Washington to write to Congress that he hoped it would be more guarded in the future in the matter of promotions.

Muhlenberg joined Weedon in his vocal and written protests against official recognition of Woodford's equally vociferous claim. The argument became so hot that Washington, on March 4th, was obliged to order all the major and brigadier generals, except those officers directly concerned in the quarrel, to assemble at General Stirling's quarters in an effort to decide the matter. The discussions consumed much time, but finally the matter was put to a vote; and Woodford's claim to seniority was upheld by the scant margin of a single ballot. So narrow was his triumph, that the Board of Generals declined to rule in the matter, and so informed the Commander-in-Chief. Washington thereupon was forced to refer the matter to Congress.

Muhlenberg, informed of Woodford's possible victory as a result of the Board's election, threatened his resignation if Woodford's claim was upheld; and was only prevented from taking precipitate action by a direct personal plea from Washington that Muhlenberg should be patient, and shelve his threat at least until the quarrel was finally adjudicated. Muhlenberg reluctantly consented, but requested that tentative consideration be given toward his eventual replacement. Weedon did not prove so docile. He presently went home to Virginia, though he subsequently rejoined the army. Scott's claim, being the least tenable, was given little consideration by either Washington or Congress, and Scott wisely permitted it to lapse.

Congressional Resolves

In an effort to guarantee the continued services of military and naval officers by firmly attaching them to the American cause by legal as well as by spiritual means, a proposal was made in Congress that Oaths of Allegiance to the United States should be required of all officers, without exception, in present and future service of the United States. After lengthy consideration of the matter, Congress, in February, resolved unanimously "That every officer who holds or shall hereafter hold a commission or office from Congress, shall take and subscribe" an oath or affirmation of allegiance to the national government. Twenty days from the date of the passage of the resolution were allowed for taking the oaths. Congress directed that if any officers refused to accede to the oaths they were to be immediately "cashiered, and forfeit two months' pay . . . and be rendered incapable of serving" again in "any office under Congress," civil or military. Congress also recommended that the individual states similarly disqualify these officers.[20]

During the same month, February, Congress was able to erase from its agenda several other military matters. It resolved that the Board of War be "directed to be very cautious in recommending or giving any encouragement" to the foreign officers who were constantly deluging Congress with applications for employment and promotion.[21]

Next, Congress decided to renege on the stipulation of the Saratoga Convention that guaranteed the return of the prisoners of Burgoyne's army to England. Congress ordered the prisoners removed from Cambridge, Massachusetts, to a place of greater safety from possible enemy recovery.[22] Congress feared that the return of these troops to England would simply release the garrisons in that country for service in America. Another Congressional directive in February requested Washington to send a replacement to Rhode Island for the aging, ill and retiring Major General Joseph Spencer in order to continue surveillance of the British troops occupying Newport.[23] This would force Washington to sacrifice a scarcely dispensible major general from his already depleted corps of general officers. Major General Sullivan would receive the appointment.

On the matter of the proposed exchange of prisoners, Congress directed that no exchange could be effected until the enemy prisoners' financial accounts were completely settled to Congress' satisfaction.[24] Since war-time conditions frequently caused unavoidable delays in this business, Sir William Howe had suggested to Washington that the financial accounts of the prisoners be settled only at the earliest convenient time, and that the as yet unpaid accounts should prove no hindrance to early discussions concerning the exchange. Howe guaranteed that the British debt would be paid in gold. The Congressional resolution ignored Sir William's proposal, and as a result the prisoners of both sides continued in durance.

On the subject of recruiting, Congress requested the states to complete their regiments through drafts from the state militias. The states, in an effort to fill their quotas of men, especially in the case of New England, had to resort to high bonuses and to inequitable systems of substitutes whereby a draftee could escape induction by paying a fellow citizen to assume his place. Both these methods produced considerable evils, the worst of which resulted from those unprincipled persons who alternately joined and deserted the army for repeated bonus and substitute money.

The final major resolve of Congress during February was an order that all persons seizing or murdering civilian citizens of the United States would be automatically subject, on apprehension, to the death penalty. Washington had complained to Congress that reports were frequently reaching Headquarters that Loyalists in the vicinity of Philadelphia were murdering, or abducting to the enemy, innocent civilians simply because they opposed the Loyalists' political point of view. Congress extended this penalty to include persons accused of guiding enemy troops or acting as spies. Congress appended to this directive an order that no enemy military parties be permitted to proceed beyond the enemy lines "on pain, if taken, of being treated as marauders and punished with death."[25]

This concluding directive was understandable in the case of enemy troops in disguise (such as the raiders who had recently taken the cattle), but if the enemy troops were in uniform the directive was of course contrary to the accepted rules of war. Washington, in strict adherence to these rules, and to protect American soldiers in like circumstances, refrained from employing this penalty against regularly uniformed enemy captives. The usual imprisonment was all the penalty he exerted. Irregular raiders such as the Doanes were a different matter, and subject to the extreme penalty when caught.

Not one of the above Congressional resolutions that marked the February business was designed to alleviate the perilous condition of the troops. By the middle of the month Washington was still describing the state of the troops as indeed dreadful; but "Naked and starving as they are," the Commander-in-Chief pridefully wrote to Governor George Clinton of New York, "we cannot enough admire the incomparable patience and fidelity of the soldiery . . . All the magazines provided in the States of New Jersey, Pennsylvania, Delaware and Maryland . . . will not be sufficient to support the army more than a month longer . . . [and] When the forementioned supplies are exhausted, what a terrible crisis must ensue."[26] Washington pleaded for New York's assistance in averting the imminent ruin. Similar pleas were extended to Governor William Livingston of New Jersey and to other governors.

Although life in camp was desultory, there was occasional activity in the surrounding country. "This Season produces nothing worth mentioning," General Lachlan McIntosh was writing to Governor Richard Caswell of North Carolina, "save Little skirmishes . . . of no account."[27] The skirmishes were mostly unintentional, resulting from unexpected clashes between the contending scouting parties. These attacks and counterattacks were often so minute as to be scarcely remembered even in local history.

On February 17th a detachment of Pennsylvania Militia attempted "to surprise the enemy's pickets" on the west side of the Middle Ferry near Philadelphia. The British had constructed a pontoon bridge across the Schuylkill at this point in order to link their fortifications on the Lancaster Road with the city. The enemy pickets quickly posted themselves in a convenient stone building and successfully rebuffed the Militia's attack.[28] On the same day "a detachment of [British] light infantry," which had been ordered from the city "to protect the country people who venture everything to bring fresh food" to Philadelphia, "surprised a troop of rebels" west of the Schuylkill River in the eastern part of Chester County, "killing four and takin eighteen prisoners."[29]

Royal partisans also received their rebuffs from the Americans. A particularly heroic instance was the defense of his home by the patriot Squire Andrew Knox, of Philadelphia County, against a gang of pro-British ruffians. The squire's house "was surrounded early in the morning" by the attackers, who demanded entry. Although the gang half-forced the door, the elderly Squire, who had hastily grasped a cutlass, assisted by his son armed with a fusil, successfully defended the house even though the cutlass was broken in the fracas and the fusil refused to fire. The attackers, having failed to force the door, put seven shots through the panels, one of which grazed the Squire's knee. The gang, having failed to intimidate the defenders, gave up its attempt and retreated.[30]

In England during the latter part of February, the full import of the recent Franco-American treaties had struck painfully. Lord North reluctantly recognized the need of a new Peace Commission which would be sent to America with full powers to negotiate all the complaints that had distilled the American rebellion. The commissioners, his lordship notified Parliament, must be vested with full powers to suspend hostilities and such laws as had given offense to the Americans; grant pardons, immunities and rewards (the last of which, his lordship could privately hope, would induce American leaders to consult personal interest); restore the Colonial constitutions that Britain, in American opinion, had wantonly negated; and nominate governors and other officials who would prove satisfactory to the Americans, with the proviso, of course, that these officials were also satisfactory to His Majesty.

In lieu of direct taxation, the attempt at which had so enraged the Americans, the commissioners would endeavor to negotiate some reasonable and moderate contribution towards the common defense of the empire. Although Britain considered such a contribution only equitable, if the Americans balked, the commissioners were not to insist on it. Lord North's proposed concessions would become the gist of the Conciliatory Acts that the Prime Minister, with private reluctance, suggested for parliamentary consideration.

CHAPTER VII

STEUBEN

Accepted by Congress

Congress had resolved in January that "whereas the Baron Steuben, a lieutenant general in the foreign service has . . . offered his services to these states . . . Congress cheerfully accepts his service."[1] These facts concerning Frederich Wilhelm Augustus Henry Ferdinand Baron von Steuben, which were transmitted in a Franklin-Deane letter to Congress from Paris, were partly inaccurate. Steuben was not a baron; he was not a lieutenant general and his family name was not Steuben but Steube. The Franklin-Deane letter did, however, report more accurately when it described Steuben as being well versed in military matters.[2]

Congress, in examining Steuben's credentials, in advance of his arrival at York, was pleased to learn that Steuben "desires no rank, is willing to attend General Washington and be subject to his orders; does not require or desire any command . . . but will serve occasionally as directed by the General; [and] expects to be of use in planning encampments . . . and promoting the discipline of the army." He heard before he left France of the dissatisfaction of the Americans with the promotion of foreign officers and Steuben "therefore makes no terms, nor will accept of anything but with general approbation, and particularly that of General Washington," as a result of earned merit.[3]

Steuben was advised regarding his journey from his port of arrival, Portsmouth, New Hampshire, to York, that he should "keep as far from the coast as possible lest he should be sur-

prized by parties of the enemy." Steuben was accompanied by Pierre Duponceau and Louis Dupontiére, his aides; Pierre L'Enfant, Théveneau de Francy (a nephew of Caron de Beaumarchais, and his agent to Congress) plus Carl Vogel, Steuben's German servant. "Crossing the States of Massachusetts, Connecticut, New York" and into Pennsylvania, Steuben and his party proceeded to York to submit his person to the appraisal of Congress. The journey "employed three weeks," because of the difficulties of traveling and some time spent in Boston.

"The fame of Baron Steuben preceded him" to York, where "he was welcomed, and courted by all," and was royally entertained at the parties and balls that "were then at their height." The social season was in full swing despite undeniable knowledge of the miseries the army was experiencing at Valley Forge. "General Gates in particular, paid him the most assiduous court . . . and even invited him to make his house his home," an invitation that Steuben "prudently declined" so as not to appear under obligation to an officer who, as Steuben had been apprised, had pretensions of rivaling Washington.[4]

At York, however, business not pleasure was Steuben's principal aim. "Congress appointed a Committee" of its members "to confer with him on the subject of his pretensions" in the American service, and were not a little surprised, when he told them that all his ambition was to serve as a volunteer in the army. The committee had been prepared for more inflated pretensions on Steuben's part than the plenipotentiaries' letter had intimated. "All the favor he asked" was that his two aides, Duponceau and Dupontiére, should have the rank of Captain, "which was immediately granted."[5] Steuben himself neither requested nor was offered immediate rank in the army.

Having attained his objectives, Steuben and his party departed from York on February 19th, reaching Lancaster "early in the afternoon," where he was "waited upon by Colonel Gibson," commandant of the town, "and other gentlemen, who invited him, and his family [i.e., staff] to a Subscription Ball" which was "to take place that evening." Steuben accepted the invitation, and he and his party "accordingly went."[6] Such festivities, as Steuben would soon learn, had little in common with the conditions which were being experienced at Valley Forge, where "the love of freedom which once animated the breasts" of officers and men was being "controlled by hunger."[7]

Conditions at Valley Forge continued so bad that some officers were strongly recommending the immediate removal of the army westward. If food and clothing could not be brought to the army, the army must go to its sources of supply. For example, Colonel Mark Bird of the Militia, ironmaster of Hopewell Furnace, had collected 1,000 barrels of flour at Reading. Some of it was shipped down the Schuylkill until falling water put an end to the business. The balance remained at Reading, since wagoners could not be found to undertake the journey by land. Washington, again desperate to keep his army together, ordered Colonel Ephraim Blaine, one of the Deputy Commissary-Generals for Purchases, to proceed at once to Maryland with 50 wagons in the hope that some untapped source of food might be encountered. Seven meatless and nearly flourless days faced the troops during the closing days of February.

In the midst of this desperate situation, Steuben arrived at Valley Forge on February 23rd.

The Commander-in-Chief was impressed by his first interview with the newcomer, though their communication was considerably hampered since Steuben spoke no English. German, his native tongue, and French were his only familiar languages. However, John Laurens, proficient in French as a result of his youthful studies in Switzerland, translated the conversation. At the conclusion of the interview, Steuben recalled, "the Commander-in-Chief accompanied me to my quarters, where I found an officer with twenty-five men as a guard of honor. When I declined this saying that I wished to be considered merely as a volunteer the General answered me in the politest words, that the whole army would be gratified to stand sentinel for such volunteers . . . On the same day my name was given as watchword" to the outposts of the camp.[8] As a result of this initial interview, Washington reported to Congress that Baron Steuben "appears to be much of a Gentleman, and as far as I have had an opportunity of judging, a man of Military knowledge."[9]

Steuben was initially quartered at Abijah Stephens' farmhouse, beyond the east perimeter of the camp, in the quarters recently vacated by DeKalb, who was absent with Lafayette on the Canadian expedition.[10] How long Steuben remained at the Stephens house is not known. Tradition assigns him quarters elsewhere, including an unusually large log cabin especially constructed for him on the Maurice Stephens farm at the edge of the Grand Parade, the scene of his principal duties.[11]

Very soon "Baron Steuben," as Washington persisted in calling him instead of von Steuben, was riding about the encampment, giving "an impression of the ancient fabled god of war . . . a perfect personification of Mars. The trappings of his horse, the enormous holsters of his pistols, his large size," powerful but not obese, "and his striking martial aspect all seemed to favor the idea."[12]

Steuben's Assessment of Army

On his first inspection tour, Steuben was shocked by the scenes he witnessed in camp. The men, he wrote, "were literally naked, some of them in the fullest extent of the word.

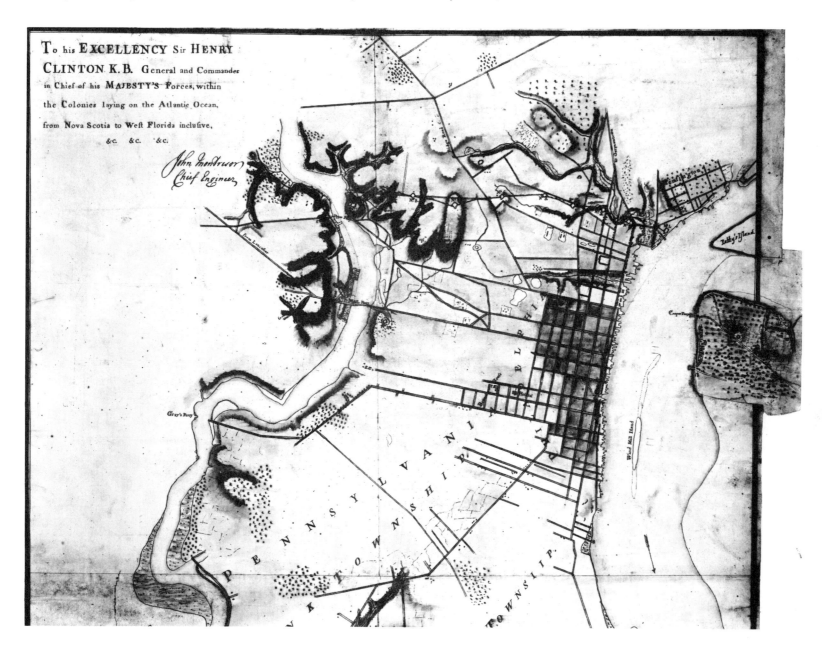

PHILADELPHIA AND ADJACENT AREAS. *Section of map showing in the upper portion the line of redoubts and abatis constructed by the British from the Schuylkill River to the Delaware River during the British occupation of Philadelphia; also the defenses of the Middle Ferry across the Schuylkill, and other points pertinent to the text. Map drawn by Captain John Montrésor, Chief of British Engineers. Courtesy William L. Clements Library, Ann Arbor, Michigan; Clinton Map 252; Brun Guide 540.*

The officers who had coats, had them of every color and make," rather than of the uniform dye and cut with which Steuben had been familiar in Europe. "I saw officers . . . mounting guard in a sort of dressing gown, made of an old blanket or woolen bed cover. With regard to their military discipline I can safely say no such thing existed." No two regiments contained equal numbers of platoons nor equal numbers of men. Officers drilled their men according to personal fancy, and by varying systems; and marched them in the single file "mode of marching used by the Indians" rather than in closed ranks.

Absenteeism among officers was rife, despite the Commander-in-Chief's cancellation of all furloughs except those of the most pressing nature. Steuben "found a Massachusetts regiment commanded by a lieutenant," the superior officers of the regiment all being absent on one excuse or another. The equipment of the troops, Steuben discovered, was in "a horrible condition, the arms covered with rust, half of them without bayonets, many from which a single shot could not be fired . . . A great many of the men had tin boxes instead of pouches" in which to port their ammunition, "others had cow horns" for porting powder; "and muskets, carbines, fowling pieces and rifles were to be seen in the same company." As for bayonets, "The American soldier, never having used this arm" in most instances, "had no faith in it." Mostly, the soldier "never used it but to roast his beefsteak" or disposed of it entirely.

In the succeeding days, Steuben's repeated inquiries into the state of the army only served to expand his criticisms. The various military departments, copied from the British system, were, in Steuben's scoffing opinion, only "bad copies of a bad original." Steuben further noted that "The eternal ebb and flow of men engaged for three, six, and nine months, who went and came every day, rendered it impossible to have either a regiment or a company complete." Because of this unhealthy system, neither the Commander-in-Chief nor any officer in the army could be expected to have precise knowledge of the number of men present for duty in any unit. The varying sizes of the regiments prevented the proper maneuvering of regiments, brigades and divisions alike.

Army financial accounts were still conspicuously absent, and pay and provision returns were lost in a sea of disorganization. Muster rolls were equally confused and out-of-date. Steuben was "sure that . . . a general would have thought himself lucky to find a third of the men ready for action whom he found on paper." Many of the men who were capable of active duty "were scattered about in every direction . . . Several thousand soldiers" were employed as officers' servants. Often these officers were assigned to detached duty and took their soldier-servants with them, thereby depriving the army of many men. Officers were not much better trained than the rawest recruits, and were little advised in the nature of some of their simplest duties. Steuben also took note of the frequent stealing in the Commissary Department, which was costing the nation untold sums of money.[13]

Steuben, having fully digested the defects that plagued the army, sought a plan by which to create an effective and well-supplied fighting force. The most urgent need as far as his own prospective duties were concerned was to produce a system of drill well suited to the native individuality of the American soldier, and simplified enough to produce results in the scant time before active hostilities recommenced. Indeed, Steuben admitted that it was "exceedingly difficult to find an arrangement likely to succeed." He was, he later noted, "often obliged

to abandon ideas I had formed" since he was much "in want of information and advice" concerning the best system to inaugurate.[14] Nathanael Greene, John Laurens and Alexander Hamilton, who had acquired more than a smattering of military learning, proved of assistance in solving Steuben's perplexities.

Partially depending on advice of these officers, Steuben commenced the composition of a drill manual which he titled *Regulations for the Order and Discipline of the Troops of the United States.*[15] Well aware that time was exceedingly precious, Steuben worked long hours on its completion. When the text was finished and translated from French to English, Steuben showed it to Greene, Laurens and Hamilton; and made such final alterations as they considered advisable before presenting a copy to Washington. When approved by him, the manual would be copied and re-copied until every general and field officer possessed a transcript.

Accompanying the manual was a set of military proposals intended for the guidance of the Commander-in-Chief and Congress. In the latter, Steuben suggested that a more active and better trained Inspector-General than Conway be immediately appointed; and further that the new Inspector-General ought to establish a uniform system of drill and duty throughout the army. Steuben proposed that all the military departments, particularly the Commissary, be placed on an equally uniform system of management.

As Steuben became better acquainted with the army, the army became better acquainted with him. John Laurens soon arrived at the opinion that the Prussian soldier was "the properest man we could choose for the office of inspector general." Laurens observed that he had "the highest opinion of the service" Steuben "would render in this line, as he seems to be perfectly aware of the disadvantages under which our army has labored . . . and is not so staunch a systematist as to be averse from adapting established forms" of regulations and drill "to stubborn circumstances. He will not give us the perfect instructions, absolutely speaking, but the best which we are in a condition to receive."[16]

Temporary Inspector-General

Steuben received an appointment from Washington as temporary Inspector-General of the troops at Valley Forge; and the Commander-in-Chief, with whom Steuben frequently dined in order to discuss the *pro tempore* Inspector-General's ideas, directed him to institute his new system of drill as soon as possible. Steuben was given free choice of methods and procedure. He "commenced operations by drafting 120 men from the line" whom he judged would be most proficient in learning his system, and whom he "formed into a guard for the general-in-chief."[17] These new men were actually added to the remnant of the old Commander-in-Chief's guard which continued to function. Since the old Guard consisted entirely of Virginians, Washington suggested that the recruits be drawn from other regiments, thereby avoiding any resentment in the army that only Virginians were being given preference.

The new recruits became Steuben's "military school." Once these men were trained to his satisfaction, he planned to distribute them among the army to act as drill-masters to the rest of the troops. Steuben commenced his task by systematizing his personal habits. He rose at dawn, shaved, drank a cup of steaming coffee when the beverage was available, and smoked his pipe until the moment of duty arrived. By sunrise Steuben's stableman-servant, Carl Vogel, had his master's horse saddled, and weather permitting, Steuben galloped his mount to the Grand Parade where he expected the trainees to be already assembled and prepared for their exercises.

The men drilled twice a day, "and to remove the English prejudice which some officers entertained, that to drill a recruit was a sergeant's duty and beneath the station of an officer," the Prussian drill-master "often took the musket" in his own hands "to show the men the manual exercise which I wished to introduce."[18] Steuben's initial efforts at drilling the trainees were considerably hampered by his ignorance of the English language. His first attempts to communicate his commands in German and French received little understanding from his English-speaking soldiers despite his efforts to pantomime the drill intended.

Fortunately, French-speaking Captain Benjamin Walker, of the 2nd New York Regiment, came to the Inspector-General's rescue and offered his services as interpreter until Steuben could acquire at least partial command of English. Steuben later remarked concerning Walker's saving offer, "If I had seen an angel from Heaven, I should not have been more rejoiced."[19] Steuben, however, by-passed Walker when particularly exasperated at the clumsy efforts of the trainees, and reverted to a multi-lingual tirade to express his exasperation. The explosions were only received with laughter by the rustics who were the objects of his irritation, a merriment in which Steuben himself consented to join despite his usually grave and "imposing countenance" that was generally set with "calm dignity." Although his nature was described as "affable" on most occasions, he rejected any real "familiarity."[20]

Sub-inspectors, to act in each brigade, were appointed and required to be present on the drill ground in order to learn the intricacies of the Steuben-devised manual of arms and field maneuvers. After a "fortnight" of drilling, the initial trainees

GENERAL VIEW OF THE GRAND PARADE *looking toward Mount Joy, which lies to the left. The inner line of defense was located on Mount Joy and the hills to the right. The only identified grave at Valley Forge, that of Lt. John Waterman of Rhode Island, is located among the small clump of pines. Steuben drilled the troops on the Grand Parade. It was also the scene of the French Alliance celebration on May 6, 1778.*

"knew perfectly how to bear arms, had a military air, knew how to march, to form columns, deploy and execute some little maneuvers with excellent precision." Time was of the essence. Steuben remarked, "In our European armies a man who has been drilled for three months is called a recruit; here, in two months I must have a soldier."[21]

When the initial company had been drilled to Steuben's reasonable satisfaction, he "paraded them in the presence of all the officers of the army." The company "formed in column, deployed, attacked with a bayonet, changed front," and performed other maneuvers. The demonstration, Steuben declared, "afforded a new and agreeable sight" for every witness. At the conclusion, "having gained my point," Steuben wrote, "I dispersed my apostles" among the army. As soon as efficiency in drilling by companies was well advanced, Steuben noted, "I lost no time in extending my operations . . . I applied my system to battalions, afterwards to brigades."[22]

As with the rank-and-file, Steuben permitted no neglect of duty to pass unnoticed among the officers, high and low. The strictness of his methods at times appeared high-handed in the light of near famine in camp; and as a result, several brigadiers threatened to "quit the service" unless he relaxed his strictness.[23] Steuben refused to accede to their demands.

CHAPTER VIII

MARCH LION

Valley Forge Versus Philadelphia

The approach of March witnessed no improvement in the weather or in the Commissary and Quartermaster Departments. During the seven days that concluded February, General Greene recorded, not a scrap of meat was available to the troops, the men existing on whatever fragments of food were still available. Near the conclusion of this ghastly week many of the soldiers notified their officers that they could not continue in camp "unless fed."[1]

The conditions at Valley Forge were far from the comparative luxury that the enemy troops were experiencing in Philadelphia where "one hundred and twenty-two new stores" dispensing almost every need and many luxuries had been opened in the city for the convenience of the British Army and its Loyalist friends who still possessed hard money. The occupation of the city had witnessed an influx or pro-British speculators to replace the patriot merchants who had fled at the British approach in September. These new stores were proprietored one "by an Englishman, one by an Irishman, one by an American the remainder being one hundred and eighteen, by Scotchmen or Tories from Virginia."[2]

The influx of basic supplies and even luxuries to Philadelphia had greatly increased since the removal of the impediments in the Delaware River by the capture of Forts Mifflin and Mercer in November. Although the supplies transported to Philadelphia via the river route were far from fresh, the British Army was certainly not faced with the starvation conditions prevalent at Valley Forge. General Sir William Howe, therefore, could leisurely await the acceptance of his resignation by King and Ministry, which, he had learned from Lord Germain, had already been presented to His Majesty.[3]

With the beginning of March, Washington was impelled once more to reassure his soldiers of his personal feelings toward them. "The Commander in Chief," General Orders on the first day of the month read, "takes occasion to return his warmest thanks to the virtuous officers and soldiery of this Army for that persevering fidelity and Zeal which they have uniformly manifested in all their conduct." This "clearly proves them worthy the enviable privilege of contending for . . . the Freedom and Independence of their Country. The recent Instance of uncomplaining Patience during the scarcity of provisions in Camp is a first proof that they possess in an eminent degree the spirit of soldiers and the magnanimity of Patriots."

He assured his troops that every possible effort was being exerted to forward supplies to camp. He noted that the present adversities were "trifling indeed when compared to the transcendent Prize" of liberty which would "undoubtedly crown their Patience and Perseverance," and would afford them "the Admiration of the World, the Love of their Country and the Gratitude of Posterity."[4]

In later years Lafayette would recall that the "patient endurance of both soldiers and officers was a miracle which each moment served to renew."[5] A soldier writing to his wife said, "I miss your cooking. Here we have to change the order of our courses to get variety. For breakfast, we have bacon and smoke; for dinner, smoke and bacon; and for supper, smoke."[6]

Health was still a serious problem. Dr. Benjamin Rush could see only the physical, not the spiritual, aspect of the camp. He saw it as dirty and stinking, and the hospitals "sinks of human life."[7] Anthony Wayne noted to Richard Peters, "I am not fond of danger but I would most cheerfully agree to enter into action once every week in place of visiting each hut of my encampment (which is my constant practice), and where objects strike my eye and ear whose wretched condition beggars all description. The whole army is sick and crawling with vermin."[8]

Greene Quartermaster-General

Conditions became so bad at Valley Forge that on March 2nd Nathanael Greene, despite his initial objections, accepted the long vacant post of Quartermaster-General. Greene recognized that his new office would be far from agreeable to him. "My rank in the army and the splendor of command which I am obliged to discontinue for a time are no inconsiderable sacrifices, and what I have in return [are] a troublesome office to manage and a new set of officers in the different districts to seek for."[9] Greene had exacted one condition from Congress on which his acceptance of the post was predicated. The moment a prospect of battle became evident he was to be reinstated in his command of a division of the army until the emergency was over. To this condition both Congress and the Commander-in-Chief acceded.

Greene determined to exert every possible effort in his new post. He had lived firsthand with the terrible conditions at Valley Forge, and knew that the principal source of these was the Quartermaster Department. In order to be near the Quartermaster departmental headquarters, which he expected to establish, Greene transferred his private quarters (and Mrs. Greene) to Moore Hall. Since the Committee on Conference was still quartered and held its sessions in the mansion, the comparatively spacious building was for the time rather crowded. Greene next set up Quartermaster and subsequently Commissary Department headquarters at the Black Bull Tavern, now simply called The Bull, a mile and a half west of the encampment on the road to Pottsgrove and Reading.

Conciliatory Acts

In Britain, on the same day as Greene's appointment, March 2nd, Parliament, in obedience to Lord North's exhortation of February 17th, passed the Conciliatory Acts. From Britain's standpoint, the terms of the Acts were more than equitable and would surely negate the Franco-American Alliance. The Acts guaranteed to the Americans the "removing [of] all Doubts and Apprehensions concerning Taxation by the Parliament of Great Britain in any of the Colonies, Provinces, and Plantations" in America, and repealed the duty on tea that had so incensed Americans.

The Acts also unequivocally restored the Massachusetts Charter by repealing the Act of 1774, which had been designed "for the better Regulating the Government" of that Colony; removed the Restraining Acts against American commerce; and enabled the King "to appoint Commissioners with sufficient Powers to treat, consult, and agree" with the Americans "upon the Means of Quieting the Disorders now subsisting in certain of the Colonies."[10]

His Majesty, though displeased with the Acts, presently appointed Frederick Howard, Earl of Carlisle, as chief Commissioner. Also appointed to serve were Admiral Sir Richard Howe, Sir William Howe, Sir Henry Clinton, (Sir William's expected replacement), George Johnstone, (late governor of West Florida) and William Eden. Both Howes declined the appointment. Johnstone and Eden were considered by the Ministry as ideal choices since through long residence in America they had presumably established close relations with many of the principal "rebels," and had frequently reproached the Ministry for its anti-American actions.

The proposed American irruption into Canada having proved a failure, Congress directed the Board of War to notify Lafayette that he was "to suspend for the present [the suspension would prove permanent] the intended irruption."[11] The only material result of the whole affair had been a relatively fruitful consultation between Lafayette and the Oneida Indians, a tribe of the Six Nations. As a result of this conference, the Oneidas promised that when spring arrived they would provide a strong war party to act as scouts for the patriot army in Pennsylvania. With this information in hand, Congress empowered Washington "to employ . . . a body of Indians, not exceeding 400."[12]

A "thin C[ongre]ss," so-called because many of its members rarely attended the sessions, and a delinquent Board of War continued to embarrass Washington by their dilatory actions toward forming the magazines so necessary to the subsistence of the army. The noticeable lack of attendance on the Congressional sessions permitted the faction opposed to Washington to hamper his efforts. Congressman William Duer pleaded with the absent members of Congress to return to their duties and put more force in Congressional actions.[13] Washington, at the same time, was writing to the Board of War, "As the season approaches fast when we may expect to draw together a considerable reinforcement to the Army I cannot help having apprehensions that we shall be at a loss for Arms and Accoutrements for them" as well as supplies for the troops at present in camp.[14]

Hardships Continue

The almost constant lack of supplies, especially food, at Valley Forge, continued to force the Commander-in-Chief to dispatch foraging parties into the countryside in an effort to unearth some hitherto hidden caches of food and fodder. Numerous complaints reached Pennsylvania's President Wharton from civilian patriots that the foraging parties were frequently seizing their property without offering payment or even promissory certificates, contrary to the Commander-in-Chief's express orders. Wharton passed these complaints on to Washington.

The Commander-in-Chief, after conferring on the subject with Pennsylvania Congressman Joseph Reed, a member of the Committee on Conference, replied to Wharton, "There is nothing I have more at Heart, than to discharge the great duties incumbent on me with the strictest Attention to the Ease and Convenience of the People. Every Instance, therefore of Hardship or Oppression, exercised by the Officers of any Department under my immediate Controul gives me the most sensible Concern, and should be immediately punished, if complaints were properly made and supported." There had been, Washington admitted, "some Foundation for such Complaints," but stern measures were necessary as a result of "the great Delay and Backwardness of the People in forwarding Supplies and affording the Means for Transportation."

Washington took the occasion of his letter to remind Wharton that it had been at the insistence of the Pennsylvania authorities that the army, contrary to the Commander-in-Chief's desire, was wintering in the eastern part of the state. It was therefore incumbent on those authorities to assist in solving the logistical problems facing the army in a location where "with unparallel'd Patience" the troops "have gone thro' a severe and inclement Winter, unprovided with any of those Conveniences and Comforts which are usually the Soldier's Lot, after the Duty of the Field is over." Washington added, "We are distressed even in small matters but our sufferings in Camp for want of Forage and Waggons is beyond all description."[15]

Washington had been able to obtain for the transportation of supplies "few carriages [i.e., wagons] but what he took by force" from local inhabitants. Many of these people "hid their waggon wheels" in order to render their wagons useless. The Americans soon "compelled them to produce" the missing wheels by threats of reprisal. Some Loyalist sympathizers "disabled their waggons" in an effort to keep the vehicles out of American hands.[16]

As mid-March approached, the weather continued undecided. There seemed, as General Varnum wrote home to Rhode Island, "no Distinction of Season. The Weather frequently changes five time[s] in Twenty four Hours. The Coldest I have perceived has been in this month. Snow falls; but falls only to produce Mire and Dirt." Varnum then grew philosophical. "But for the virtuous few of the Army" throughout the harsh winter "I am persuaded That This Country must long before this have been destroyed. It is saved for our sakes; and its Salvation ought to cause Repentence in us for all our Sins, if evil and Misery are the Consequences of Iniquity. For my own part, I believe they are; And expect by this Pennance to emerge into the World, after leaving this Place, with all Accounts fully ballanced."[17]

Despite the casual hints of spring, the spells of cold outweighed the "gentle breezes and cooling zephyrs" that Varnum occasionally noted in the air. The men were still "obliged to sleep by turns for want of blankets to cover the whole, and the rest keeping watch by the fires. There is hardly a man" who, at one time or another, a soldier noted, "has not been frostbitten."[18] Both officers and men continued to grumble against

nature, the Commissary Department, the Quartermaster Department, Congress and the Board of War. A Congressional recommendation that the troops should observe Lent was greeted with sarcastic comments. The men had already been fasting and worse for months.

General Gates, President of the Board of War, put in an appearance at Valley Forge to confer with the Commander-in-Chief and the Committee on Conference, among other matters, on the subject of the proposed exchange of prisoners. Washington had been promoting this business with General Howe with a double motive in view: first, the relief of the American prisoners, and second, the return of Maj.-General Charles Lee, captured in 1776. Both the proposed general exchange and that of General Lee (for British Maj.-General Richard Prescott who had been captured by an American raid on Rhode Island) had been postponed indefinitely because of the Congressional order that the financial accounts of the British prisoners in American hands must be settled first.

Washington did not hesitate to condemn this Congressional stipulation as "diametrically opposite both to the spirit and letter of the propositions made on my part" to the enemy commander, "and acceded to on his. The public, as well as my own personal honor and faith are pledged for the performance." Washington feared that much "dissatisfaction and disgust" would prevail both in the army and in the country in general, as well as "resentment and desperation" among the American captives in British prisons, if Congress refused to cancel its recent prohibition.

Washington, as a result, had been forced to request Howe to agree to a postponement of the scheduled meeting of Commissioners at Germantown. Howe wrote to Lord Germain that since the Americans had cancelled the meeting "without assigning any satisfactory reason," he was led "to believe that neither" the American commander "nor those under whose authority he acts, are sincere in their professions to carry an exchange into execution at this time."[19]

On March 10th Washington, "in pursuance to a Resolve of Congress," directed General Sullivan "to proceed with all convenient dispatch" to Rhode Island to replace the recently resigned Major General Joseph Spencer,[20] whose troops were keeping the enemy force, which occupied Newport, under surveillance. The Americans had hopes of eventually driving the enemy from their Rhode Island stronghold.

Sullivan's departure from Valley Forge denuded the army of another high ranking officer, but the prospect of Lafayette's and DeKalb's early return from Albany would eventually offset this loss, though neither Lafayette nor DeKalb had orders from the Board of War or Congress to return to the army. Lafayette, fretful at his inactivity and the failure of the expedition, worriedly wrote to the Commander-in-Chief. In answer, Washington replied, "You seem to apprehend," that the failure of the Canadian expedition "will fall upon you." On the contrary, Washington was fully "persuaded that every one will applaud your prudence in renouncing a Project, in pursuing which you would vainly have attempted Physical Impossibilities."[21]

Quintin's and Hancock's Bridges

Shortly after the middle of March Washington was notified that a major enemy force was foraging in Salem County, New Jersey. A detachment under the command of Lt.-Colonel Charles Mawhood, consisting of some 1,500 men, including "the 17th, 27th and 46th regiments," Major John Graves Simcoe's "Queen's Rangers and one hundred Royal Pennsylvania Militia," had sailed south from Philadelphia via the Delaware River under convoy on the 11th and had landed in Salem County on March 17th.

The raiders "took with them four heavy pieces" of cannon "and two howitzers, and provisions for two weeks. Six empty transports followed them to Salem to take on forage and cattle, the *Camilla* frigate acting as convoy."[22] On receiving this information Washington immediately dispatched Colonel Israel Shreve and the 2nd New Jersey Regiment from Valley Forge to lend support to the New Jersey Militia who were hastily gathering at Hancock's and Quintin's Bridges on Alloway's Creek in Salem County to oppose the enemy incursion.

At Salem, Colonel Mawhood published a stern demand that the Militia should "lay down their arms and depart, each man to his own home," in return for which the British would refrain from all unnecessary depredations and confine their business entirely to foraging. "If, on the contrary, the militia should be deluded and blind to their true interest and happiness," Mawhood threatened to put weapons "into the hands of the inhabitants well affected" to the British cause and "attack all such of the militia as remain in arms, burn and destroy their houses and other property, and reduce them [and] their unfortunate wives and children to beggary and distress."

Colonel Elijah Hand, who had assumed command of the Militia, memorably replied to Mawhood, "After expressing your sentiments of humanity, you proceed to make a request which I think you would despise us if we complied with. Your proposal that we should lay down our arms we absolutely reject. We have taken them up to maintain rights which are

dearer to us than our lives, and will not lay them down till either success has crowned our cause with victory . . . or we meet with an honorable death."

Hand then reproved Mawhood for the slaughters, which the British had perpetrated at Quintin's Bridge on March 18th and at Hancock's Bridge on the night of the succeeding day. The Quintin's Bridge slaughter had resulted from a British ambush sprung on a column of the Militia which unwarily pursued a feigned British retreat. The enemy, by "denying quarter" to those militiamen "who surrendered themselves prisoners" had acted little in accord with the accepted laws of war. At Hancock's Bridge Simcoe's Rangers, by a night march, had surrounded the Hancock house and bayoneted "in cold blood" some twenty or thirty militiamen "who were taken by surprise in a situation in which they neither could nor did attempt to make any resistance."[23] The frightened militiamen had fled to the attic where Ranger bayonets ended their lives. The Rangers, refusing to bother questioning their victims, had even killed old Hancock himself and two other staunch Loyalists, one of them Hancock's brother.

The British raiders returned to Philadelphia on March 29th bearing their booty and leaving in their wake a considerably devastated Salem County. American patriots were outraged by these bloody attacks.

CHAPTER IX

SALUTE TO SPRING

A Retrospect

During the latter half of March the worst scenes at Valley Forge were ending. The weather became warm, and the "appearance of verdure" across the land, gave assurance that spring was near.

In retrospect to the severe winter, General Lachlan McIntosh was obliged to report to Governor Richard Caswell of North Carolina, "I am sorry to have to inform you the men of my Brigade," the North Carolinians, "have suffered severely this winter. Fifty of them died in and about camp since the beginning of January last." The brigade had reached the encampment in December as the most undermanned brigade in the army. By late March the brigade had "near two hundred sick" in camp and nearby hospitals, "besides as many more reported sick absent in different hospitals" in other parts of the state and in New Jersey.

McIntosh described the condition of his brigade as "most distressing," especially since the brigade could boast only one doctor present "to attend the whole of them." The brigade's other doctor had taken permanent leave without McIntosh's permission, and the general could not "help charging him with inhumanity in leaving so many of his brave country men to perish without assistance."[1] In all, 214 North Carolinians of the 1,072 who arrived at Valley Forge, died either in camp or in the various hospitals during this period, which was nearly half the deaths the North Carolina troops sustained during the entire war.

The northern troops had not fared much better despite being more accustomed to severe winters. By early spring some three thousand men from all the states represented at Valley Forge were either sick with, or convalescent from, smallpox despite the Commander-in-Chief's untiring efforts to have all the men

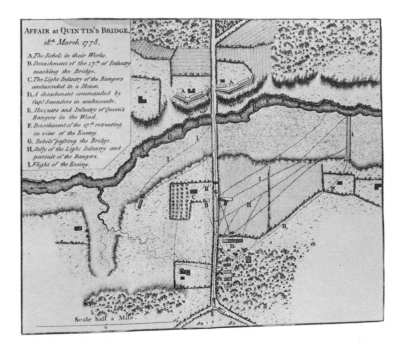

ATTACK AT QUINTIN'S BRIDGE. *Map drawn by Major John Graves Simcoe of the Queen's Rangers (Loyalists) to illustrate the action at Quintin's Bridge, Salem County, N. J., March 18, 1778. The map shows, top to bottom, the American fortifications on Aloes (Alloways) Creek, the New Jersey Militia's pursuit of the feigned British retreat, the British ambush commanded by Capt. Saunders of the Rangers, and the American flight. Several Americans were drowned while attempting to recross the creek below the bridge. This map was published in Simcoe's* JOURNAL OF THE OPERATIONS OF THE QUEEN'S RANGERS, *Exeter (England), 1787.*

inoculated against the disease. Although the death rate began to lessen as the days passed, the humble mounds that littered the encampment testified to the constant burials that had taken place and were still continuing. As a result of the scarcity of clothing, many of the dead had been buried naked in unmarked graves, and their tattered clothing reused. Lieutenant John Waterman, Quartermaster of the 2nd Rhode Island Regiment and Commissary of Varnum's Brigade, gained lasting fame by occupying the only identified grave at Valley Forge.[2]

Toward the last of March supplies began to arrive on a regular basis now that the roads were clear. The waters of the Schuylkill increased enough to permit shipments down the river to Valley Forge, from Reading, where large quantities of supplies had accumulated. Reinforcements, too, began to arrive, particularly from the southward, and Steuben's drill methods were in full employment. Washington busied himself with plans for a spring campaign. Officers' furloughs, already severely limited, were cancelled and the fortifications at Valley Forge were placed in a more defensible state, after consultations with staff officers concerned.

As the soldiers became healthier, some of the old camp grumbles reappeared. The inter-Colonial jealousies that had been prevalent prior to and during the early stages of the war became evident once more. Pennsylvanians spoke scathingly of the New Englanders' "miserable appearance, and what is worse, the miserable behavior of the Yankees. Among them is the strangest mixture of Negroes and Indians and whites, with old men and young children, which, together with a nasty, lousy appearance, makes a most shocking spectacle."[3]

The Rhode Island troops in particular relied on Negroes to fill their ranks. Nor did the Virginians and North Carolinians hold a more exalted opinion of the Pennsylvanians. There were ethnic antipathies, too, which resulted in a near-riot on St. Patrick's Day when the Pennsylvania-Germans erected a derisive "Paddy" that aroused Irish tempers. Only the soothing influence of Washington prevented an intra-army battle.

On March 19th Washington, noting the efficiency with which Baron von Steuben was drilling the troops, officially appointed him Inspector-General *pro tempore* of the troops at Valley Forge, pending Congressional confirmation. The Commander-in-Chief also directed the various brigade commanders "to make choice of a Major" from each brigade "whose activity, Intelligence, Address and decided Taste for the kind of employment, qualify him in a superior degree for the office" of sub-inspector to his brigade.[4]

With the coming of warmer weather, Washington ordered that the camp be strictly policed of its refuse, and that closer heed be paid to sanitary conditions. Officers were directed to "be very attentive to the water their men drink. The little springs about the camp from which [the soldiers] have been accustomed to supply themselves during the winter will in their present state become extreamly impure and pernicious in the approaching warm season." The old springs and wells were to be capped, and new wells "sunk in proper places with barrels to preserve them." The new wells were to be frequently "cleansed to prevent an accumulation of Filth."[5] He also directed that sulphur or gunpowder should be frequently burned in each hut to purify the atmosphere. The huts were to be kept as clean and neat as possible. When continued warm weather was assured, the mud-and-stone chinking between the logs of the huts was to be removed to fumigate the interiors more fully and keep the air circulating and fresh.

By March 20th, Washington was informed that the annual General Meeting of the Quakers in Philadelphia was scheduled, and that many Quakers in the areas surrounding the city had none too secretly indicated their intention to attend the meeting provided they were able to elude American patrols. The Commander-in-Chief immediately notified General Lacey of the Militia that "Sunday next, being the time" set for the Quaker meeting, "a number of that Society will probably be attempting to go into Philadelphia. This is an intercourse that we should by all means endeavor to interrupt, as the plans settled at these meetings are of the most pernicious tendency." Also, if the rural Quakers were allowed to proceed to the city, supplies and information might be borne to the enemy. "I would therefore have you dispose your parties in such a Manner as will most probably" permit the Militia to "fall in with these people." The offending Quakers, when discovered, were to be arrested or turned back, and as punishment their horses were to be confiscated and sent to the army.[6]

Patrols from Morgan's riflemen at Radnor and other regular troops were ordered to block those roads south of the Schuylkill that the Militia was unable to cover. The remnant of Lachlan McIntosh's North Carolina Brigade was ordered across the Schuylkill to support the Militia, and to oppose an enemy column reported to be scouting on the Germantown Pike west of Germantown.

Washington's precautions, which he had taken care to publicize, prevented most of the rural Quakers from slipping into the city. Nevertheless, a rump meeting of the urban Friends was held. The meeting unanimously lamented "the present prevailing Calamities [which] have been suffered to fall so heavy amongst us in this Land." The meeting also spiritually conveyed its prayers to those Quakers and other Philadelphians "who are in Bonds" as exiled prisoners of the Americans at Winchester, Virginia.[7] These exiles had been arrested as supposed enemies of the American cause and had been transported south in September.

By January 1778, Congress was already privately reconsidering the exiles' status and "offered to them their Liberty" on condition that each should affirm an oath of allegiance to the United States.[8] The affirmation of oaths being contrary to Quaker principle, the prisoners refused this demand. Yet, there was a general inclination in Congress and among the Pennsylvania authorities (who at the direction of Congress had actually made the arrests) to free the exiles.

Several of the exiles' wives (principally Mesdames Israel Pemberton, Henry Drinker, Henry Pleasants and Owen Jones) determined to take the matter of their husbands' release into their own hands. If American and British passes could be obtained, they planned to proceed to Lancaster and York to lay petitions for amnesty before the Pennsylvania Council and Congress respectively. With a British pass readily obtained from Howe, the four ladies accompanied by a single male Quaker escort left Philadelphia by carriage on April 5th.

They proceeded ten miles west on the Lancaster and Old Gulph Roads in the direction of Valley Forge, where they became the overnight guests at the home of a fellow Quaker, John Roberts, in Mill Creek Valley. The guests were welcomed by Roberts' wife alone, since her husband had fled to Philadelphia, having been designated by the American authorities as an enemy sympathizer.[9] An American scouting force

45

"of near one hundred men" discovered the ladies, but on being told of their mission, refused to interrupt their journey.

The following morning the petitioners drove to the advance American picket at The Gulph where, after a brief detention, their passage to Valley Forge was facilitated by a temporary pass and a token guard of soldiers. They arrived at Headquarters "about 1/2 past one" in the afternoon and immediately "requested an audience with the General." While awaiting an answer to this request they "sat with his wife (a social, pretty kind of woman) until he came in. It was not long before" the American commander entered and, as Elizabeth Drinker, the diarist of the expedition, recorded, "discoursed with us freely, but not so long as we could have wished, as dinner was served, to which he invited us . . . We had an elegant dinner" under the circumstances, "which was soon over, when we went out with the Genls. wife to her Chamber and saw no more of him."[10]

Mrs. Pemberton had been permitted time to present a letter to the Commander-in-Chief pleading on behalf of themselves and the wives and families of the other exiles for the release of the prisoners. Two of the prisoners, she verbally informed Washington, had already died, and the rest were reported in ill health despite the considerable leniencies permitted by their captors. The letter also requested that a wagon-load of supplies be allowed to proceed unmolested to Virginia for the exiles' relief. Since the prisoners were under the jurisdiction of the civil authorities, Washington was obliged to deny these requests, but promised to forward the letter to the Pennsylvania Council at Lancaster for consideration.

Besides this verbal promise, the Quaker women received a pass in the form of a personal letter from Washington to Thomas Wharton, Jr. "Mrs. Jones, Mrs. Pleasants and two other ladies," the Commander-in-Chief notified the President of Pennsylvania, "waited upon me this day for permission to pass to York Town, to endeavour to obtain the release of their Friends. As they were admitted by the Officer of the advanced picket to come within the Camp, I thought it safer to suffer them to proceed, than to oblige them to return immediately to the City . . . You will judge the propriety," Washington conceded to Wharton, "of permitting them to proceed further than Lancaster, but from appearances I imagine their request" to proceed to York "may be safely granted. As they seem much distressed, humanity pleads strongly in their behalf."[11]

Leaving camp, the petitioners "crossed ye large bridge" erected by General Sullivan "over Schuylkill" and lodged at Fatlands, the residence of Quaker James Vaux, a short distance beyond the river. The following morning they drove west via Pawling's Ford to the Nutt and Ridge Roads which lead west to Lancaster.

As early as March 10th Wharton had written to Congress that nothing dangerous need be anticipated from the Quaker prisoners' release. Wharton also suggested the release of former governor John Penn and Chief Justice Benjamin Chew. "The dangerous example which their long continuance in banishment may afford . . . has already given uneasiness to some good friends" who were critical of the arbitrary methods employed in arresting them.[12] Congress presently forwarded orders to the Virginia authorities to release the prisoners and return them to Pennsylvania. Thus, the four wives who had been permitted to proceed to York were united with their husbands, and the entire party returned to Philadelphia where "the joy amongst the members" of the Quaker sect "over the unexpected return of their brethren was extremely great."[13]

On their return to the city, the ex-prisoners found conditions considerably changed. By the latter part of March, Robert Proud was noting, "The Vigilance of the Rebel Party by Means of the Country Militia supported by Washington's Army has on every Side distressed the Inhabitants of this City to a high Degree, by preventing Provisions coming in from the Country (tho' the Royal Army appear to be in want of nothing) . . . Hard Money is scarcely to be got or borrowed; unless in trade; and the Expense of Living enormously high. Most Employments are entirely stopped, unless what relates to the Military, and desolation is laying waste the Country especially around the City. We wait for a Change, to relieve great Numbers from otherwise inevitable Beggary and Ruin, and which indeed have already happened to many." In the stores the "sales are Small and principally in the Hands of European Adventurers."[14] Gold and silver specie were the only mediums of exchange readily acceptable and civilian coffers now contained little money other than "the old legal paper money" in Colonial and Continental currency which had been declared void by the British authorities.

Steuben Takes Charge

At Valley Forge, by the latter part of March, food and clothing began to reach camp in such comparative abundance that "multitudes of soldiers," were accused of "selling their clothes for drink" or of "otherwise wasting them."[15] Gen. Steuben, learning of this, immediately ordered a "regular muster of clothing" among the troops in an effort to arrest the practice.

Steuben also "introduced a number of salutary regulations" in the camp and the hospitals "which contributed more to the health and comfort of the troops than did the utmost efforts of all the medical staff."[16] Sanitary measures were strictly supervised by the omnipresent Inspector-General who admonished all officers that, "There is nothing which gains an officer the love of his soldiers more than his care of them" whether they were in sickness or in health, but especially "under the distress of sickness."

The Inspector-General ordered that, since the weather was moderating, "two or three tents should be set apart in every regiment for the reception of the sick" rather than sending the mildly sick to the overcrowded hospitals. This practice was to be followed wherever the army camped as long as the weather remained conducive to the practice. Stricter supervision of the sanitary conditions in all the hospitals was instituted. "When a soldier dies or is dismissed the hospital," Steuben directed, "the straw he lay on is to be burnt, and the bedding," too precious to be destroyed, was to be "well washed and aired before another is permitted to use it."[17]

By March 24th, Steuben reported to the Commander-in-Chief that the training of the troops had progressed to such a state as would permit the regiments of the army to proceed with regimental drills under the supervision of their own officers. Washington ordered that thereafter, or until further notice, "at nine o'Clock precisely all the Brigades will begin their exercise, in each Regiment on its own parade and the Inspector General will attend the Exercise." The drilling, after a decent break for dinner, was to be continued until 5 p.m.[18] With campaigning weather imminent, long hours of drill were imperative; and the training of brigades and divisions in large-scale maneuvers had yet to be accomplished.

Also, on March 24th, Washington wrote to the President of

Congress, "I have this whole Winter been clearly of opinion that General Howe's movement would be very early this Spring to take advantage of the Weak state of our army." It was therefore "our indispensable duty to reinforce and arrange our Army as speedily as possible, that we may . . . be prepared for defence [or] take advantage of any favourable circumstance, which may happen to injure the enemy." He again begged Congress to concur in "a speedy adoption" of the rearrangement of the army he had recently recommended, and to appoint sufficient General officers, "as I am convinced that we shall be plunged into a Campaign before our arrangements are made and the Army properly organized."[19]

Congress' delay in complying with Washington's recommendations was somewhat favorably offset by news that arrived from another quarter. "A number of trading vessels" loaded with military supplies had "arrived to the Southward" from France.[20] If the supplies and weapons could be hastened north, they might arrive in time to equip the troops in camp as well as expected recruits. Washington, on the advice of the foreign officers, especially Steuben, was extremely anxious that as many soldiers as possible be armed with the Charleville-type musket, standard weapon of the French Army. A uniform shoulder arm might eventually eliminate the logistic difficulty posed by different gun calibers necessitating various sizes of ball. Instead of depending in great measure on the troops for the manufacture of cartridges, production and storage of ammunition could be centralized.

Although Washington was as anxious to acquire recruits as to acquire weapons with which to arm them, he was obliged to prohibit a particularly reprehensible mode of recruiting. "Several of the towns" in Massachusetts "had hired British Deserters" from Burgoyne's interned army "and had sent them on" to Valley Forge as substitutes since Massachusetts had been unable to complete her quota of recruits from patriot ranks. "I shall be obliged to send them back," Washington notified General William Heath, the American commander at Boston, "or they will most certainly . . . desert again to the Enemy and carry off their Arms." The Commander-in-Chief "desired the [Massachusetts] council to put a stop to this practice" in obedience to "a late Resolve of Congress" which had ordered "an absolute prohibition to the inlistment of Deserters, it being better to be deficient in the quota than to have such Men."[21]

In preparation for military activity, Washington directed that all officers reduce the quantity of personal baggage. In the past, the superabundance of baggage had not only considerably hampered the army's movements but had proved costly to the public safety and purse by taking troops from battle service to guard the baggage train. Washington "expected that the General and Field Officers will set the Example and see that it is strictly followed by all those under their respective Commands."[22] All officers were "to provide themselves with necessaries only which cannot be dispensed with," and the omission of cumbersome "Chests and Boxes" to port personal belongings was strongly recommended. "Portmanteaus and Valises made of strong Duck" were suggested as replacements.[23]

To preserve the army as a cohesive unit in anticipation of any precipitous move, Washington directed that no scouting parties other than those directly ordered by Headquarters were to be permitted. The interior lines of defense were ordered completed against a possible enemy offensive.

Despite the fact that many states were providing additional troops, Pennsylvania was proving rather backward on this score.

Wayne complained to President Wharton that he had "but little hopes of being Supplied with many Recruits unless the Officers" sent on the recruiting service "in the Back Counties meet with more success than those in Phil'a. and Chester [Counties]—an Officer from the Latter came in yesterday after being out five weeks without a single Recruit."[24]

Wharton replied that the State Council was "of opinion with you that a greater number of officers should be employed on the recruiting service," though he was personally "a good deal astonished to find that an officer could be five weeks in Chester County, and not have it in his power to recruit one man." Wharton expressed doubt that this officer had "been very attentive to that part of his duty," but was able to assure Wayne that "the accounts" concerning recruiting "that Council receives from most of the Counties are, upon the whole, favourable."[25]

Wayne should not have been completely disappointed at the lack of success in recruiting in his home County, Chester, since he had long known that the remaining patriots in the County were in a minority to Loyalists and pacific Quakers. The same condition was true of the eastern parts of Philadelphia County. Nor was eastern Pennsylvania the sole culprit in failing to produce its quota of men; several sister states had "proceeded but very little way in recruiting;" and Washington was fearful that "the augmentation of the army" would suffer as a result of the non-completion of the regiments.

Although the American commander had only recently (March 24) expressed his opinion to the President of Congress that Sir William Howe would soon initiate military operations, he was also "fully of opinion that the enemy depend as much or more upon our divisions and the disaffection that they expect to create by sending their emissaries among the people, than they do by force of arms." Two of these emissaries had already been apprehended and hanged at Lancaster.

The Commander-in-Chief found "the situation of matters in this state melancholy and alarming," and ripe for British subversion. "We have daily proof that a majority of people in this quarter are only restrained from supplying the enemy with horses and every kind of necessary thro fear of punishment, and although I have made a number of severe examples I cannot put a stop to the intercourse."[26] An inhabitant detected in this traffic by Lacey's Militia was sentenced "to be hanged Dead, Dead, Dead,"[27] and other rustics had suffered similar or lesser punishments, including confinement for the duration.

A British officer out of uniform had been detected as far west as Lancaster County purchasing horses for enemy use and had been summarily hanged. The British officer prisoners, held in supposed durance at Reading and Lancaster, had been permitted excessive liberty and had thereby "converted many ignorant people" to pro-British sympathies "by their Stories of the power of Britain." Washington, therefore, was distinctly hopeful that a "general exchange" of prisoners was "not far off, by which means we shall be rid of all that set" of enemy officers, "and I am convinced that we had better, in future, send all Officers" taken prisoners back to the enemy "upon parole than keep them among us."[28]

The most urgent reason for an early exchange of prisoners, however, was the reportedly sorrowful condition of the American captives in Philadelphia where "several hundred prisoners" were sardined into the Walnut Street Gaol in space originally designed for the comparatively few civilian delinquents imprisoned in normal times. An American occupant wrote, "A few small rooms were sequestered for the officers . . . Each room must contain sixteen men. We fully covered the floor when we lay down to rest, and the poor [enlisted] soldiers were shut into rooms of the same magnitude with double the number."

"The soldiers were soon seized with a jail fever and in the course of three months it swept off four hundred men, who were all buried in one continuous grave" in Potter's Field, now Washington Square, "without coffins." The Reverend James Morris, an American chaplain who shared the sufferers' captivity, recorded, "Such a scene of mortality I never witnessed before . . . Death was so frequent that it ceased to terrify, it ceased to warn, it ceased to alarm survivors."[29]

Prisoner Exchange Commissions

On March 28th, having procured assent that he might ignore Congress' recent stipulation concerning the British prisoners' accounts, Washington appointed as American commissioners to deal with their enemy counterparts on the subject of the proposed exchange, Colonel Elias Boudinot, the Commissary of Prisoners, Colonel William Grayson and two of the Commander-in-Chief's personal aides, Lt.-Colonels Robert Hanson Harrison and Alexander Hamilton. Although Boudinot had recently requested acceptance of his resignation as Commissary of Prisoners, at the direct request of Washington he agreed to continue in that office until the present negotiations were reasonably well accomplished. Representing the British, General Howe appointed Colonel Charles O'Hara, Colonel Humphrey Stephens and Captain Richard Fitzpatrick.

The initial meeting between the commissioners was scheduled at Germantown on March 31st. Congress had empowered the American representatives "to adjust all differences," and "to fix the exchange and accommodation of prisoners of war upon a more certain, liberal and ample foundation" with respect to the "principles of justice, humanity and mutual advantage" to both sides.[30] With the exchange now seemingly in firm prospect, both contestants had their "hopes and wishes that nothing will cause further delay" in the negotiations.[31] Washington renewed his pledge to Howe "that German Town shall be considered a neutral place" during the negotiations, "and that, no Troops shall be permitted to enter it" while the conference lasted "except the guards mutually sent to attend" the conferees.[32]

Sir William had notified Washington that he intended to send "a commissioned Officer, a Sergeant and twelve dragoons" as escort for the British commissioners, and would agree to the presence of an equal number of American guards in the village. Howe added that, in addition to his three commissioners, "Joshua Loring, my Commissary General of Prisoners, will give his occasional attendance" at the meetings if his presence should be required.[33] The first meeting occurred as scheduled on March 31st, but made little progress, then adjourned until the following day. The British commissioners returned to Philadelphia to confer with Howe and Loring.

On the morning of April 1st the Americans re-opened the proceedings with a discussion of American objections to several points in the paper submitted by the British commissioners on the previous day, the principal objection being that the paper did not include a "recital of authority" by which Sir William Howe was acting in instituting the discussions. The Americans maintained that the British Ministry might, at a future date, negate any agreements to which Sir William affixed his assent. After some discussion, the British commissioners informed the Americans that it would be necessary for them to confer with

Howe on the subject; and that they would therefore again retire to Philadelphia.

The British noted that General Howe "expected the commissioners on both sides were always to retire, after the business of the day, within their respective lines, and that the neutrality of German Town was only to continue during the time of actual negotiations, as, on account of the proximity of that place to Philadelphia, many inconveniences might attend" the American commissioners' "constant residence there." This request gave the appearance that Howe distrusted the Americans, who might trespass on the agreements regulating the negotiations and communicate with patriot agents whom Howe was aware were loose in the city.

This proposal, the American commissioners reported to Washington on their return to camp, "was equally unexpected and surprising" to the American commissioners, and they "considered it contrary to the tenor of the correspondence" between the Commanders-in-Chief "for the appointment of a place of treaty." The British requirement would certainly delay the daily negotiations since the American commissioners would be forced to travel "seventeen miles" twice a day. "For the dispatch of business" the Americans thought it necessary for the commissioners of both sides to "constantly remain together."[34]

Washington immediately notified Howe that he was "sorry to learn" of this unfortunate "interruption to a business, which we are mutually interested should proceed without more delay." He "had no idea, but that the Gentlemen on both sides were to remain constantly at German Town 'till the conclusion of the treaty." If the location of the negotiations at Germantown was the only adverse specification, Washington was "perfectly agreeable" that the two commanders "fix upon some place not liable to" Sir William's objection. "Newtown," in Bucks County, Washington observed, "appears to answer this description" since the place was remote enough from Philadelphia to allay any scruples the British commander entertained.[35] Sir William presently gave his consent to this proposal.

Commissary and Medical Departments Reappraised

At Valley Forge, Washington was earnestly pressing the resurrection of the American Army. With the regiments nearly prepared to perform maneuvers on brigade and divisional levels under the aegis of Steuben, the continuing lack of general officers had become more apparent. Without proper officers of sufficient rank, the brigades and divisions, in conjunction with the artillery, could not properly practice major maneuvers. Washington therefore directed Generals Knox, Woodford, and Weedon to return immediately to camp; Knox from Massachusetts, Woodford and Weedon from Virginia. Knox presently appeared. Woodford also returned to camp, but Weedon, fretful that Congress had finally decided in favor of Woodford's claim to seniority, remained in Virginia.

In an effort to assure a constant supply of provisions in camp and to stock magazines for a possible early campaign, General Greene directed the Commissary Department, over which he as Quartermaster-General had assumed supervision, to preserve a proper deportment toward the civilians with whom they dealt. Such deportment had been too frequently ignored in the past, and many persons with whom the Commissary Department wished to continue dealings had been antagonized.

To this end, Greene directed, "punctuality in payment for such articles as shall be purchased, will be highly necessary."

SMALL COMMISSARY QUARTERS AT VALLEY FORGE. *The building is noted on maps as located on property belonging to "the Estate of John Wilkinson" in Revolutionary times, but its actual occupants at the time of the encampment are unknown.*

Greene expressed his desire "to accommodate the whole business" of both the Quartermaster and Commissary Departments "to the ease and convenience of the inhabitants of the country, as far as shall be consistent with the good of the service." He hoped thereby that he and his agents would acquire the inhabitants' "cheerful aid and assistance on all occasions in promoting the common cause."[36]

On April 9th, Congress relieved Greene of the responsibility of the Commissary Department by appointing Colonel Jeremiah Wadsworth of Connecticut to the post of Commissary-General. Wadsworth had acquired considerable experience in this line, having acted as Deputy Commissary-General in his native state. Washington was certain that the new Commissary-General "possesses the most useful quality of great activity and address in the business," and was pleased with the appointment.[37]

Wadsworth's duties included supervision of the Clothier-General's Department under the direct supervision of James Mease. Anthony Wayne nevertheless continued to by-pass the Continental Clothier-General and deal directly with Paul Zantzinger in Lancaster as his personal clothing agent for the Pennsylvania Line. Wayne, who had gone to Lancaster in January to further his arrangements with Zantzinger, at the end of March directed Lt.-Colonel Stephen Bayard to proceed to Lancaster and assist Zantzinger, who was experiencing difficulties. Linen overalls, shirts, shoes, gaiters, garters and "one black Stock and hair Comb for each man" were needed for the troops, "together with Infantry Caps and other Clothing, but the Overalls, Shirts and Gaiters were most Essential."[38]

Wayne, still not despairing of an influx of Pennsylvania recruits, directed Zantzinger and Bayard to plan on clothing at least three thousand men. Bayard replied that the best he and Zantzinger could accomplish at present was to purchase enough linen from the Continental Clothier-General "for Twelve hundred shirts" which would be manufactured in Lancaster and forwarded to camp within a few days. No more acquisitions of clothing could be expected in the foreseeable future. Bayard

soon requested Wayne's permission to return to Valley Forge. He was "heartily tired of Lancaster" and its political atmosphere and "wou'd much rather be in camp."[39]

In camp at Valley Forge, despite a still unbalanced diet, full stomachs improved the health of the troops, and sickness began to wane. Furthermore, the Medical Department was beginning to effect more efficacious measures for caring for the men and preventing new outbreaks of disease. By April the hospitals were functioning relatively smoothly despite the continuing crowded conditions. Medicines were in better supply. Their growing quantity permitted the department to commence preparing the medical chests that would accompany the regimental surgeons when the army marched from Valley Forge. The apothecary store was moved from Manheim to Yellow Springs in order to locate it nearer the camp; and by the middle of April, this dispensing store was ready for business. Surgeon-General Dr. John Cochran sent orders that representatives of Greene's Division "bring their chests first" to Yellow Springs.

The apothecaries thereafter "propose going thro' the whole army," filling the regimental chests division by division. The work proved slow, since supplies of medicine from Carlisle arrived tardily; and considerable time was consumed in delivering the chests from Valley Forge over the dozen miles of rough and often muddy road that separated the camp from the apothecary store. Dr. John Brown Cutting suggested that the business might be facilitated by the purchase of new chests which should be smaller and lighter than the ones presently in use. The new chests could be pre-filled and shipped to Yellow Springs ready for immediate use. Here they could be traded for the old chests, which would then be used in the hospitals.[40]

The cost of the Medical Department was now consuming some $20,000 per month; and Dr. Jonathan Potts, Purveyor-General of the Middle Medical Department, was frequently obliged to appeal to Congress for funds to keep the department in business. The department's coffers were often empty. Joseph Shippen, Paymaster of the Medical Department, was embarrassed to notify Dr. Potts early in May that the Paymaster had been "writing with the greatest impatience for 50 or 60,000 dollars" from Congress "to pay off the pressing demands from Lancaster and every other part of our Department." Potts had requested that $3,000 should be immediately forwarded to him for the departmental expenses at Reading. "If I had a single shilling," Shippen observed, "the Credit of our Hospitals should not suffer by any detention of payment nor would I omit any thing in my power to serve you if I could invent the ways and means to come at it."[41]

Even when money was available, the hospital agents experienced difficulties in purchasing foodstuffs, since they were forced to compete with the army's purchasing agents. Dr. Potts complained of this competition to Colonel Ephraim Blaine, Deputy Commissary-General of the Army, and requested Blaine to institute some arrangement whereby foodstuffs would be mutually purchased for the troops and the hospitals.

Blaine replied by blaming the hospital purchasing agents, whom he accused of inattention to duty. He then notified Potts that the army agents would lend what assistance they could on condition that Dr. Potts would "dismiss all those persons whom you have appointed to purchase" food for the hospitals. The competition had only served to escalate the cost of provisions a full ten per cent. Blaine promised to discuss the whole matter with the Commissary-General when Colonel Wadsworth returned to Valley Forge.[42] Despite these difficulties, Dr. James

Craik was pleased to notify Potts that "the hospitals are in fine order," and that "if they are well supplied I hope they will keep up their character."[43]

Although the beginning of April was rainy, the showers were not so constant as to prevent military matters at Valley Forge from blooming, along with the blooming of spring. The Commander-in-Chief's old guard had been dissolved and the men returned to their regiments, and a new guard was instituted, still commanded by Captain Caleb Gibbs. The new guard was Steuben's creation and still consisted mostly of infantry, though some were mounted, and was closely associated with the new mounted Provost Guard commanded by Captain Bartholemew von Heer. The latter guard was recruited from horsemen of repute, particularly Germans from Berks and Lancaster Counties in Pennsylvania. Von Heer, like Steuben, had served under Frederick the Great and was an equally strict disciplinarian.

Further attention was given to the camp defenses. The Commander-in-Chief, having inspected the lines, was forced to note, "The works of the New Line" defending the heights to the rear of the encampment, "being very carelessly executed in many Parts," and General Duportail's remonstrances to the officers "commanding fatigue Parties" who were constructing the fortifications having "been of no Avail, the General calls on the several Brigadiers to inspect the Parts which have been allotted to their Brigades and order the defects to be remedied." The principal weakness of the entrenchments appeared to be the stakes supporting the embankments, "those of the exterior face being placed too perpendicularly" to sustain the weight of the earth especially during excessively rainy periods.[44] Washington also directed, "As the stumps and brush in front of the New Lines afford an excellent obstacle to the approaches of an Enemy," he forbade "that any of it should be burnt by the fatigue parties or any others for the distance of extreme musket range in front of the Lines."[45]

The Exchange of General Lee

Although the business of a general exchange of prisoners had not been consummated, Washington on April 4th posted a letter to General Howe in which the American commander expressed his "pleasure, that you have directed General Lee's releasement on parole." The parole would continue in effect until the captured General Prescott was returned to the enemy, thereby completing the exchange. Lee had already arrived in Philadelphia from New York. "Lieut. Col. Meade, one of my Aids," Washington notified Howe, "with a small escort of Horse, will meet General Lee at your Picket near Schuylkill Bridge," the floating bridge at the Middle Ferry near Philadelphia, "on Sunday Morning" April 5th.[46]

General Lee departed from the enemy lines on the date specified by Washington, but did not arrive in the vicinity of Valley Forge until the following day, having dallied en route for reasons unknown. At Valley Forge "the greatest preparations were made for his reception, all the principal officers of the army were drawn up in two lines advanced of the Camp about 2 miles" east on the Gulph Road. "Then the troops with the inferior Officers formed a line quite to head Quarters. All the Music of the Army attended." The Commander-in-Chief, "with a great number of principal Officers and their Suites, rode about four miles" nearly within sight of The Gulph "and waited till Genl. Lee appeared. General Washington dismounted and received General Lee as if he had been his brother."

INNER LINE OF ENTRENCHMENTS *occupied by Gen. McIntosh's North Carolina Brigade overlooking the Schuylkill River. The entrenchments were dug with a dry moat in front, the dirt being thrown up in the rear to form the parapet. The remains of the entrenchments are now about 2 feet high, though originally considerably higher. They are exactly as the passage of time through nearly 2 centuries has left them.*

Lee, escorted by Washington and followed by other generals, then "passed thro' the lines of Officers and the Army, who paid him the highest military Honors," until the cavalcade reached Headquarters, where he was greeted by "Lady" Washington "and was entertained at an Elegant Dinner" to the accompaniment of music. A room on the second floor at Headquarters "was assigned to him" temporarily until permanent quarters could be appointed. (Lee subsequently quartered at David Havard's, southwest of the encampment, displacing officers of the Commissary Department who moved across the Schuylkill to "Mill Grove," which later became John James Audubon's first home in America, and to nearby "Walnut Hill.")[47]

The next morning, Washington appointed Lee to command the right wing of the army as soon as his parole expired. Lee, however, "requested leave to go to Congress at York Town," a request that was "readily granted" by Washington. Prior to leaving for York, Lee paused for a private conversation with Elias Boudinot concerning a startling plan that Lee had devised in New York and previously presented to Boudinot during Boudinot's visit to American prisoners in that city, with the request that Boudinot transmit the plan to Congress.

Lee, firmly of the idea that the Americans could not withstand the enemy militarily, had proposed to Boudinot that Congress, accompanied by the army and the patriot populace, should retreat to Pittsburgh in western Pennsylvania. There the American cause could be defended from a wilderness fortress until attrition destroyed the enemy forces. Lee inquired if Boudinot had mentioned this plan to Congress. On receiving a reply that Boudinot had not considered the plan worth mentioning to anyone, Lee insisted that he himself would present the plan to Congress, though he would fail to do so. Boudinot claimed that Lee pointed out to him the necessity of implementing this plan, since upon his return to service Lee "found the army in worse condition than expected."[48]

CHAPTER X

APRIL PREVIEW

Expected Re-organization of Army

On April 8th Lafayette rejoined the army, ending further attempts against Canada. DeKalb had been left behind at Albany in temporary command on the Hudson until the arrival of Gates, who had been appointed to succeed the ailing Mc-Dougall as commander of the Hudson River area. On reaching camp, Lafayette discovered that the Committee on Conference was at last ready to report to Congress concerning the re-organization of the army.

Washington could now expect that it would be "the choice of Congress [that] upwards of forty thousand Continental Troops, exclusive of Artillery and Horse," would be provided "for the Service of the ensuing Campaign," and that "provision" in the form of a pension would be made "for the officers," since, he assured Congress, "without it, your Officers will moulder to nothing." In fact, Washington warned Congress that he had "not the least doubt, that until the Officers consider their Commissions in an honorable, and interested point of view" which guaranteed them a compensated estate after the war, that no order or interest in their duties would prevail.[1]

Early in April, the commissioners for arranging the general exchange of prisoners re-met at Newtown. The talks were protracted and, although they initially held some hope of productiveness, were adjourned indefinitely by the middle of the month without reaching a final agreement. The American commissioners had again objected that the powers conferred on the British commissioners were not sufficiently binding, and might be altered at the whim of the British Ministry. Howe refused to expand his commissioners' powers without ministerial sanction, thereby negating the present negotiations. Washington feared that there was little "good prospect" that a cartel would "ever be formed, or at least for a great while, on a liberal and extensive plan."[2]

Three days after the cessation of the conversations at Newtown the Commissaries of Prisoners of the two armies, Elias Boudinot and Joshua Loring, met privately at Germantown to effect the final exchange of Maj. Gen. Charles Lee (who was still technically on parole) for Maj. Gen. Richard Prescott as well as for the exchange of certain other officers. During the course of this conversation Boudinot and Loring discussed a renewed attempt to effect a general exchange.

As a result of this conversation, negotiations were resumed at Newtown. Lafayette took advantage of this occasion to visit his former friend, Captain Fitzpatrick, one of the British commissioners, who queried Lafayette "how he could bring himself . . . to leave France" and come to America "to choose by no means the best company and surroundings." Lafayette replied that Captain Fitzpatrick "might rather ask him how he could ever deliberately make up his mind to sail away from America, ever regretting afterwards . . . the loss of his rare and pleasant associations with General Washington."[3]

News From England

The packet from England, which arrived at Philadelphia on April 9th, bore a letter officially notifying Gen. Howe of royal assent to his requested resignation. A second packet, which arrived on the 14th, brought other significant dispatches. Their substance was publicly announced on the following day by "printed proclamations [that] were posted everywhere" in the city "announcing that England was giving up all taxation of America and that in the future the several provinces would be taxed according to their ability to pay" taxes collected internally and voluntarily granted to the Mother Country for the general support of the Empire.

This announcement was the earliest official confirmation in America that the long-rumored Conciliatory Acts had received the reluctant blessings of King and Parliament. Many citizens of Philadelphia were inclined to doubt that the announcement would "make an impression" on the rebellious Americans. The passage of these acts, it was said, had come too late to be effective. In the hope of implementing the Acts, a Peace Commission was "expected from England who will make a formal declaration" of the altered position of the British Government, and the Commission would attempt to open negotiations with Congress for a British-American rapprochement.[4]

The second packet also brought from England a letter from George Johnstone, ex-Governor of West Florida, addressed to Robert Morris. Johnstone, who had been appointed a member of the Peace Commission, was attempting to initiate a personal correspondence with certain members of Congress with whom he had considered himself intimate before the war, and whom he hoped to influence in favor of American acceptance of the peace proposals. "A reconciliation between Great Britain and the American Colonys upon the footing of the most Perfect Freedom as fellow Subjects," Johnstone wrote to Morris, "is the object on earth I have most at Heart." Johnstone fully agreed with Joseph Galloway's 1774 Plan of Government which had proposed a political entente between Britain and America as co-partners in the Empire. Both Britain and America, however, had rejected the plan.

"Tho' I am not in the Secrets of the Government Here," Johnstone continued, "& have Strongly opposed all those measures which are Deem'd oppressive to America & have constantly supported those claims against British Taxation & the altering the Charters of [Colonial] Government by the mere authority of Parliament . . . Yet I have had a hint & have good reason to believe a Proposition will be made to Parliament in four or five days by Administration, That may be a ground for reunion."

At the time of Johnstone's writing, the Conciliatory Acts had not been publicized in England. Nevertheless, the tenor of Johnstone's letter would indicate that he was not only fully apprised of the Acts but may actually have been requested by a person or persons in or close to the government to compose his missive. Johnstone then suggested, or rather begged, that Morris use his influence to prevent any precipitate Congressional acceptance of a treaty with France until Congress might at least have the time to study the British propositions.

Johnstone concluded his letter, "I am conscious from your Integrity & Patriotism wch. I have long admired That as nothing but necessity forced you [Morris and his fellow Americans] to take up Arms, so nothing but necessity or honorable engagements . . . will force you to adopt a final Separation of Interests" between America and Britain. Johnstone's letter was opened, read and approved at British Headquarters in Philadelphia prior to transmittal of the letter to Morris.[5] Shortly after the announcement of the Conciliatory Acts in Philadelphia the news of the Acts arrived at Valley Forge. Both officers and men expressed themselves as in no mood to accede to the enemy propositions.

Amusements in Camp

These expressions of continuing determination were a scant relief from the monotony of constant drill that began to grate on morale. Lighter amusements were sought, and sometimes mischief. Officers and men, when duty would permit, occasionally indulged in an ancestral form of baseball called "base," or in "wicket" (*i.e.,* cricket) which was a particular favorite of the officers. Even the Commander-in-Chief occasionally paused in his rounds of duty to take a turn at bat in the latter game. The mischief, though not of a malicious kind, could nevertheless be dangerous. On one occasion "some Rogueish chaps tied a sheaf of straw to the tail" of a Brigade Quartermaster's horse "and set it on fire and let him run, which very much offended" the outraged owner, who sought out his commanding officer, General Maxwell, "to enter a complaint."[6]

Such petty as well as large troubles frequently afflicted the camp. One such minor incident affected the Commander-in-Chief's own household. Patrick McGuire had been hired in the previous spring "to act as steward" to Washington and his staff. McGuire had proved increasingly "given to liquor, and where he dares take the liberty, very insolent." McGuire also, it was discovered, was stealing food designed for the Commander-in-Chief's table. Washington, therefore, was at last "obliged to dismiss" the errant Irishman.[7]

Military activities continued mostly abortive in April although both Pennsylvania and New Jersey were the scenes of small enemy raids. A considerable amount of what activity did occur consisted of spying. American agents spied in Philadelphia; Loyalists spied on the American camp and the country around. An otherwise anonymous "Mr. Parker, a merchant in Virginia now in Philadelphia" had even taken the unapprehended leisure on his way to the city to sketch a rough and rather inaccurate map of the Valley Forge defenses. On reaching the city he delivered the map to the British commander.[8]

Covert messages sent into the city by outlying Loyalists were frequently detected by American scouts, but this was only a small portion of the information that flowed into the city. At first the Americans were comparatively lenient with apprehended enemy agents. The first offense resulted only in a warning. The second, however, could lead to the gallows. As the flood of information reaching the enemy became more obvious it became necessary to inaugurate stricter measures than mere warnings for initial offenses.

William McKay, an enemy agent, employed the subterfuge of selling fresh meat to the Americans as a means of observing the camp at Valley Forge, and having satisfied his curiosity, carried his observations to the enemy. McKay's career as a spy suddenly ended on the gallows at Valley Forge on April 15th in the presence of the whole army. American spies were similarly active in Philadelphia. Even British Headquarters seemed scarcely immune to American infiltration since the Americans were early apprised of a rumor that the Ministry had ordered an evacuation of the city.

With the evacuation rumors increasingly rampant, and in preparation for a proposed council of war to consider alternative plans for the prospective campaign, Washington requested his generals to write out their opinions as to possible counter moves.

Knox, Muhlenberg, Poor and Varnum favored an attack on New York City, an attack which, they argued, would necessitate an immediate enemy withdrawal from Philadelphia to protect the principal British base in America. The defenses of Philadelphia, they noted, were too strong to warrant an attack. Other officers, notably Wayne, were inclined to an assault on Philadelphia despite the strength of its fortifications. Lafayette, Steuben and Duportail urged caution in any decisions and suggested that time should be the governing factor in arriving at any conclusions.

Washington was formally notified of the British Conciliatory Acts by the receipt of a batch of handbills from Sir William Howe each containing a précis of the Acts. Howe requested public distribution of the handbills. Howe had received the handbills from Major General Sir William Tryon in New York. The American commander immediately forwarded copies to York for Congressional consideration. Washington's aide, John Laurens, having studied the enemy handbill, observed to his father, the President of Congress, "unless properly counteracted [the acts] will indubitably tend to foment disunion, perhaps the only and evidently the surest method of destroying us."[9]

At nearly the same time Washington also received a copy of Loyalist publisher James Rivington's *New York Gazette* in which the latter had printed copies of what he claimed were letters written by Washington two years earlier. These letters, Washington promptly announced, were frauds composed by an unknown British forger. They intimidated that Washington disfavored American independence. Washington forwarded the *Gazette* to Henry Laurens, noting that the forgeries might afford the President of Congress "some amusement," though the Commander-in-Chief was as much provoked as amused. "Among the many villainous arts practiced by the enemy to create divisions and mistrusts, that of forging letters from me is one."[10]

Congress and the Conciliatory Acts

On receiving copies of the Conciliatory Acts, Congress erected a committee, consisting of its own members, to study the Acts as far as the condensed text would admit. The committee presently reported that in its opinion the Acts were only intended to create divisions among the Americans, and recommended that there should be no negotiations except on terms of independence or a complete withdrawal of the enemy fleets and armies from American territory. Congress immediately confirmed the committee's report.

Washington, agreeing with this report, considered the moment more imperative than ever to rehabilitate the Continental Army. "The necessity of putting the army upon a respectable footing," the Commander-in-Chief observed, " is now become more essential than ever" since the enemy was showing his desperation by "endeavouring to ensnare the people by specious allurements of Peace. It is not improbable" that the enemy "had such abundant cause to be tired of the War, that they may be sincere, in the terms they offer, which, though far short of our pretensions, will be extremely flattering to Minds that do not penetrate far into political consequences: But, whether they [the British] are sincere or not," the enemy proposals "may be equally destructive . . . Nothing can be more evident, than that a Peace on the principles of dependence . . . would be to the last degree dishonourable and ruinous" to America.[11]

Congress, in an effort to hasten the rehabilitation of the army, proclaimed a universal pardon for all deserters provided they would rejoin the colors within a stipulated period of time.[12]

By late April, the troops having been drilled to as near excellence as time would permit, General Steuben, seeking a partial respite from his burdens, changed his quarters from the immediate vicinity of the encampment to the more pleasant surroundings "at the house of Jimmy White" on the bluff overlooking the peaceful Schuylkill River a mile or so west of Headquarters.[13] Although Steuben's personal efforts had brought the troops to a reasonable degree of excellence, all his work might be of no use if resignations of officers continued.

The Virginia Line received the most "violent shock" of any of the Continental Lines as a result of the resignations of nearly ninety officers because of continued Congressional failure to implement the pension plan. These officers also feared that the proposed re-organization of the army would leave considerable numbers of officers stranded without commands, and without future governmental recognition of their past services. Washington despairingly informed Congress that unless it expedited the proposed pension and other provisions for the officers, the Commander-in-Chief had "just grounds to fear" the present rate of resignations would "shake the very existence of the army unless a remedy is soon, very soon, applied."[14]

The Commander-in-Chief could not refrain, under the stress of the moment, from privately criticizing Congress for its frequent "indecision and delay in coming to determinations" especially in military matters. Washington partially blamed this procrastination on "the *jealousy* which Congress unhappily entertains of the army. This jealousy," he deduced, "stands upon the common opinion . . . that standing armies are dangerous to a state." The Commander-in-Chief observed that the American Army was basically a civilian army, and readily expected disbandment at the earliest possible moment after the cessation of hostilities. "We should all be considered," Washington concluded, "Congress, army" and general public, "as one people, embarked in one cause," and as a unit "acting on the same principle and to one end."[15]

On April 21st the long-expected council of war was held at Headquarters. Besides the Commander-in-Chief, only Generals Knox, Greene, Wayne, Poor and Paterson attended. After the various opinions, which Washington had solicited in written form (including those from absent officers), had been read to the assembled officers, verbal discussion ensued. Greene and Poor sustained an opinion that an attack on New York, after leaving a holding force commanded by General Lee to keep the enemy in Philadelphia under surveillance, was probably the most effective plan proposed.

Wayne advocated immediate offensive operations by attacking the enemy wherever and whenever such an attack appeared feasible. Paterson was of an opinion that the army should remain in camp for further training and better equipping. Knox, while opposing a purely defensive war such as that proposed by Paterson, nevertheless opposed an attack on Philadelphia, and was none too enthusiastic concerning operations directed against New York. Washington, as was his frequent custom, reserved his decision.

Meanwhile the ministerial orders for the exacuation of Philadelphia had been approved and signed in London without the knowledge of the already appointed Peace Commissioners, and some three weeks before they sailed from England. The Ministry had been informed that a powerful French fleet commanded by Count D'Estaing, with land troops aboard, had been assembled at the Mediterranean port of Toulon, and was preparing to sail for American waters. The ministry feared a naval blockade of the British fleet and army stationed at Philadelphia.

Although weeks passed before any definite knowledge of an enemy evacuation of Philadelphia would reach patriot ears, the constant rumor exalted American spirits. Congress, as it often had done on other occasions, "set apart Wednesday," April 22nd, to be universally "observed as a day of Fasting, Humiliation and Prayer, that at one time and with one voice the righteous dispensations of Providence may be acknowledged, and His Goodness and Mercy towards us and our Arms supplicated and implored." The Commander-in-Chief, in obedience to this directive, ordered "that the day shall be most religiously observed in the Army, and that no work be done thereon, and that the Chaplains prepare discourses suitable to the Occasion."[16]

Notification of French Alliance

The closing days of April brought "important intelligence" to Valley Forge. A French war-vessel, *La Sensible,* had recently arrived at Falmouth, now Portsmouth, Maine, in 35 days from France, which she left the 8th of March with dispatches from the American plenipotentiaries at the Court of Versailles. These reports informed America that France at last had recognized America as "free and Independent States," and more importantly, that treaties between the two nations, which could implement that recognition, had been negotiated and signed.[17] Simeon Deane, the American courier from France and brother of plenipotentiary Silas Deane, had brought copies of the treaties for the ratification of Congress.

On hearing the news, Washington's adjutant general, Alexander Scammell, expressed what would be the prevailing sentiment among Americans. An alliance with France, despite a lingering repugnance of a number of patriots toward her as a former enemy, would be far "preferable" to a reconciliation "with a proud, cruel people who would watch the first opportunity to crush" their former Colonists should America accede to British overtures, and who would only "render America miserable" in such an event.[18]

CHAPTER XI

FORTUNES OF WAR

The Crooked Billet

Although unofficial, Simeon Deane's news of the French Alliance spread through the army with astonishing speed. Even the report of the Pennsylvania Militia's defeat at the Crooked Billet on May 1st failed to dim the high hopes that prevailed in camp.

Brigadier General John Lacey and his Pennsylvania Militia had headquartered at the Crooked Billet Tavern in northern Philadelphia County. Loyalist spies had informed the British of Lacey's principal station, and that the Militia was constantly undermanned. An excellent opportunity was therefore offered to the British to eliminate or at least rebuff the continuing nuisance of the Militia's presence in a district from which British raiders drew much of their fresh supplies. General Howe directed Colonel Robert Abercrombie with twelve companies of Light Infantry, the Queen's Rangers and ninety Light

Horse to attack the Militia. The British column left Philadelphia between 10 and 11 p. m. on the night of April 30th and "proceeded up the Old York Road" in the direction of the Crooked Billet with the intention of surprising the Militia the following dawn.[1]

As the British attackers, led by Loyalist guides familiar with the roads and terrain, approached their destination under cover of darkness, the force was divided in an effort to surround the sleeping Americans. The principal column under the personal command of Abercromby bore left on the Easton Road so as to strike at the American right. The Queen's Rangers, under Major John Simcoe, had been ordered to flank-march to reach the American left and rear. The dragoons were to attack the American front and occupy its attention while the flanking columns completed their maneuvers. Despite the fact that Lacey had directed his scouts to watch the approaches from Philadelphia attentively, the British attack came as a complete surprise. Because of the raw weather and light rain that was falling, the scouts failed to cover the roads properly.

The first intimation the Militia received of the enemy's presence was a sharp fire of British muskets and carbines. Lacey, awakened from his sleep in the Gilbert house across the road from the camp, was informed by a sentry that both the camp and the house were completely surrounded. Not waiting to dress completely, Lacey quit the house so precipitously and so out of uniform that the enemy dragoons failed to recognize him as the American commander, and rode after the Militia instead.

The general was able to join the retreating militia and endeavored to fashion some order out of the confusion. Since the dragoons had broken through the American camp and were blocking the only road leading to apparent safety, Lacey ordered the Militia to attack the blockading force. Fortunately, most of the Militia succeeded in breaking through the enemy.

Lacey admitted the loss of 26 men killed, eight or ten wounded, and several missing who were undoubtedly prisoners in enemy hands. British Capt. Montrésor erroneously reported that "between 80 and 100" Americans were left "dead on the field," and that "between 50 and 60 prisoners" were taken.[2] If this British claim had been true, Lacey's small force would have been virtually wiped out, which it was not. Lacey later reported that five enemy dead were discovered on the field after the enemy withdrawal.

The disproportionate number of American dead to the wounded resulted from the fact that "many of the unfortunates" who had been severely wounded, and "who fell into the merciless hands of the British were cruelly and inhumanly butchered." A number of Americans, in an effort to escape enemy detection, had hidden themselves in piles of buckwheat straw and were burned alive when the enemy set fire to the ricks. "Others," Lacey reported, "after being wounded by a ball had received near a dozen wounds with cutlasses and bayonets."[3]

Two days after the action, Washington rebuked Lacey, "You may depend that" such a misfortune "will ever be the consequence of permitting yourself to be surprised," and if it "was owing to the misconduct of the officer" in command of the advance pickets "you should have him brought to trial."[4]

On May 4th Lacey, in obedience to the Commander-in-Chief's suggestion, ordered the offending officers court-martialed. The court sat in a house at the Cross Roads on York Road several miles north of Crooked Billet. Lieutenant Neilson, in command of the scouts, was declared guilty and summarily dismissed from the service. His subordinate, Ensign Laughlin, was acquitted

with honor. Several militiamen and local citizens, accused of having contact with the enemy, were likewise tried, and those found guilty flogged and some of the more flagrant cases sent to Lancaster for confinement. Although Lacey was the recipient of considerable criticism as a result of the ill-conduct of the Militia in this affair, investigation exonerated him from personal blame. He was even commended by the Pennsylvania Executive Council for his cool conduct.

May Poles and King Tamany

May Day at Valley Forge was a far different scene than that at the Crooked Billet. "May poles were Erected in everry Regt in the Camp and at the Revelle." The camp was awakened "by three cheers in honor of King Tamany.[5] The day was spent in mirth and Jollity, the soldiers parading marching with fife & Drum and Huzzaing as they passd the poles their hats adornd with white blossoms." The 3rd New Jersey Regiment, having cheered itself hoarse before its own May pole "Marchd of[f] to Head Quarters to do Honor to his Excellency but just as they were descending the hill to the house an Aid" rode up from Headquarters and "met them and informed them that the Genl was Indisposd and desird them to retire which they did with the greatest decency and regularity." The regiment then "marchd from right to left of Lord Stirlings Division Huzzaing at every Pole they pasd and then retird to their Regimental parade taking a drink of whiskey which a Generous contribution of their officers had procurd for them."[6]

Alexander Graydon observed many of the officers engaged in a May Day celebration in the afternoon "at a barbeque on the banks of the Schuylkill." The Commander-in-Chief and his aides, though invited, did not attend. Many officers became "joyous and pretty full of liquor . . . The drummer and fifer who made the music" for some strange reason, since there were plenty of patriot musicians in the army, "were deserters from the enemy" who, as the party progressed, "were sneering at some of the gentlemen who did not entirely preserve the dignity of their station."[7] In the evening, other officers of a more sober disposition merely "had a song and dance in honour of King Tamany," which lasted to the mid-night hour, at which time they "retird to rest."[8]

Congress and the French Alliance

In York on May 2nd, Congress commenced its discussions concerning the French treaties. Both Washington and Lafayette had expressed their delight with the treaties in letters addressed to Henry Laurens. Washington congratulated Congress "with infinite pleasure . . . on the very important and interesting advices brought" from France, and notified the President of Congress that "as soon as Congress may think it expedient I shall be happy to have an opportunity of announcing to the Army with the usual ceremony, such parts of the intelligence as may be proper."[9] Lafayette was even more exuberant in his congratulations. "Houra, my good friend . . . a very good treaty will assure our noble independence."[10] Already Lafayette spoke and wrote of "his *new country*—America," though his love for France was undiminished.

Although Congress had adjourned for a week-end holiday, on Saturday May 2nd the President hastily called the members into session so that the dispatches brought by Simeon Deane from France might be read. On Monday, the 4th, Congress took the treaties into full consideration after resolving "That this Congress entertain the highest sense of the magnanimity and wisdom" of the French sovereign as exemplified by the treaties. Congress directed the American plenipotentiaries in France to "present the grateful acknowledgments of this Congress to His Most Christian Majesty."

Having tentatively ratified the treaties, Congress appointed a committee consisting of Richard Henry Lee, Francis Dana and William Henry Drayton to compose the official ratification. The result of the committee's labors was presented to Congress on the following day and readily approved. On reflection, Congress inserted a request that France agree to expunge Articles XI and XII from the Treaty of Amity and Commerce since Congress was somewhat apprehensive that differences might arise between the parties concerning complete negation of import duties on trade between the United States and the French West Indies. These duties might become a lucrative source of income to the United States. The request, however, was not of such major importance that Congress would hesitate to accede to an otherwise unqualified ratification of the treaties. If France failed to agree to the suggested deletions, Congress would not argue the point.

On May 6th Congress publicized its ratification of the treaties and "recommended to the inhabitants of these United States that they regard and treat the subjects of France as those of a magnanimous and generous Ally" whose sovereign had "generously treated" with the United States "on terms of perfect equality and mutual benefit."[11] Congress only permitted the publication of Articles I, II and VI of the Treaty of Alliance, which Articles respectively stated that in the event of a war between Britain and France the United States would make that war a "common cause" with France; that France recognized American independence; and that France forever renounced any claim to territory on the North American continent. Article VI was made public in order to quiet the fears of those patriots who were concerned about a possible French attempt to regain Canada. The other Articles were temporarily suppressed because Britain and France still maintained official relations.

Celebration at Valley Forge

On May 5th a courier from Congress arrived at Valley Forge with dispatches that notified the Commander-in-Chief that the treaties had received the full assent of Congress, and that official ratification was expected on the same day that the dispatches had been sent. Although the General Orders for the following day had already been issued, Washington immediately drew up "After Orders" to the effect that "it having pleased the Almighty ruler of the Universe propitiously to defend the Cause of the United States . . . by raising us up a powerful Friend among the Princes of the Earth to establish our liberty and Independence . . . it becomes us to set apart a day for gratefully acknowledging the divine Goodness and celebrating the Important Event which we owe to his benign Interposition."[12] The following day, May 6th, was appointed as the date for the celebration. Although directions for the ceremonies were explicitly explained in the "After Orders," Washington placed their administration and execution in the hands of Steuben.

The morning of May 6th was "excessively hot" by the time the troops were assembled at 9 a.m. on their respective brigade parades to witness the official announcement of the alliance and its ratification, and to hear their chaplains deliver discourses

"suitable to the occasion." At 10:30 precisely a single cannon shot boomed across the encampment as "a signal for the men to be under arms" and ready for inspection by their respective Brigade Inspectors. At 11 a.m., a second shot directed the troops to march to the Grand Parade where Lord Stirling would take command of the right wing of the front line, Lafayette the left, and DeKalb, who had finally returned from Albany, the second line.

When the troops had assembled, the Commander-in-Chief and his suite appeared from the direction of Headquarters, and Washington accompanied by Stirling, Greene, Lafayette, DeKalb "and the other principal officers" reviewed the troops. At the conclusion of the review, a third cannon shot announced the official commencement of the *Feu de Joie,* or "Fire of Joy," which was "conducted with great judgment and regularity."[13] The cannon commenced the ceremony by roaring a thirteen gun salute in honor of the thirteen states; which salute was followed by a "running fire" of musketry that commenced on the right of the front line, ran to the left of the line, and was then taken up left to right along the second line.

The brief silence that followed was broken by a huzza from every throat "Long Live the King of France." The same performance, cannons and muskets, was pursued a second time, followed by the huzza "Long live the friendly European Powers." (There was rumor that Spain and perhaps other European nations would soon follow France's decision and ally themselves with America.) A third time the sound of firing echoed among the hills, concluded by the huzza "To the American States."[14]

At the conclusion of the ceremony, the Commander-in-Chief and his suite retired in the direction of Headquarters. Now and again Washington paused, turned around in his saddle, and lifted his hat to the troops in recognition of their continuing cheers. The field and line officers followed the Commander-in-Chief on foot, linked arm-in-arm thirteen abreast in honor of the thirteen states.[15] A cold lunch had been laid outdoors in

THE SITE OF GEN. KNOX'S ARTILLERY PARK *at the foot of Mount Joy appears in the near distance. In the far distance appears the high ground that marked the outer line of defense. The cannon are reproductions.*

55

the vicinity of Headquarters for the officers, at which the guests "spent the afternoon enjoying all desirable mirth and jolity."[16]

Not until "about six o'clock in the evening [was] the company broke up, and his Excellency returned to Headquarters." During the long repast at which many toasts were drunk the French officers "seemed peculiarly pleased with this public approbation" of the alliance; and Washington was noticeably wearing "a countenance of uncommon delight and complacence." Nor were the troops, who had "never looked so well, nor in such good order since the beginning of the war," forgotten in the festivities that followed the official ceremonies.[17] A gill of rum was issued to every man.

During the course of the ceremonies, a member of Washington's suite had been informed that a Loyalist spy had been captured while observing the proceedings, but the officer to whom the report was made "cooly observed to the gentleman who gave the information that he thought it best to take no further notice of the spy." The spy was to be allowed to return to Philadelphia since the enemy "must feel more pain from his account" of the excellent condition and rigid drilling of the patriot army "than grief on hearing" of the spy's "detection and death."[18] Nor was this occurrence the sole exhibition of humanity that marked this happy occasion. "The Commander-in-Chief being more desirous to reclaim than punish Offenders . . . and that as many as can may participate in the pleasure of this joyfull day," was pleased to release all offenders from the Provost-Marshal's stockade, including a couple of deserters who had been sentenced to be hanged.[19]

Washington, as he wrote to Robert Morris, could indeed "rejoice most sincerely." The "dark and tempestuous clouds, which at times appeared ready to overwhelm" the patriot cause, seemed on the verge of disappearing. "The game, whether well or ill played hitherto, seems now to be verging fast to a favourable issue . . . unless we throw it away by too much supineness on the one hand, or impetuosity on the other."[20]

CHAPTER XII

BUSINESS AND PLEASURE

Commissary and Quartermaster Improvements

Despite the favorable prospects of the French Alliance, Washington considered that "no change has happened in our affairs, which will justify the least relaxation in our military preparations."[1] Now that the army was increasing in numbers and had proved its basic military skill, the Commander-in-Chief was particularly anxious that the Commissary and Quartermaster Departments exhibit an equal polish, and urged Nathanael Greene and Jeremiah Wadsworth to push their exertions "in their fullest vigor and extent."[2]

Greene's and Wadsworth's efforts were proving productive, and Lt.-Colonel Samuel Ward of the 1st Rhode Island Regiment, before leaving to join General Sullivan in Ward's native state, could report to his wife, "I live very well . . . I rise with the sun. After adjusting my dress, we begin our exercises at 6 o'clock which last till 8 in the morning. Then we breakfast upon tea or coffee." After breakfast the officers "walk, write, read, ride or play till dinner time, when we get a piece of good beef or pork, tho generally of both, and we have as good bread as I ever eat."

The afternoon was also "ours till 5 o'clock, when we begin our exercises and leave off with the setting sun . . . We have milk and sugar in plenty . . . Our Regiment begins to grow healthy."[3] With spring and improved general conditions, disease was slowly dying out. While the hospitals were still overflowing, patients were soon reduced in number.

On May 8th the Commander-in-Chief received a report that a British expedition was raiding north on the Delaware River, and that the enemy had succeeded in burning the remnants of the Continental and Pennsylvania Navies that had been scuttled by the Americans near Bordentown, New Jersey. The scuttling had been inadequately handled, since the shallowness of the water left much of the hulks visible above the surface. One battalion of British Light Infantry had embarked aboard a pair of gallies and several accompanying flatboats, and had stolen up the river under cover of night and set fire to the American frigates *Effingham* and *Washington* and several lesser craft.

The British raid also resulted in the incineration of a number of houses along both sides of the riverfront at Bordentown, including that of patriot Joseph Borden, and of considerable American military stores. Had the scuttling been done effectively, Washington admonished the national and state Naval Commissioners, the enemy would have had little inducement to raid Bordentown and elsewhere along the upper river.[4]

Council of War

Washington's primary present concern was a new council of war for which both Gates and Mifflin (representing the Board of War) had been invited to Valley Forge. These two officers on their arrival were quartered at the Moses Coates house[5] some miles west of the encampment near the present Phoenixville.

The council of war convened at Headquarters on May 8th. Present besides Washington, Gates and Mifflin were Greene, Stirling, Lafayette, DeKalb, Armstrong, Steuben, Knox and Duportail. Washington commenced the proceedings by informing the council that the British had at present in Philadelphia roughly 10,000 effective troops "exclusive of Marines and New Levies" of Loyalist volunteers; at New York about 4,000 effectives; and at Rhode Island another 2,000. The total effective strength of British and Hessian regulars in America, exclusive of troops in Canada, he therefore estimated at at least some 16,000 men, an estimate he would later learn was less than the actual number.

To oppose these enemy forces the Americans could at present muster some 11,800 troops at Valley Forge including "such of the sick present and on command, as might be called into action on any emergency." General Smallwood could count 1,400 men at Wilmington including his semi-invalids. Only 1,800 effectives were stationed on the Hudson River, a force scarcely adequate to protect that vital waterway and the Highland defenses should the enemy be inclined to attack them.

The Commander-in-Chief was not exceedingly hopeful concerning reinforcements large enough to oppose enemy movements or attack enemy posts unless new dispositions of American troops, supported by additional recruits, were made at the risk of weakening other vital posts. Washington continued by stating that prospects now offered by the Commissary Department were "tolerably good," thereby relieving total anxiety on the department's account and permitting American operations to proceed without excessive fear of a collapse of supplies.

"Having stated these particulars for the consideration of the

Council," Washington requested "that after a full and candid discussion . . . each member would furnish him with his sentiments in writing on some general plan, which . . . ought to be adopted for the operations of the next campaign."[6] The Commander-in-Chief then outlined various alternatives of action for discussion, after which the council adjourned to consider the matter individually. The decision at which the conferees would arrive was in agreement with Washington's own opinion "that the line of conduct was most consistent with sound policy, and best suited to promote the interests and safety of the United States, was to remain on the defensive and wait events, without attempting any offensive operations of consequence unless the future circumstances of the enemy should afford a fairer opportunity than at present."[7]

Washington was pleased to announce to the council before it broke up that Steuben's official appointment as Major General and Inspector-General of all troops in the Continental service had been confirmed by Congress. (Major General Conway had resigned the post of Inspector-General, though, on learning of the French Alliance, he attempted to rescind his resignation, which request was tabled by Congress.)

Re-organization of Army

In expectation of a possible precipitate removal from Valley Forge, and with a satisfactory number of major generals in camp, Washington undertook a major re-organization of the army by dividing the troops into five divisions. The first division was placed under the command of Charles Lee as the senior major general. Major General Mifflin, who had requested active duty, and Major Generals Lafayette, DeKalb and Stirling were given the commands of the second, third, fourth and fifth divisions respectively. With this organization in effect, the divisions, brigades and regiments could be placed on a more proper footing.

Prior to the council of war Washington had left camp to inspect the sick in the hospital at Yellow Springs and while on his short tour paused to speak "to every person in their buncks which pleased the sick exceedingly."[8] He issued orders that the Medical Department was "to have all the sick of the army," both those at Valley Forge and those in the outlying hospitals, "taken care of in case the army should make a Sudden move." All the surgeons and medical assistants who could "be spared" from the distant hospitals were to be sent to Valley Forge "to attend the sick that would be left on the grounds," as no less than "fifteen or seventeen hundred" patients might be expected to be left behind if the army soon proceeded to its next destination.[9]

On May 11th Washington received a note from Sir William Howe offering to renew negotiations for a total exchange of prisoners. Howe expressed his personal worry concerning the health of the American prisoners in Philadelphia as the weather warmed toward summer. His private motive, however, was undoubtedly to divest the British Army of the difficulty of transferring the prisoners to New York in view of the recent orders received from London to evacuate Philadelphia at the earliest possible moment. Marching prisoners across New Jersey would be next to impossible, and the evacuation ships would be loaded beyond normal capacity even without the presence of the prisoners. Washington immediately sent a copy of Howe's communication to Congress for its decision in the matter.

Although the planned evacuation of Philadelphia had not yet been made public, rumor of its imminence had become so omnipresent in Philadelphia that merchants commenced offering their goods at depressed prices in an effort to be rid of their stocks and convert them to more portable specie. Many merchants ransacked the neighboring waterways for small vessels in which to transport themselves and their unsold goods to New York. The British Army and Navy, however, had, in obedience to Howe's orders of the previous fall, sequestered or destroyed most of the vessels of a size capable of facing the open sea; and shipping rates on the few vessels that remained in private hands skyrocketed.

Several of the more desperate Loyalists living in the neighborhood of the city appeared at Valley Forge, and on being admitted to Washington's presence "requested to be pardoned, but he sent them on" to Lancaster to deal with the Pennsylvania authorities.[10] The matter, the Commander-in-Chief informed the supplicants, was not of a military nature and he had no authority to make a decision.

On the evening of May 11th, Washington and his lady together with Lord and Lady Stirling and their daughter Lady Kitty Alexander, General Greene and his lady, and as many other officers and ladies as could crowd into the temporary open-air theater erected near the banks of the Schuylkill, witnessed a performance of Addison's *Cato,* staged in belated celebration of the French Alliance. "The scenery," it was noted, "was in Taste" despite the difficulties presented by the rustic neighborhood, and the performance of the amateur actors enlisted from the officer corps was indeed "admirable." The hero "did his part to admiration" and at the closing curtain "made an excellent *die.*"[11]

The play was chosen for the occasion by the producers for its pertinent lines, i.e., Cato: "It is not now a time to talk of aught but chains or conquest; liberty or death." Also, "What a pity is it that we can die but once to serve our country," and "What dire effects from civil discord flow."

Oaths of Allegiance

Washington, on the following day, complied with the February 3rd resolve of Congress that officers of all ranks were required to subscribe to Oaths of Allegiance to the United States or face dismissal. The twenty days originally allowed by Congress from the date of its resolve for taking the Oaths had long since expired. The condition of the army and other pressing matters, notably the resignations and resultant confusion in the officer corps, had prevented an earlier activation of the Congressional resolve either at Valley Forge or at other installations occupied by the military forces.

"In order to accomplish this very interesting and essential" business as quickly and smoothly as possible Washington designated Generals Stirling, Lafayette, DeKalb, McIntosh, Knox, Poor, Varnum, Wayne and Muhlenberg to supervise the oath-taking among the inferior officers.[12] Printed forms of the Oaths had been sent to Valley Forge by Congress, and each general was directed to witness each Oath in duplicate with his personal signature. One copy was then to be returned to Headquarters, the other to remain in the possession of the affirming officer as a means of identification and proof of loyalty.

Although the Commander-in-Chief designated May 12th as the official date on which the oath-taking was to commence at Valley Forge, several Oaths were subscribed on the previous day. On the 12th the proceedings officially began when the

THE SO-CALLED "BAKE HOUSE," *the home of ironmaster Col. William Dewees of the Pennsylvania Militia, co-owner of the Valley (or Mount Joy) Forge with Isaac Potts. The house received its designation because Baker-General Christopher Ludwig constructed ovens in the cellar to bake bread for the army. Courts-martial and the signing of the generals' Oaths of Allegiance sworn to by officers of the army took place in the house, which dates from about 1760.*

generals present in camp assembled at the Ironmaster's House (the Dewees mansion, now designated the Bake House) near Headquarters of General Washington.

Washington, as senior officer, after laying his hand on the Bible, was the first to affirm by repeating aloud the words that Congress had prescribed. "I George Washington, Commander-in-Chief of the Armies of the United States of America [this much of the printed Oath and two subsequent blanks he had filled in in his own hand] do acknowledge the United States of America to be Free, independent and Sovereign States, and declare that the people thereof owe no allegiance or obedience to George the Third, King of Great-Britain; and I renounce, refuse and abjure any allegiance or obedience to him; and I do Swear that I will to the utmost of my power, support, maintain and defend the said United States, against the said King George the Third, his heirs and successors and his or their abettors, assistants and adherents, and will serve the said United States in the office of Comr. in chief as aforesd. which I now hold, with fidelity, according to the best of my skill and understanding."[13] General Stirling witnessed the Commander-in-Chief's signature. Washington subsequently witnessed those of his assembled subordinates.

When the moment arrived for General Lee to affirm his Oath, the officers present noticed that he momentarily lifted his hand from the Bible. When Washington queried Lee concerning this unusual action, Lee replied that he had no compunction affirming an oath against the current British sovereign but had some qualms against refuting the Prince of Wales. Fortunately for Lee, the assembled officers treated his remark as a witticism, and the ceremony continued.

Possibly Lee's conscience was pricked, when he recalled the campaign plan he had submitted to Sir William Howe during his incarceration in New York suggesting a British attack on Virginia and Maryland via Chesapeake Bay;[14] or what he had

said when he "had been closeted" in a private discussion with Howe just before leaving for Valley Forge.[15] According to Elias Boudinot, Lee had received considerable presents from the British commander. These presents had been "stored in the cellar of the house where he [Lee] lodged," but their liquid nature had attracted the attention of British soldiers who broke in "and stole the whole of it." All this, Boudinot concluded in his journal, "increased my suspicions of Genl. Lee exceedingly,"[16] although Lee did complete his Oath of Allegiance.

The subscribing to the Oaths by the field and junior officers continued through subsequent days with an activity that was only briefly marred. The officers of Woodford's Virginia Brigade expressed an objection to taking the Oaths, since they considered that the directive requiring the Oaths sullied the many proofs they had already given of devotion to the patriot cause. They also feared that by inscribing their present ranks on the Oaths they might be signing away their chances for future promotion or resignation. Lafayette, whom Washington had assigned to witness the Oaths of this brigade, since the brigade was attached to Lafayette's Division, immediately informed the Commander-in-Chief of the difficulty, at the same time delivering to Headquarters a paper signed by the hesitant officers "listing their reasons for not taking the Oath."

Washington at once replied in writing to Lafayette, "As every Oath should be a free act of the Mind, founded on the conviction of the party, of its propriety [a somewhat specious argument considering that Congress had voted dismissal of any recalcitrant officers] I would not wish, in any instance, that there should be the least degree of compulsion exercised . . . The Gentlemen therefore . . . will use their own discretion in the matter . . . as their conscience and feelings dictate." Washington averred the Oath "is substantially the same with that required in all Governments, and therefore, does not imply any indignity . . . The objection, founded upon the supposed unsettled Rank of the Officers is of no validity (rank being only mentioned as a further designation of the party swearing); Nor can it be seriously thought, that the Oath is either intended, or can prevent their being promoted, or their resignations."[17] Lafayette immediately relayed this appraisal to Woodford's officers who acceded to the Oaths without further demur.

British Evacuation Preparations

In Philadelphia considerable activity had commenced among His Majesty's troops. "Ye heavy cannon are ordered on board ye Ships, and some other things look mysterious," a worried citizen recorded.[18] This activity might have appeared mysterious to the uninformed, but there was no mystery at British Headquarters. It was a prelude to quitting the city.

The embarkation of the enemy's artillery was the first visual indication that the evacuation might be under way. The moment at which this event would occur was of great interest to Washington, but for the time being confirmation of the event and the moment of implementation were well-kept secrets at British Headquarters; secrets that American spies and Loyalists alike failed to penetrate. Loyalists who had been in the city and were later captured by the Americans could give little information regarding British activities.

Among the Loyalist captives taken by the Americans at this time was the famous Germantown printer and publisher, the younger Christopher Saur (or Sower as the name is often Anglicized), who was brought to Valley Forge by Captain

Allen McLane's scouts. Saur had no useful information on the evacuation, and was released at the intercession of General Muhlenberg, an old friend.

Additional indications of British evacuation intentions were reports that the enemy transports "were taking in wood and water" and that the enemy were deliberately burning a number of vessels under construction on the waterfront stocks in the city. Colonel Stephen Moylan, who now commanded the dragoon regiment stationed at Trenton, replacing Pulaski, endeavored to get more information than rumor afforded.

Moylan "sent a woman into Philadelphia" in an attempt to determine a fuller explanation of the enemy's conduct. The feminine patriot could only report back "that there was great talk of the Troops embarking," but that she could not ascertain whether an evacuation or an offensive operation was intended. She had heard frequent mention "that war was certainly declared" between Britain and France, that Clinton was superseding Howe in a matter of days, and that a "Grand *Fete Champetre*" was to be given in honor of the departing commander.[19] This "grand fete" would be the famous Meschianza or medley.

Although the report of Anglo-French hostilities was unconfirmed, knowledge that a French fleet-of-war commanded by Count D'Estaing was about to sail for American waters had preceded the actual sailing. With this knowledge in hand Lafayette, certain that hostilities would soon occur between the garrisons of the various West Indies islands in French and British possession, enthused, "If my compatriots make war in several corners of the world I would fly to their colors," and he would "leave for the field" in the West Indies unless otherwise ordered by his sovereign.[20]

Although Lafayette's anxiety to fight under French colors is understandable, he witnessed with pride the divisional maneuvers of the Continental Army on the Grand Parade at Valley Forge on May 14th. These maneuvers were the first involving the whole army in concert. Steuben's ceaseless efforts reached their apex in this event, which proved "a sight that would charm" any beholder.[21]

So nearly perfected had the army's drill and maneuvers become that Washington on the same day ordered "the Troops are in future to be exempt from exercise every Friday afternoon." The Friday vacation, however, was not to be entirely devoted to rest and pleasure. It was to be partly employed in washing clothes, sprucing up the camp and bathing in the Schuylkill River. The officers who supervised the ablutions were "to be particularly careful that no man remains longer than ten minutes in the water"[22] for fear of getting a chill.

On the day of the army's divisional maneuvers a party of Oneida Indians, some sixty strong, commanded by the half-breed Louis Toussard, arrived in camp from New York. These were the Indian scouts that the Oneida sachems had promised Lafayette during his conference with the Indians at the time of his aborted Canadian expedition. They were immediately placed under the supervision of Daniel Morgan and assigned to cooperate with his Rifle Corps in scouting duties. Frontiersman Morgan had been long familiar with Indian habits of warfare. Prior to engaging in their assigned duties, the Indians were escorted through the camp to view the army, and were saluted at the Artillery Park by thirteen guns.

Matters were not as friendly with other Indians. On the western frontiers of Pennsylvania, Indian attacks on the settlers were growing in intensity and ferocity. Frequent imploring complaints were reaching the Pennsylvania authorities at Lancaster of the inability of the frontiersmen to defend themselves against the Indians. The complaints were forwarded to the Commander-in-Chief, who was obliged to order General Lachlan McIntosh to proceed at once to Pittsburgh in an attempt to control these attacks. McIntosh was also under orders to counteract the influence of British agents circulating among the Ohio tribes and inducing them to warfare. Washington had scant desire to dispense with McIntosh's efficient services, especially with a campaign imminent.

At the same time Brig.-General James Potter, having completed his requested winter furlough, returned to the Militia and replaced the youthful and less experienced John Lacey.

Benedict Arnold, still limping heavily from the bullet wound he had received at Saratoga the previous fall, had by now, in obedience to orders, arrived in camp. Unable to ride, he had been transported in a chaise from his home in New Haven, Connecticut, where he had spent the winter recuperating. Arnold was still a hero and was welcomed as such in camp. Arnold, however, was still unfit for active duty, and was given restful quarters at the Moses Coates residence west of the encampment where Gates and Mifflin had recently quartered.

The Meschianza

Although Loyalists were complaining of British inactivity, the British Army in general, despite recognizing its failure to achieve any outstanding success under Sir William Howe's command, was far from critical of its retiring commander. Sir William was a charming gentleman who had always been careful to retain the confidence and affection of his troops. Most of the British officers, therefore, (there were some exceptions) determined that their feelings for Sir William should not pass unnoticed before their retiring commander retreated from the scene of American history, and planned the Meschianza in his honor.

For several days prior to the date (May 18th) set for the extravaganza, preparations were made for "as splendid an entertainment as the shortness of the time" preceding Howe's departure "and our present situation" in a city that little afforded materials for decorative effects "would allow us," Captain John André, one of the prime promoters of the extravaganza, recorded. "Twenty-two field-officers joined" in underwriting the cost, four of whom (Sir John Wrottesley, Colonel James O'Hara, Major Gardiner and Captain John Montrésor) "were appointed managers."

On the day designated for the festivities "a grand *regatta*" on the Delaware River, commencing at Knight's Wharf at the northern fringe of the city, "began the entertainment."[23] As the barges bearing General and Admiral Howe, Sir Henry Clinton, the inferior generals, other officers, and many ladies decked in all their finery, were rowed south along the line of flag-draped ships of His Majesty's Royal Navy, "the frigate *Roebuck* greeted the sloop of the brothers Howe with a salute of nineteen guns, and many transports responded." Music "was heard everywhere" from the various military and naval bands.[24]

The principal entertainment was scheduled for the Wharton Mansion south of the city. The building had been requisitioned for the occasion from its Loyalist owner, and the grounds and interior had been lavishly decorated for the affair. The interior was especially gorgeous, having been draped with countless festoons and graced with candelabra. Its walls were studded

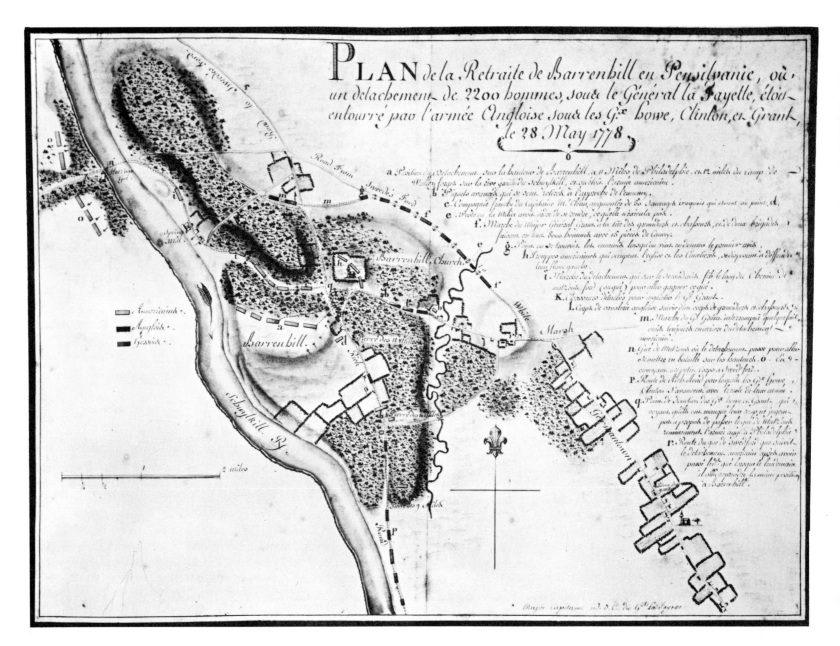

THE RETREAT AT BARREN HILL. *Plan of Lafayette's retreat May 20, 1778 (the map is misdated May 28) drawn by Michel Capitaine du Chesnoy, one of the French engineers serving with the American Army. Du Chesnoy correctly indicates the positions and marches of the American and British forces except General Grant's route, which is believed to have extended in a far wider northern arc. The Marquis De Chastellux visited Barren Hill and the surrounding area with Lafayette on Decem-* ber 12, 1780 at which time Lafayette told him that General Grant "made a long detour, marching first out Frankford road, then turned [westward] at Oxford," to reach Whitemarsh and Barren Hill. Lafayette in his Memoirs says of Grant's route, "that corps proceeded on the road to Francfort, and, by a circuitous movement, fell into that of Whitemarsh." Map printed through Courtesy of John Carter Brown Library, Brown University, Providence, Rhode Island.*

with mirrors borrowed for the occasion. John André had designed and personally aided in the decorations. With such a pleasurable port-of-call in view, the barges bearing their festive passengers wasted no more time on the water than was necessary, and proceeded to the Old Fort Wharf as the landing-place giving them closest access to the principal scene of diversion.

Debarking, the revelers formed a procession in the wake of the guest of honor and other principal officers "and advanced through an avenue formed by two files of grenadiers, and a line of light-horse supporting each file. This avenue led to a square lawn" where the merrymakers discovered "two pavilions with rows of benches rising one above the other," which had been constructed for their accommodation, and on which the pleasure-seekers were presently seated.

When the audience was settled, a mock tournament ensued between the Knights of the Blended Rose and the Knights of the Burning Mountain, vieing for the favors of selected local belles. The ladies, designated the paragons of feminine beauty, were dressed in pseudo-Turkish costumes designed by the imaginative André. The knights were clad in imitation armor as fragile as the whole pleasurable affair. The tournament happily concluded in a bloodless draw, the demoiselles representing each faction being declared equal in beauty. The company then adjourned from the scene of mock strife to the Mansion, passing through two triumphal arches.

Dancing began immediately and continued till midnight, at which time a supper consisting of countless delicacies was offered in "a magnificent saloon" especially constructed for the occasion. When the guests had finished eating, fireworks lit the sky for the amusement of all, after which further dancing occupied the guests till the approach of dawn.

Not all fireworks on this memorable evening were furnished

by John Montrésor's engineering ingenuity. Captain Allen Mc-Lane and his American scouts, who had learned of the festive occasion, and that a large majority of British and Hessian officers would be occupied with duties other than military, profited by the opportunity to slip close to the British lines north of the city under cover of darkness and apply torches to the abatis fronting the enemy breastworks. The attack was more of a prank than anything serious. Although a few shots were fired by the British and Hessian defenders, no American casualties resulted. Nor were the festivities at the Wharton Mansion for a moment interrupted.

The Meschianza caused considerable sneering amusement among the American patriots when descriptions of the revel seeped through the enemy lines. In Philadelphia, Quakers expressed disgust at the frolic. "How insensible do these people appear, while our Land is so greatly desolated, and Death and sore destruction have overtaken, and now impend, over so many."[25] Some of His Majesty's officers felt a like disdain, and had refrained from attending the affair. Said an artillery major, "the Knights of the Burning Mountain are tom-fools, and the Knights of the Blended Rose are damned fools," and queried, "What will Washington think of all this?"[26] Nevertheless, Sir William Howe was deeply appreciative of the honor bestowed on him.

CHAPTER XIII

BARREN HILL

Lafayette Reconnoiters Enemy

On the day of the Meschianza, May 18th, Lafayette received the following important orders from Washington. "The detachment under your command with which you will immediately march towards the enemy's lines is designed to answer the following purposes: to be a security to this camp" by giving warning of any meditated enemy attack, "and a cover to the country between the Delaware and Schuylkill."

Further objectives were "to interrupt the communication" between the country and Philadelphia, "obstruct the incursions of the enemy's parties, and obtain intelligence" of British "motions and designs." This last objective, Washington noted, "is a matter of very interesting moment, and ought to claim your particular attention," since it was "of the utmost importance" that the Commander-in-Chief be instantly notified of any confirmation of an impending British evacuation. Washington was especially interested in "the time of intended embarkation, so that you may be able to fall upon the rear of the enemy in the act of withdrawing" from the city if such appeared feasible.

Lafayette was reminded that his "detachment" of above 2,000 men, including two platoons of the Commander-in-Chief's Guard, with Brigadier General Enoch Poor second in command, was "a very valuable one, and that any accident happening to it would be a severe blow to this Army." Lafayette was to use every precaution " for its security and to guard against a surprise. No attempt should be made nor anything risked without the greatest prospect of success." Washington was particularly emphatic that Lafayette should frequently change the position of his detachment since "a stationary post is unadvisable, as it gives the enemy an opportunity of knowing your situation and concerting plans successfully against you."[1]

Colonel Stephen Moylan at Trenton was ordered to detach

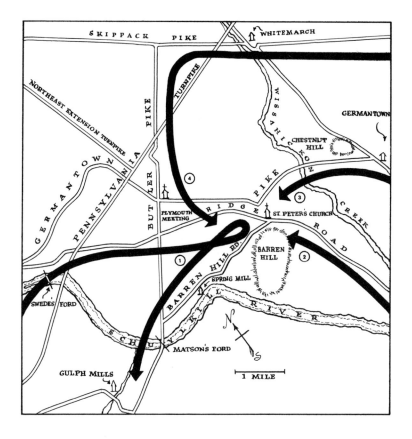

INTERPRETATION OF DU CHESNOY MAP OF BARREN HILL ACTION. *1. Lafayette's advance over Swede's Ford and his retreat down Barren Hill Road. 2. Howe's route on the Ridge Road. 3. Grey's route on the Germantown Pike. 4. Grant's route.*

"a select party of fifty dragoons,"[2] which was to proceed immediately to the vicinity of Whitemarsh to act in concert with Lafayette. The Pennsylvania Militia under General Potter was also ordered to render Lafayette every possible assistance.

Lafayette's column, accompanied by five pieces of light artillery, marched from Valley Forge "about midnight" the 18th/19th. The troops crossed the Schuylkill River at Swede's Ford (now Norristown), reaching the Ridge Road in Norriton Township. The column then marched in the direction of Germantown via the Ridge Road until the troops arrived at Barren Hill. On reaching this position Lafayette "bivouacked . . . waiting for daybreak."

The division's front stretched from the bluffs overlooking the Schuylkill on the south, north-eastward across the Ridge Road as far as the Germantown Pike, the latter thorofare marking the left flank. In order to protect this flank, the militia, with the help of Moylan's dragoons when they would arrive, were to block the Bethlehem Pike at Whitemarsh. Allen McLane's scouts, assisted by Daniel Morgan's Oneida Indians, were to patrol the roads leading to Philadelphia in front of Lafayette's position. The division remained motionless on the 19th while its commander sought to discover patriot citizens who would be willing to slip into Philadelphia and acquire whatever information was available concerning the enemy's intentions.

Howe Plans Surprise

Instead, information concerning Lafayette's strength and position had been quickly borne into Philadelphia "by spies amongst our men."[3] Howe immediately conferred with his principal officers regarding the feasibility of attacking Lafayette's force.[4] The consultation resulted in a plan whereby the Americans would be encompassed by several attacking columns in an endeavour to capture the whole American force. So certain was Sir William Howe that his strategy would succeed that, in advance of departing for the field, he invited friends to a dinner to be held the following evening at which he expected to present to the company the captured French marquis. The strategy evolved by Howe and his ranking subordinates necessitated employing nearly the whole British-Hessian garrison. The troops were to march by night in three columns, one each to Falls of Schuylkill and Germantown, and the third through Whitemarsh via Frankford.

The Falls of Schuylkill column, under the direct command of Howe (accompanied by General Clinton and Admiral Howe) took the Ridge Road route that led directly to the American front. The column that marched to Germantown under Major General Charles Grey proceeded along the Germantown Pike in an effort to strike the American left. The third column under Major General James Grant marched northeast to Frankford, then swung in a wide arc westward through Whitemarsh where, according to British intelligence, no American troops were present. Grant on reaching Whitemarsh would circle the American rear, and thus complete the intended noose.

Grant, having the furthest distance to march, had started first and had reached Whitemarsh undiscovered by the Americans, since the Militia, for reasons never elucidated, had failed to take its assigned position and Moylan's dragoons were still en route. Fortunately a local militiaman carried the warning to the American camp where he awakened the Chevalier Pontgibaud, Lafayette's aide, and reported the enemy advance. "Lafayette, awakened by the sound of our voices" joined the conference. Presently the news was confirmed by the arrival of a post-rider from Allen McLane whose scouts had captured two enemy soldiers and discovered the peril presented by Howe's column in front. By then, morning of the 20th was breaking.

Lafayette "was admirably cool, and showed that presence of mind so valuable in a commander in a time of danger." He immediately ordered Pontgibaud to scout in front and verify the truth of the information. Pontgibaud presently "saw the head of a moving column" of the enemy and "returned at full speed" to his commander with a confirming report.[5] Meanwhile Lafayette had roused the camp, and began to set the troops in marching order. He also placed several infantry companies in Barren Hill (St. Peter's Lutheran) Churchyard to give the impression that the Americans intended to defend the position.

Grant's enclosing column arrived on the scene too late to surprise Lafayette, Grant having dallied for breakfast at Plymouth Meeting. To meet this new threat, Lafayette projected "heads of columns" from the surrounding woods, which effectively brought Grant's advance to a halt while the British general formed a formal line of battle. This halt gained Lafayette the extra moments he needed to free his division from the planned encirclement.

Lafayette Escapes Trap

While Grant's force was forming, Lafayette withdrew all his troops and marched rapidly down Barren Hill and proceeded some three miles to the safety of Matson's Ford, the nearest possible route across the Schuylkill. By noon, the weather became "exceedingly warm," but the troops never relaxed their pace as they passed through Spring Mill and achieved the road to the ford. Reaching the ford, they commenced crossing the river in water arm-pit deep.

Despite their haste, the Americans crossed the ford "in good order . . . [and] as fast as the troops crossed they formed" a line of battle on the heights above the ford "and prepared for action" should the enemy attempt to follow.[6] The two platoons of Washington's personal guard brought up the rear, and assisted in getting the artillery safely across.

At Valley Forge Washington, on being informed of Lafayette's peril, sent messengers to warn him of the impending danger. They arrived in the vicinity of the threatened action only in time to discover Grant's column interposed between themselves and Barren Hill, and were forced to return to Valley Forge without delivering their message. Washington, in the meantime, had ordered signal guns fired at Valley Forge in an effort to convey a warning to Lafayette.

Grant, unaware that Lafayette had slipped away while he was forming his line of battle, commenced a slow advance. Meanwhile, Howe and Grey were rapidly approaching Barren Hill via the Ridge and Germantown Pikes respectively. Neither force, however, could ascertain more than small covering parties of Americans hovering on their fronts. McLane's scouts were attempting to delay the enemy advance by a show of force. The Oneida Indians, hidden in a woods to observe enemy movements, were approached by a column of British dragoons. The Indians, startled at the appearance of these wondrously clad horsemen, rent the air with a war-whoop and fled. The dragoons, frightened by this unfamiliar and savage sound, likewise decamped. The Indians were presently observed swimming to safety across the Schuylkill. On reaching the further shore and counting their numbers, they discovered one of their men missing, whereupon they commenced a mourning ceremony. However, the supposedly lost warrior soon reappeared, and the red-men happily continued their retreat.

THE HOME OF JOHN BROWN, JR., *occupied by Gen. Maxwell as his quarters. The house is now only part of the kitchen and servants quarters for the larger house (hidden to the right) built by Philander C. Knox, Attorney-General under President Theodore Roosevelt and Secretary of State under President Taft.*

The only American casualties in the whole affair occurred when several of Grant's dragoons approached Matson's Ford while the rear-guard of Lafayette's force, consisting of two platoons of the Commander-in-Chief's Guard, was crossing. The dragoons opened a scattered fire that resulted in four or five Americans struck. A return fire from the Americans on the far bank dropped a couple of British horsemen.

The British, having ascertained that the American position covering the ford appeared too strong to warrant the cost of an attack, and receiving an unverified report that the whole American Army was in motion from Valley Forge toward the point of danger, returned to Philadelphia "at about 2 o'clock" p.m. on the 20th.[7]

Lafayette, after observing that the British declined to attack his position at Matson's Ford, encamped for the night in the vicinity of The Gulph. The following morning he recrossed the Schuylkill at Swede's Ford, three miles west of Matson's, and, on receiving a report that the enemy had returned to Philadelphia, marched his troops, with Washington's consent, back to Barren Hill. Here he remained unmolested until the 23rd, on which date he "returned to camp."[8] On his arrival there Lafayette received "a good deal of praise,"[9] including Washington's congratulations for a timely and skillful retreat.

CHAPTER XIV

THE END DRAWS NEAR

Half-Pay Pension Approved

On May 18th, the day Lafayette left Valley Forge for Barren Hill, Washington announced to the officers of the army the Congressional resolution of May 15th, which guaranteed that "all military officers commissioned by Congress who are or who hereafter may be in the service of the United States and shall continue" in that service "during the war, shall after the conclusion of the war be entitled to receive annually for the term of seven years, if they live so long," the half-pay pension for which the officers had so long clamored. As a result of this resolution, the hitherto continuous offers of resignations almost ceased. A few days later, Congress ordered the re-organization of the army in conformity with the agreements reached between the Commander-in-Chief and the recent Committee on Conference. The Commander-in-Chief hastened to express his gratitude to Congress.

In anticipation of an expected enemy movement, Washington directed General Smallwood to abandon Wilmington and join the army at Valley Forge. An unforeseen delay in removing the supplies cached at Head of Elk (now Elkton, Maryland), and Smallwood's objection that Wilmington might be attacked if left totally undefended, induced the Commander-in-Chief to order Smallwood to send only the First Maryland Brigade to Valley Forge.

The Second Brigade, bolstered by the old and newly recruited Delaware troops, was directed to march only as far as Chad's Ford on the Brandywine where, under Smallwood's immediate command, it could continue to cover both Wilmington and Head of Elk, yet remain within reasonable marching distance of Valley Forge. In early June, however, the Second Brigade would also be ordered to proceed to Valley Forge, leaving the defense of Delaware in the hands of the local militia.

On May 21st Congress resolved its final objections to British proposals concerning the exchange of prisoners, and ordered Washington to expedite the business. The Commander-in-Chief at once requested Elias Boudinot to return to camp to forward the exchange before the recommencement of military operations. Boudinot was at his home in New Jersey, having stopped en route from a brief visit to New York City under a flag of truce to investigate numerous complaints concerning the maltreatment of American prisoners.

While awaiting Boudinot's return, Washington transmitted a copy of the Congressional resolution regarding prisoners to General Howe. Since Howe was on the verge of retiring, he transferred the matter to General Clinton's hands, and Clinton directed his Commissary of Prisoners, Joshua Loring, to meet with Boudinot at Germantown and hammer out the final arrangements for an exchange of prisoners.

Since Boudinot was delayed in reaching Valley Forge, Washington substituted his personal aide, Lt.-Colonel Alexander Hamilton, as his acting emmissary to meet with Loring. This meeting revealed that Clinton's notions concerning an exchange somewhat varied from those of Howe. Another meeting was arranged; and Boudinot, who by this time had returned, accompanied by his intended successor as Commissary of Prisoners, Major John Beatty, met with Loring at Germantown to resolve the differences of opinion concerning the exchange.

Farewell to General Howe

On May 24th the British Army, amid scenes of unabashed regret and sorrow, witnessed Sir William Howe's departure from America. A few dissenting officers refrained from showing grief, but the great majority of the British Army exhibited a "universal regret" at the loss of its commander. The army's feelings were perhaps best expressed by John André. "We see him taken from us," André wrote to a friend in England, "at a time when we most stand in need of so skillful and popular a commander" whose three years' experience in America had constantly added "to the confidence we always placed in his conduct and abilities . . . I do not believe there is upon record an instance of a Commander-in-Chief having so universally endeared himself to those under his command; or of one who received such signal and flattering proofs of their love."[1]

Howe was honored by a last departing salute of nineteen guns and by an added personal sign of respect shown by Clinton, who ordered the password of the day to be "Brandywine" and the countersign "Howe" in remembrance of Sir William's September victory. General Clinton and Admiral Howe, followed by all the officers not on duty, accompanied the departing general to the city waterfront. Hessian General Baron von Knyphausen "was so moved" by the scene "that he could not finish a compliment he began to pay" Sir William "in his own name, and that of his Officers who attended him." The tearful ceremony of parting concluded at "1/2 past one" in the afternoon, as, arm-in-arm, the Howe brothers stepped into the Admiral's barge and were rowed to the flagship *Eagle* where they dined in private and bade each other a family farewell.[2]

That evening the vessel bearing Sir William to England slipped south to the neighborhood of Billingsport, New Jersey. At ten o'clock in the evening Sir Henry Clinton issued an order for the embarkation of the "Baggage of the Army" not directly needed by the troops, "the whole to be completely on board by one o'clock to-morrow in the afternoon." The transports recently arrived from New York and not needed to feed the army "would fall down the River at that hour."[3] Orders were also issued to dismantle the fortifications of the last heavy cannon.

None of these scenes escaped the notice of American spies in the city; and reports thereof were hastened to Valley Forge. Not only did the signs in Philadelphia point towards an evacuation, but Washington was also informed of increasing enemy activity at Cooper's Ferry on the Delaware River shore, opposite the city, which surely gave indication of a British retreat across New Jersey. If this was true the American commander might find a favorable opportunity to strike a blow at the retreating enemy. Washington, therefore, alerted the New Jersey Militia, directing them to make every possible effort to delay the enemy march, should it occur, by demolishing bridges, felling trees across the enemy's line of march, and sniping at the enemy's flanks. Washington also detached General Maxwell to proceed to New Jersey with the two remaining regiments of the New Jersey Brigade, and there unite with Maxwell's two regiments previously sent to New Jersey.

Washington did not dare to "detach [a force] largely to harrass the enemy . . . before they have actually crossed the Delaware . . . [since] the number of our sick (upwards of 3,000 in camp), [and the] security of stores, which are covered by our present position," prevented major detachments from the army. Under these circumstances the army would not be free to "take such a Post in Jersey" as would enable it to effectively block an enemy retreat.[4]

Reports emanating from Philadelphia depicted colossal British haste in preparation for evacuation. The enemy troops, a report stated, had been issued "three days provision and had their canteens filled with rum, [and] that the women and children" of enemy officers and fleeing Loyalists "had embarked" on the transports, as also had the enemy's invalids. "The number of transports" available, the report continued, "amount to 180 vessels," which did not "appear adequate to the number of troops" stationed in Philadelphia. This report led Washington to assume that the principal body of enemy troops intended to march across New Jersey.

"A general despair among the Tory inhabitants" of the city was daily becoming more manifest. Loyalist pleas to accompany the fleet to New York deluged British Headquarters. "The inhabitants [were] anxious to know whether their persons and property" would receive British protection "from the rage of the American soldiery."[5] Already various Loyalist families who preferred permanent or temporary exile to exposing themselves to possible American retaliation had "given in their names" at British Headquarters in the hope that places could be found to accommodate them in the anchored transports.[6]

In the expectation that the city would presently return to American control, Washington appointed the invalid Benedict Arnold to assume command in Philadelphia the moment the enemy left. Arnold celebrated his appointment with an outdoor feast in the cherry grove adjoining the Moses Coates' residence where he quartered. Twenty-one guests including General and Mrs. Greene, General and Mrs. Knox, and Foragemaster-General Colonel and Mrs. Clement Biddle attended. Lafayette and Wayne arrived late and stayed only long enough to sip a glass of wine.

Washington Alerts Army

In preparation for an evacuation of Valley Forge in the face of a possible enemy retreat, Washington commenced withdraw-ing the major outposts of the army. In particular, Daniel Morgan was directed to abandon his principal post at Radnor. His rapidly marching riflemen would be needed to scout ahead of the army the moment the troops decamped. No officers or men were "under any pretence whatever (unless duty requires it) to be absent from Camp, that they may be ready to march at an hours warning."[7] Exact returns of the number of sick in camp were ordered from the regimental surgeons so that "a sufficient number of proper officers" could be "left in charge" of the invalids when the camp was abandoned.[8]

Orders were issued to General Lee that his division consisting of Poor's, Varnum's and Huntington's Brigades would precede the main force and march directly "to the North [Hudson] River" in the event the enemy's retreat across New Jersey aimed at crossing to New York City at or near Elizabethtown. Lee, however, was to "halt on the first strong ground after passing the Delaware at Coryell's Ferry, till further orders."[9]

The supposition that the British march across New Jersey might commence at any moment was supported by the numbers of enemy troops who had already crossed the Delaware into New Jersey and were stationed under the command of General Leslie within the temporary fortifications erected in the vicinity of Cooper's Ferry. Other enemy troops were crossing constantly. Daily, too, the enemy transports were falling down the river in preparation for seeking the open sea en route to New York.

Having received copies of the finalized Conciliatory Acts from General Tryon at New York, and with the impending arrival of the British Peace Commissioners who were to implement the Acts, General Clinton requested a personal interview between Clinton's representative, Colonel Patterson, and the American Commander-in-Chief. Patterson, Clinton notified Washington, would bring with him the definitive copies of the Conciliatory Acts, which Clinton desired Washington transmit to Congress.

Obviously, Washington had no desire for the presence of an enemy officer in camp at this stage of American preparations, and rejected Clinton's request. Nevertheless he assured Clinton that if either he or Admiral Howe "have any dispatches [relative to the Peace Commission] for Congress and think fit to transmit them to my care" through the usual channels of flags of truce, "they shall be forwarded by the earliest Opportunity." Any communications "of a military nature" for the American commander would be likewise received, but only if committed to writing. This method of communication had answered past purposes and would continue to answer "all the purposes you may have in view."[10] Since delivery of the Conciliatory Acts had been ordered by the Ministry, and since American receipt of the Acts was imperative to British interests, Clinton could only accede to Washington's directive.

Even at this late hour, Washington requested Congressman Joseph Reed, formerly Adjutant-General and recently a member of the Committee on Conference, to repair to Valley Forge and assist in the final re-organization of the army. Reed was eminently suited for the task both as a former military man and as an accredited member of Congress. Francis Dana, who had chairmanned the Committee on Conference, also arrived to assist, thereby lending further prestige to any changes the Commander-in-Chief might see fit to institute. Meanwhile, Washington, in consultation with Steuben, had prepared and published the order of march from Valley Forge.[11]

On discovering that many civilians intended to flee from Philadelphia, Washington expressed deep concern that "hundreds, nay thousands of people, and among them valuable Artisans, with large quantities of Goods" of value to the patriot cause and American commerce, "will be forced from Philadelphia" unless the state authorities acceded to "the generous policy, recommended by Congress" for the forgiveness of unintentional or only meager anti-American acts.

Frequent well-confirmed reports had reached Valley Forge that much of the civilian populace still in the city was no longer pro-British. Many persons, it was reported, were expressing increased reluctance to continue as subjects of a British crown and government that could no longer protect them, and would prefer civilian oaths of allegiance to the United States rather than depend on the increasing uncertainty of British victory. Washington reported to Henry Laurens that the distress of these civilians because of the insecurity of their prospects was "scarcely to be paralleled."[12]

A British Spy Attempt

Sir Henry Clinton was quite as interested in the condition of the American Army and in Washington's possible ability to counteract British intentions as Washington was in Clinton's plans. This enemy interest precipitated an episode at Valley Forge involving Thomas Shanks, "formerly an officer in the 10th Pennsylvania Regiment," who had been cashiered by an American court-martial the previous autumn when judged guilty of stealing a superior officer's shoes. Shanks "as a consequence went in to the enemy" in Philadelphia and had offered his services to the British.[13]

General Clinton accepted the offer and directed Shanks to proceed to Valley Forge in an effort to spy on the American camp. Shanks was accompanied on the preliminary leg of his journey by a British sergeant who had been instructed to guide the spy through the British lines and see him safely on his way, after which the sergeant was to return. The sergeant, however, had different thoughts concerning his destination. While Shanks "took one road" toward Valley Forge "the Sergeant [took] the other," having determined to take advantage of this opportunity to desert from the British Army. The sergeant "arrived first" at Valley Forge and "gave the necessary information" to the Americans concerning Shanks' mission.[14]

On Shanks' arrival, he was immediately apprehended and court-martialed, the British sergeant acting as the principal witness against him. Shanks was induced by the evidence presented to confess his crime and was hanged in view of the whole army. "His body hung from 10 o'clock in morning till retreat beating [and] was then cut down and his Body was sent to the surgeons."[15]

While Shanks was awaiting his fate, the booming of cannon from the direction of Philadelphia caused the American camp considerable puzzlement. The sounds, it was later learned, only emanated from the enemy's celebration of His Majesty's birthday. During this ritual the "shipping fired" its guns, and there were "royal salutes from the artillery park" on the city Commons,[16] but the celebration lacked its usual luster. Nevertheless, "All the generals and staff officers who were in the city had dinner with General Clinton,"[17] and there were fireworks in the evening for all to see.

On the same day, Washington received via "a flag from Sir Henry Clinton" a packet containing copies of the Conciliatory Acts as finalized by Parliament, together with letters from Clinton and Admiral Howe requesting the American commander not only to transmit copies to Congress but also to distribute copies abroad for public information. Although the American commander immediately posted "by express" those copies destined for Congress, he refrained from public distribution until the sense of Congress in the matter could be ascertained.[18]

Clinton's messenger also informed Washington of the imminent arrival of the British Peace Commissioners in America. The Commissioners, in view of the Ministry's ordered evacuation of Philadelphia, had actually been directed to sail for New York, though not informed of the reason. On approaching American shores, the Commissioners, seeking to hasten their negotiations by establishing themselves in closer proximity to Congress, prevailed on the ship's captain to alter his course for Philadelphia.[19] In fact, almost at the moment that Washington was notified of their impending arrival, the Commissioners' ship, the frigate *Trident,* was sighted in Delaware Bay, and the next day could be seen from Philadelphia. Lord Cornwallis, returning from his winter furlough in England, was also aboard the vessel.

CHAPTER XV

THE PEACE COMMISSION

Admiral Howe Briefs Commissioners

As the Peace Commissioners sailed up the Delaware River, Lord Carlisle, the Commission chairman, noted that America was "a beautiful country covered with wood" that was more extensive than the forests of England, "and to all appearance extremely rich." However, Lord Carlisle was "grieved . . . to tell" his wife in England "that both sides of the river are in possession of the enemy, who are well armed, and absolutely prevent any intercourse whatever with the land except at Philadelphia and its immediate vicinity."[1]

Adverse tides and winds prevented the Commissioners from setting foot on American soil at Philadelphia until June 6th, on which date Lord Carlisle, Johnstone and Eden (the last accompanied by his wife) were personally greeted by Clinton as they stepped ashore.

The Commissioners, weary from their long six weeks' voyage and glad to set foot on land again, "supp'd with Lord Admiral Howe" that evening. At the table, their host explained the present aspect of American affairs. As a result of this and conversations with other persons, William Eden soon observed that "American Politics are a wretched story — We were surprized on our arrival," Eden lamented, "to find every thing prepared for a total desertion of Pennsylvania in consequence of Orders" from the Ministry "which had preceded us. This Circumstance . . . in the Prosecution of which the Commanders in Chief," General Clinton and Admiral Howe had no discretion, "has thrown much cold water upon the fermentation" which Loyalist reports had erroneously assured the Commissioners "was otherwise taking place in the Colonies from the Love of English Concessions & the dislike of French Alliances."

Eden reported to England, "what will happen I cannot say . . . My forebodings are not good." He assured his correspondent "I shall try hard however to do my duty" in the delicate mission, but "as to Disgraces & Disappointments I must bear them as well as I can in common with my Countrymen."[2] The rains on the night of the 6th were in keeping with Eden's feelings and the sodden condition of British hopes and aspirations for victory.

Less than twenty-four hours later, Washington, through his agents in Philadelphia, was informed of the arrival of the enemy Commissioners. The American commander immediately so advised Congress and questioned whether from a military standpoint the Commissioners' arrival would "make any alteration in the intentions of the Enemy." Such alterations were not yet obvious, but if the Commissioners' residence in Philadelphia was extended "even a short time" Clinton would be obliged to revictual his army since he "had retained but a very small quantity of provisions" in the city, "and scarce any Baggage."[3]

Efforts to Bring on Talks

On June 9th, the Commissioners attempted to open negotiations with Congress. The distinguished Scotch scholar, Adam Ferguson, because of his notable reputation in both Europe and America, had been appointed secretary to the Commission in the hope that he might prove an acceptable intermediary between the Commission and the American authorities. On June 9th, therefore, Ferguson appeared under a flag of truce at an American outpost bearing a letter from Clinton, requesting Washington to issue a pass which would permit the Commission's secretary to proceed to York to consult with Congress.

Although Ferguson was not allowed to enter the camp, at his earnest request Clinton's letter was borne to Headquarters. Washington sent a message to Ferguson that though he would be pleased to forward a copy of Clinton's letter to Congress for its approval or disapproval, Ferguson himself would be obliged to return to Philadelphia until Congress was heard from. Washington also sent Ferguson a letter of explanation directed to Clinton, which informed the enemy commander that, "I do not conceive myself at liberty, to grant the passport which you request for Doctor Ferguson, without being previously instructed by Congress on the subject. I shall dispatch a Copy of your Letter to them; and take the earliest opportunity of communicating their determination."[4]

At this point George Johnstone recommenced his suborning letters to members of Congress that had begun with his February letter to Robert Morris. Although Johnstone composed epistles to Morris and Francis Dana (both of whom he had previously known) the principal object of his attention was General Joseph Reed. Long before leaving England Johnstone had become friendly with Reed's brother-in-law, Dennis de Berdt, and had informed Reed of this acquaintance by letter dated April 11th, from London. Johnstone now employed this friendship in an effort to influence Reed.

Johnstone began his second letter to Reed with a fulsome appraisal of the latter's "great worth and consequence in the unhappy disputes that have subsisted" between the Mother Country and her Colonies. "Your pen and your sword have both been used with glory and advantage in vindicating the rights of mankind," though Johnstone could only view the present rebellion with regret. "Such a conduct," he further averred, "must ever command my warmest friendship and veneration. In the midst of these affecting scenes my feeble voice has not been wanting to stop the evils . . . that every subject of the empire might live equally free and secure . . . not one part dependent on the will of another . . . My wishes have ever been that America might so far prevail, as to oblige" the Mother Country to see her error in attempting to impose her arbitrary will on America.

Now, as the presence of the Peace Commission made evident, Great Britain was "at length convinced of her folly and her faults," and having recovered her wisdom, had instituted the Commission "for settling . . . all the differences . . . short of a total separation of interests." Johnstone concluded his letter by affirming that "Nothing could surpass the glory" that the Americans had already "acquired in arms, except the generous magnanimity of meeting" the Commissioners "on the terms of justice and equality, after demonstrating to the world, that the fear of force could have no influence in that decision."[5]

Reed received Johnstone's letter at Valley Forge, where he and Francis Dana were assisting Washington in re-organizing the army. Robert Morris had also arrived in camp on a similar errand. Reed at once presented Johnstone's letter to Washington who read it and returned it without comment. Reed then composed a reply to Johnstone, the contents of which received the approbation of Morris and, with amendments, the Commander-in-Chief. His letter unequivocally pointed out that "after the unparalleled injuries and insults this country had received from the men who direct the affairs of Britain, a negociation under their auspices has much to struggle with . . . that America would willingly exchange the calamities of war for the blessings of peace," but should the "resolution of Congress . . . leave no prospect of a happy reunion," America could hope that "Great-Britain will give up her visionary schemes of conquest and empire, for the solid benefits she may yet derive from our amity and commerce."[6]

Whether or not Reed's letter reached Johnstone's hands, Reed was never able to ascertain. Johnstone, however, failed to be disconcerted. According to Reed, Johnstone left an offered bribe of "ten thousand guineas and the best post in the government" with Mrs. Elizabeth Ferguson, a semi-patriot woman, to tempt Reed to use his influence in promoting a reconciliation.[7]

John Laurens wrote to his father that the presence of the Peace Commission only bore "the fond picture of a mother caressing her children," and he was of the "opinion that the Commissioners hope to do more by addressing themselves to individuals than public bodies."[8] Congress, presently aware of Johnstone's activities, immediately demanded that his letters to Morris, Reed and Dana be surrendered to Congress for perusal, with the result that Congress declared it a penal offense to engage in correspondence with the enemy without its specific assent and knowledge. Eventually, Congress refused to hold communication of any kind with the Commissioners as long as Johnstone remained a member of the Commission.

On June 10th, the Commissioners, chagrined at Dr. Ferguson's failure to receive a pass to York, addressed a lengthy explanation of the peace proposals to Congress. The letter passed through Washington's hands to York, reaching Congress on June 11th. Henry Laurens immediately ordered the letter read to Congress, but the reading had only "advanced to the second page when the House directed" the President "to Seal up all the Papers and adjourned to Monday Morning."[9]

The following Monday, Congress assented to listen to the completion of the reading, and directed the President to compose an intransigent reply to the British proposals. Laurens immediately wrote to the Commissioners, "The Acts of the British Parliament, the Commission from your Sovereign" enabling the Commissioners to conduct negotiations, "and your letter, suppose the people of these states to be subjects of the Crown of Great-Britain, and are founded on the idea of dependence, which is utterly inadmissible." Congress therefore would only "be ready to enter upon the consideration of a treaty of peace and commerce, not inconsistent with treaties already subsisting" with France, "when the King of Great-Britain shall demonstrate a sincere disposition for that purpose. The only solid proof of this disposition will be an explicit acknowledgment of the independence of these states, or the withdrawing his fleets and armies" from American soil and waters.[10]

With Congress' rejection of the Commissioners' letter, General Clinton no longer felt obliged to postpone the evacuation of Philadelphia. He directed the Commissioners to go aboard the *Trident,* the same vessel that had transported them from England, and informed them that all further negotiations must of necessity be conducted from New York.

CHAPTER XVI

FINAL HOURS

British Evacuation Preparations

"Our information from Phila: is that the Enemy are destroying their works: knocking the Trunions of[f] their heavy Cannon, they leave behind." By these reports on June 7th there was little doubt that the enemy evacuation of the city was imminent. Nor was the enemy route of retreat by land any longer in question. "They have a large body of Troops over at Coopers Ferry, where they have" assembled a "large number of Boats on Carriages to Transport their Men across the different creeks in N. J." The American Army "hold themselves ready at a Moments warning" to pursue the retreating enemy.[1]

The "new arrangement" of the army ordered by Congress was described at length in General Orders of June 8th so that "all officers" could readily "make themselves acquainted with the establishment and govern themselves accordingly."[2]

On the same day, Washington, observing "the very Sickly situation of the camp" as a result of the army's long residence in its huts, deemed "it improper [that] we should remain longer on the present ground." General Greene was therefore directed "to reconnoitre a new camp, with the aid of the chief Engineer," General Duportail, in a "wholesome situation . . . and at such a distance from this position, that we should run no risk" of the fortifications of the present camp "being gained by the enemy on a sudden attempt, before we could have time to repossess" the works.[3]

Greene and Duportail immediately set about the task; and on June 10th the troops "marched away from our huts" and set up tents "about a half a mile in front of our works," encamping in far more "pleasant" surroundings than the old camp could afford.[4] Some of the regiments even "crossed the Schuylkill" via Sullivan's Bridge "and encamped on the left bank of that river, just opposite to our winter quarters."[5] No longer need the men "swallow the effluvia arising from a deposite of various carcasses and filth accumulated during six months."[6]

As the fateful hour of the final British evacuation of Philadelphia approached, the city became a scene of increasing panic among die-hard Loyalists. Clinton's assurance that every person who so desired would be transported to safety in New York did little to lessen anxieties. Nevertheless many Quakers, considering their consciences clear and, trusting for their safety to Divine Providence, determined to remain in the city.

Since Clinton was fully aware that the Americans knew an evacuation was imminent, he directed that 300 men work daily to keep the British fortifications ostensibly in repair in an effort to keep the exact moment of departure a secret. American intelligence, on the 16th, reported that the last enemy baggage was being hastily packed, and even that the Peace Commissioners' linen had been "ordered from the washer-women finished or unfinished." The enemy, the report continued, had taken all the horses they could possibly collect and all the loose lumber they could find, and had loaded them on their vessels.[7]

In all the American camp only Lafayette probably appeared disconsolate. A month earlier he had received the sorrowful news of the deaths of his infant daughter and a favorite nephew, and was now writing home to his wife, Adrienne, "The distance between Europe and America appear to me more enormous than ever . . . The loss of our poor child almost constantly is in my thoughts," but in view of the imminent campaign he could give no thought to returning home.[8]

Lafayette's presence with the army was indeed required not only because of the imminence of a campaign, but also because Congress was about to begin an investigation into Thomas Mifflin's reign as head of the Commissary Department. This deprived the army of a major general, since as the prime witness in the investigation, Mifflin "obtained leave, on his solicitation, to repair to York &c in order to prepare his defence." This request, the Commander-in-Chief admonished Congress, "I thought myself under a necessity of granting, however inconvenient and injurious it may be, to permit the absence of Officers at this period."[9]

On the 15th, in anticipation of the British evacuation, some 900 American prisoners were released from Philadelphia jails. On June 16th, early in the morning, British and Hessian regiments poured across the Delaware River into New Jersey, landing at Cooper's Point and Gloucester. Captain Allen McLane, advancing his scouts close to the enemy fortifications, discovered that the last field artillery had been withdrawn from the works, though British grenadiers still exchanged a few random shots with McLane's men.

Washington Plans Action

With McLane's report in hand, Washington called a council of war on the 17th. Sixteen generals including Washington were present at the conference: Lee, Greene, Arnold, Stirling, Lafayette, Steuben, Smallwood, Knox, Poor, Paterson, Wayne, Woodford, Muhlenberg, Huntington and Duportail. The Commander-in-Chief, as was his custom, briefly reviewed the present military situation, stating that there were now some 12,500 troops on hand at Valley Forge including the semi-invalids who "might be capable of acting in an emergency." Of this grand total, only 11,000-odd "would be able to march off the ground, in condition for service."

Twenty-three hundred sick and convalescents would be left in camp and in the hospitals. The only increase in their present forces the Americans could expect was the eight hundred Continentals under Maxwell already stationed in New Jersey, plus the New Jersey Militia. Opposed to these numbers, the enemy had by the latest estimates "between 14 and 15,000" seasoned veterans capable of facing battle.

Washington then requested the assembled generals' opinions concerning three possible strategies: attacking the enemy's rear as it withdrew from the fortifications of Philadelphia; remaining in camp until the enemy had successfully crossed the Delaware; or proceeding at once towards that river. If a consensus of opinion decided against an attack on the enemy rear, Washington asked whether the army should be routed directly for the Hudson River, or attempt to overtake the enemy in New Jersey and bring the foe to battle.[10]

Although the discussion concerning these propositions was lengthy and warm, no decision was reached. Washington therefore, requested the general officers to write their opinions so that he might study them. The written opinions were unanimously against an attack on Philadelphia. The defeat of the enemy rear guard would gain the Americans little or nothing, and might result in a change in British strategy.

Wayne, Greene and General John Cadwalader, who was not present at the recent council but still wrote an opinion, favored an immediate march with the object of attacking the enemy as they crossed New Jersey. Stirling, Lafayette, Steuben, Smallwood and Knox favored merely annoying the enemy retreat without inducing a general action. Duportail agreed with this proposal but urged extreme caution lest the enemy force an action on ground unfavorable to the Americans. Muhlenberg favored an attack on the enemy only if Clinton ceased his retreat and established a defensive position in New Jersey. The opinions of the other generals were not received in time.

British Leave Philadelphia

The morning of June 18th broke hot, "the air lazy." The inhabitants of Philadelphia awoke to find that except for a few stragglers the British Army had disappeared in a "secret and still Manner" during the previous night.[11] Admiral Howe, having supervised the embarkation of the rear guard and those Loyalists who had wavered until the last moment and had finally chosen exile, was the last high British officer of either service to leave officially.

Unofficially, the last British officer to depart was Lord Cosmo Gordon, who had overslept. On being appraised of his peril, Gordon hastily dressed and dashed to the waterfront where he fortunately was able to commandeer means of passage across the river. The few British and Hessians who intentionally remained in the city had married local lasses and were determined to risk their futures as captives rather than desert the ladies of their choice.

The British-Hessian army left behind a city that "stunk abominably." Even the State House (now Independence Hall) "was left in a most filthy and sordid situation, as were many of the public and private buildings in the city. Some of the genteel houses were used for stables, and holes cut in the parlour floors" into which the stablemen shoveled horse manure.[12]

At "1/2 after 11 A.M." on June 18th George Roberts, a Militia scout, rode hurriedly into the camp at Valley Forge with word of the British evacuation of Philadelphia. Washington immediately dictated a hasty note to the President of Congress. "I have the pleasure to inform Congress, that I was this minute advised by Mr. Roberts, that the Enemy evacuated the City early this morning. He was down at the Middle ferry . . . where he received the intelligence from a number of the Citizens who were on the opposite shore" of the Schuylkill.[13] A similar message was sent to Vice President George Bryan of Pennsylvania, Bryan having assumed temporary presidency of the Executive Council at the death of the late President, Thomas Wharton, Jr.

Having received confirmation of the British evacuation from Allen McLane's scouts, Washington immediately ordered Lee's Division to march toward the Delaware, then readied his main force to follow Lee on the 19th. He directed Wayne's Division to march across Sullivan's Bridge and encamp on the north side of the Schuylkill. The moment Wayne had his Division in motion, he turned over the command of the division to his senior colonel, having received permission from Washington to proceed to Philadelphia on personal business with the stipulation that he rejoin his troops as soon as possible.

Wayne's Division would resume its march on the 19th. Lafayette's Division was to follow. DeKalb's Division was to be next in the line of march, followed by Henry Knox's artillery. Stirling's Division would form the rear. General Arnold, accompanied by Colonel Henry Jackson's Massachusetts Regiment, was directed to proceed to Philadelphia on the 19th and officially repossess the city.[14]

Washington stole a few moments from this pressing business to pay £100 in Pennsylvania currency as rent to Mrs. Deborah Hewes, whom he had displaced for six months from her home in the Isaac Potts House. Mrs. Washington had departed for home on the 9th. Had he the time, he could have summed up personal accounts for the winter and spring encampment and found that he had incurred $5,000 in expenses during the period, of which sum $450 plus £220 had been expended on his secret service watching the enemy in Philadelphia.

"At 5 o'clock" on the morning of June 19th "the general was beat" by the drums of the whole army, breakfast was hastily eaten, tents were struck, the last baggage loaded, and by 9 o'clock Lafayette's Division was in pursuit of Wayne's across Sullivan's Bridge. The march proceeded to and along Pawling's Ford Road to Egypt Road, then along the latter and the Ridge Road into Norrington (or Norriton) Township. Ahead lay the long route to Buckingham, where the main army would encamp for the night; then to Coryell's and Sherrard's Ferries and Easton, at which places the divisions would cross the Delaware into New Jersey.[15]

★ ★ ★

POSTSCRIPT

The army that marched from Valley Forge was shaping its course towards victory even though the ultimate triumph lay years in advance. The long line of march to the Delaware River crossings and into New Jersey was the real opening of the door to freedom and independence. If the Battle of Monmouth, fought on June 28th in New Jersey between the retreating British and pursuing Americans, was not a clear-cut victory for either side, the battle at least proved to Britons that America now had an army capable of meeting the best troops that Europe could offer. Although the American cause would still experience numerous doldrums and perilous moments, the spirit and training of Valley Forge would carry that cause to triumph, a triumph that through the years has become the sacred and fortunate heritage of all free men.

★ ★ ★

BIBLIOGRAPHY

Short Titles

André Journal — André's Journal, 2 vols., Boston, 1903.

Baurmeister Letters — Baurmeister, Letters from Major Baurmeister to Colonel von Jungkenn Written During the Philadelphia Campaign 1777-1778, translated and edited by Bernhard A. Uhlendorf and Edna Vosper, Phila., Pa., 1937.

Birch-Henkels — Birch-Henkels, Thomas Birch's Sons—Stan V. Henkels Auction Catalogue No. 683, Revolutionary Manuscripts and Portraits, Phila., Pa., May 5-6, 1892.

Boudinot Journal — Boudinot, Elias, Journal or Historical Recollections . . . During the Revolutionary War, n.p., 1894.

Chester Co. Hist. Soc. — Chester County Historical Society, West Chester, Pa.

Clinton Papers — Clinton, Lt-Gen. Sir Henry, Papers, William L. Clements Library, U. of Michigan, Ann Arbor, Mich.

Journals of Cong. — Congress, Journals of the Continental, Washington, D.C., 1904-37.

Papers of Cong. — Congress, Papers of the Continental Congress 1774-89, National Archives, Washington, D.C., (Micro Copy #247).

Drinker Journal — Drinker, Elizabeth, Extracts from the Diary of, Henry D. Biddle Editor, Phila., Pa., 1889, reprinted from Pa. Mag.

Duncan — Duncan, Lt-Col. Louis C., Medical Men in the Revolution, Carlisle, Pa., 1931, Army Medical Bulletin #25.

Ewing Journal — Ewing, George, The Military Journal of, privately printed, Yonkers, N. Y., 1928 (pamphlet).

Fisher Journal — Fisher, Elijah, Journal 1775-1784, Augusta, Maine, 1880 (pamphlet), reprinted Mag. of History Extra No. 6.

Fitz. — Fitzpatrick, John C. Editor, Writings of Washington, Washington, D. C., 1932.

Galloway — Galloway, Joseph, The Examination of . . . before the House of Commons, London 1779, reprinted Phila., Pa., 1855.

Germain Papers — Germain Papers, William L. Clements Library, U. of Michigan, Ann Arbor, Mich.

Graydon Memoirs — Graydon, Alexander, Memoirs of His Own Times, Phila., Pa., 1846, reprinted from 1811 edition.

Greene — Greene, George Washington, Life of Nathanael Greene, N. Y., N. Y., 1871.

Henkels-Morris Sale — Henkels, Stan V., Auction Catalogue, The Confidential Correspondence of Robert Morris, Phila., Pa., 1917.

Hillard — Hillard, Rev. E. B., The Last Men of the Revolution, Hartford, Conn., 1864.

HSP Bul. — Historical Society of Pa. Bulletin Vol. 1 (1845-47), Historical Society of Pennsylvania, Philadelphia, Pa.

HSP Ms. Colls. — Historical Society of Pennsylvania Manuscript Collections, Philadelphia, Pa.

Hunter Diary — Hunter, Dr. John, Diary, Pa. Mag. XVII 76-82.

Kapp (DeKalb) — Kapp, Friedrich, Life of Johan Kalb Major General in the Revolutionary Army, N. Y., N. Y., 1884.

Kapp (Steuben) — Kapp, Friedrich, Life of Frederick William von Steuben, N. Y., N. Y., 1859.

Lafayette Memoirs — Lafayette, Maj.-Gen. Gilbert du Motier, Memoirs, Correspondence and Manuscripts of General Lafayette, Vol. I. N. Y., N. Y., 1837.

Laurens — Laurens, Lt.-Col. John, The Army Correspondence of . . . in the Years 1777-8 . . . to his Father, Henry Laurens, President of Congress, limited ed. privately printed, N. Y., N. Y., 1867.

McMichael — McMichael, Lieut. James, Diary, Pa. Mag. XVI 129-159 (1892).

Marshall Diary — Marshall, Christopher, Extracts from the Diary of, William Duane Editor, Albany, N. Y., 1877.

Martin Journal — Martin, Joseph Plumb, Private Yankee Doodle, etc., George F. Sheer Editor, Boston, Mass., 1962.

Mass. H. S. Proc. — Massachusetts Historical Society Proceedings, Boston, Mass.

Massey Journal — Massey, Capt. Samuel, Journal, J. F. Reed Manuscript Collection, King of Prussia, Pa.

Middleton — Middleton, William Shainline, Medicine at Valley Forge, Madison, Wis., 1941, reprinted from Annals of Medical History, Third Series III 461-86.

Montgomery Co. Sketches — Montgomery County, Pa., Hist. Soc. of, Sketches II 77-91, Norristown, Pa., 1900.

Montrésor Journal — Montrésor, Capt. John, Journals of, Collections of the New York Hist. Soc. 1881, N. Y., N.Y., 1881, reprinted in Pa. Mag. V and VI, 1882.

Neisser Diary — Neisser, Rev. George, Diary, Incidents in the History of York, Pennsylvania, 1778, Pa. Mag. XVI 433-8 (1892).

N. J. Gazette — New Jersey Gazette, Burlington, N. J. (Moved to Trenton, N. J. after Feb. 25, 1778) 1777-8.

N. Y. Gazette — New York Gazette and Weekly Mercury, James Rivington Ed., N. Y., N. Y., 1778.

Niles — Niles, H., Principles and Acts of the Revolution in America, Baltimore, Md., 1822.

Paine Writings — Paine, Thomas, The Political Writings of, Vol. I, N. Y., N. Y., 1830, Crisis No. 5, reprinted from Paine pamphlet, Lancaster, Pa., 1778.

Pa. Mag. — Pennsylvania Magazine of History and Biography, Historical Society of Pennsylvania, Philadelphia, Pa.

Penn. Packet — Pennsylvania Packet, Philadelphia, Pa. (Published at Lancaster, Pa., Nov. 29, 1777-Jan. 18, 1778).

Pontgibaud — Pontgibaud, Chevalier Charles Albert de, A French Volunteer of the War of Independence, trans. by Robert B. Douglas, N. Y., N. Y., 1897.

J. F. Reed Ms. Coll. — Reed, John F., King of Prussia, Pa., MS. collection.

Reed, Jos. — Reed, Joseph, Remarks on Governor Johnstone's Speech in Parliament, etc., Phila., 1779.

Rivington Papers — Rivington, James, pub., Collection of Papers that have been Published at Different Times Relating to the Proceedings of His Majesty's [Peace] Commissioners, N. Y., N. Y., 1778.

Sang Plate — Sang, Elsie O. and Philip D., The Genesis of American Freedom 1765-1795, Brandeis U. Press, Waltham, Mass., 1961.

S. C. Hist. Mag. — South Carolina, Historical Magazine VII and VIII, Charleston, S. C., 1906-7, Formerly S. C. Hist. and Gen. Mag.

Steuben Regulations — Steuben, Baron Friedrich Wilhelm von, Regulations for the Order and Discipline of the Troops of the United States, pub. 1779, numerous later editions.

Sullivan — Sullivan, Maj.-Gen. John, Letters and Papers of, Otis G. Hammond Editor, New Hampshire Hist. Soc., Concord, N. H., 1930, vols. I and II; source mostly from Sullivan Papers in N. H. Hist. Soc.

Waldo Diary — Waldo, Dr. Albigence, Diary, Pa. Mag. XXI (1897), reprinted from History Mag. V (1861).

V. F. Ms. Coll. — Valley Forge Historical Soc., MS. collection, Valley Forge, Pa.

Warren-Adams Ltrs. — Warren-Adams Letters, Being Chiefly a Correspondence among John Adams, Samuel Adams and James Warren, 2 vols.

W. P. — Washington Papers, Library of Congress, Washington, D. C., (See Index to the George Washington Papers, President Papers Index Series, pub., 1964).

Wild Journal — Wild, Corp. Ebenezer, Journal of, Mass Hist. Society Proceedings, Boston, Mass., 1890-91, Second Series VI 78-160.

NOTES

CHAPTER I

1. J. F. Reed ms. coll., David Brearley Notes. Brearley was a signer of the Constitution from New Jersey.
2. William Penn had set aside 7,800 acres for his personal use and had called the domain Mount Joy Manor. Later he gave the estate to his daughter, Letitia Penn Aubrey, who at her husband's insistence broke up the estate and sold it in parcels.
3. The original house no longer stands, having been torn down and replaced by the Stephens family in 1811. The later house still stands though considerably altered, and is called "East Watch" because of its proximity to the eastern edge of the camp grounds.
4. Martin Journal 103.
5. Greene quartered at Isaac Walker's (later at Moore Hall); Lafayette at Samuel Havard's; Knox at John Brown's; Stirling at Loyalist Parson William Currie's; DeKalb and Weedon at Abijah Stephens'; Wayne at Joseph Walker's (Mrs. Walker was Wayne's cousin); Muhlenberg at John Moore's; Poor at Tacy Jones' (owned by the Walker family); Sullivan at Thomas Waters'; McIntosh at Joseph Mann's (a colored man) west of Valley Creek; Woodford at Samuel Richards Jr's.; Scott at Samuel Jones' (now Valley Brook Farm); Duportail at John Havard's; Pulaski at John Beaver's; Maxwell at John Brown Jr's.; Potter of the Pennsylvania Militia at Jacob Walker's; Elias Boudinot, and later Gen. Charles Lee, at David Havard's; Varnum at David Stephens'; and Huntington at Zachary Davis's (owned by David Stephens). Paterson's quarters have not been ascertained.
6. Fitz. X 192-8, Washington to H. Laurens Dec. 23.
7. Fitz. X 174, Washington to Read Dec. 19.
8. J. F. Reed ms. coll., Capt. Samuel Massey's Journal, (Pa. Militia).
9. HSP Bul. I 25, Clark to Washington, Dec. 19.
10. Montrésor Journal 132.
11. Ibid.
12. Baurmeister Letters (Jan. 20) 41.
13. Drinker Journal 74-5.
14. Kapp (DeKalb) 137-141, DeKalb to Comte de Broglie, Dec. 25.

CHAPTER II

1. Fitz. X 180, General Orders, Dec. 20.
2. Fitz. X 169 et seq., General Orders, Dec. 18.
3. Ibid.
4. Fitz. X 180, General Orders, Dec. 20.
5. HSP ms. coll., Original Broadsides in English and German.
6. Fitz. X 177, Washington to Heath, Dec. 20.
7. Journals of Congress IX 1043-4.
8. Martin Journal 103-4.
9. Ibid. 104.
10. HSP Bul. I 26, Clark to Washington, Dec. 20.
11. Fitz. X 182, Washington to Potter, Dec. 21.
12. HSP Bul. I 27, Clark to Washington, Dec. 21.
13. Waldo Diary, Pa. Mag. XXI 309. Fire cake was raw flour and water baked on hot stones or pans over an open fire.
14. Fitz. X 193, Washington to H. Laurens, Dec. 23.
15. Ibid.
16. Orders not found in Fitz. Quoted in Valley Forge Guide and Hand-Book by Rev. J. W. Riddle, Phila. 1910.
17. Huntington to Washington, Dec. 22. Not listed in W. P. but quoted in Valley Forge Guide and Hand-Book by Rev. J. W. Riddle, Phila. 1910 pg. 85.
18. W. P., Varnum to Washington, Dec. 22.
19. Baurmeister Letters (Jan. 20) 42-3.
20. Fitz. X 183-7 passim., Washington to H. Laurens, Dec. 22.
21. Fitz. X 192-8 passim., Washington to H. Laurens, Dec. 23.
22. Fitz. X 190, General Orders, Dec. 22.
23. This marquee, or tent, is now in the collections of the Valley Forge Hist. Soc. There are two other similar tents, those for eating and conference, which are now exhibited at Yorktown, Va., National Military Park.
24. Baurmeister Letters (Jan. 20) 42.
25. Ibid. 43.
26. Marshall Diary 153.
27. Baurmeister Letters (Jan. 20) 43.
28. Waldo Diary, Pa. Mag. XXI 312.
29. Fitz. X 201, Washington to Gerry, Dec. 25.
30. Ibid. 201, Washington to Caswell, Dec. 25.
31. Fitz. X 207, General Orders, Dec. 26.
32. HSP Bul. I 31, Clark to Washington, Dec. 26.
33. Ibid. 32.
34. André Journal I 134.
35. A photograph shows this building was three stories high with an attic above. The two lower stories were surrounded on three sides by a two-deck porch. Unfortunately the building was destroyed by fire in 1902. Photo in Dr. Bodo Otto by James E. Gibson 1937 opp. pg. 152.
36. Fisher Journal 7.
37. Sullivan I 604-5, Sullivan to Washington, Dec. 27.
38. Marshall Diary 152.
39. V. F. ms. coll., Wayne to Wharton, Dec. 28.
40. HSP ms. coll., Wayne Papers, Wayne to Peters.
41. Fitz. X 222-4 passim., Washington circular letter to state governors, Dec. 29.
42. Waldo Diary, Pa. Mag. XXI 314-5.
43. Ibid. 316.
44. Fitz. X 225, General Orders, Dec. 30.
45. Montrésor Journal 480.
46. HSP Bul. I 34-5, J. Clark to Washington, Dec. 30.
47. Fitz. X 225, General Orders, Dec. 29.
48. Pa. Mag. II 295, Paine to Franklin, May 16, 1778.
49. J. F. Reed ms. coll., Capt. Samuel Massey's Journal.
50. Waldo Diary, Pa. Mag. XXI 315.

CHAPTER III

1. N. J. Gazette, Jan. 21.
2. J. F. Reed ms. coll., General Orders, Jan. 1, also Fitz. X 242-3. The Varick transcript of Washington's Headquarters Orderly Book in the Library of Congress has been compared with an original manuscript Headquarters Orderly Book written in various hands dated Valley Forge Jan. 1-April 15 in the J. F. Reed collection. Except for variances in spelling and punctuation, and slight differences in text, the two Orderly Books read essentially alike. The Varick text in Fitzpatrick, has been followed for the convenience of scholars.
3. Journals of Congress IX 1067-8.
4. Ibid. 1073.
5. Journals of Congress VIII 752.
6. Fitz. X 236-7, Washington to Lafayette, Dec. 31.
7. Lafayette Memoirs I 141, Lafayette to Washington.
8. S. C. Hist. Mag. VII 64-7, Lafayette to Laurens.
9. Sullivan I 606-8 passim., General Officers' memorial to Congress.
10. Fitz. X 243-4, Washington to Congress, Jan. 1.
11. Fitz. X 246, Washington to Wharton, Jan. 1.
12. Fitz. X 234-5, Washington to Pulaski, Dec. 31.
13. Waldo Diary, Pa. Mag. XXI 317.
14. Laurens 100, J. Laurens to H. Laurens, Jan. 1.
15. "Eyewitness" account of salt herring story quoted in Annals of Philadelphia by J. F. Watson and W. P. Hazard, 1898 pg. 84; first published 1830.
16. Some of these ovens have been discovered on the grounds occupied by Wayne's Division and have been reconstructed.
17. Martin Journal 110-11.
18. Ibid. 111.
19. J. F. Reed ms. coll., Small broadsheet N. P. (England) ca. 1800.
20. Hessian captain quoted in The American Revolution by Sir George Trevelyan N. Y. 1909 Part III: 353, first printed 1899.
21. J. F. Reed ms. coll., General Orders, Jan. 8 also Fitz. X 276.
22. Laurens 99, J. Laurens to H. Laurens, Jan. 1.
23. Waldo Diary, Pa. Mag. XXI 322.

24. Sullivan II 5, Lt. Col. Nathaniel Ramsey to Sullivan, Jan. 11.
25. Woodman 87; According to Henry Woodman, born at Valley Forge in 1795, the son of a veteran of the encampment and his wife, a local lass, daughter of Abijah Stephens. Woodman received his information directly from his family, who had witnessed the encampment.
26. Fitz. X 253, Washington to Board of War, Jan. 2, 3.
27. Fitz. X 249, Washington to H. Laurens, Jan. 2.
28. Sullivan II 3, Conway to Sullivan, Jan. 3.
29. Greene I 544, Greene to Jacob Greene, Jan. 3.
30. Waldo Diary, Pa. Mag. XXI 319.
31. Duncan 243, Dr. Rush's Directions for Preserving Health of Soldiers.
32. Ibid., Dr. Rush's Observations 240-3.
33. Ibid., Dr. Tilton's report. 223.
34. J. F. Reed ms. coll., General Orders, Jan. 5, also Fitz. X 266.
35. N. J. Gazette, Jan. 21.

CHAPTER IV

1. J. F. Reed ms. coll., General Orders, Jan. 6, also Fitz. X 272.
2. Ibid., Fitz. X 273, Jan. 7.
3. Journals of Congress X 23.
4. Marshall Diary 159.
5. Kapp (DeKalb) 145, DeKalb to H. Laurens.
6. Journals of Congress X 40.
7. Fitz. X 277, Washington to Knox, Jan. 8.
8. Report of Dr. William Smith, printed in North Carolina Medical Jnl., Charlotte, N. C., 1899, and reprinted in The Care of the Sick and wounded in the Revolution, Francis R. Packard, M. D. pamphlet p. 18-19.
9. Quote from Dr. James Tilton (ibid).
10. Chester Co. HS, Minutes of the Uwchlan, Chester County, Meeting.
11. J. F. Reed ms. coll., General Orders, Jan. 9, also Fitz. X 284.
12. J. F. Reed ms. coll., General Orders, Jan. 13, also Fitz. X 300.
13. Fitz. X 285, Washington to Steuben, Jan. 9.
14. Journals of Congress X 50.
15. Ibid. 59.
16. Fitz. X 288, Washington to James Lovell, Jan. 9.
17. Congressman Philip Livingston of New York. Quoted in Valley Forge . . . by Frank H. Taylor, Phila. 1905.
18. Sullivan II 7, Washington to ?, date and address sheet missing.
19. J. F. Reed ms. coll., General Orders, Jan. 12, also Fitz. X 291.
20. Fitz. X 297, Washington to Rush, Jan. 12.
21. Laurens 108-9, J. Laurens to H. Laurens, Jan. 14.
22. J. F. Reed ms. coll., General Orders, Jan. 15, also Fitz. X 306.
23. Woodman 72-3 (see Note 26, Chapter III.)
24. During the dry summer of 1964 the author investigated the site of the bridge and could find no traces remaining other than scattered stones in the river bed that may have been used to anchor the piers. The remains of these piers were still in evidence in 1840 when a monument was placed to mark the site of the southern end of the bridge. In 1850 the marker was broken by a flood and the broken part was thereafter imbedded beside the base. Although this marker was still in evidence as late as ca. 1900 it has since been silted over and lost. A large modern marker (1907) marks the approximate site of the bridge's northern end.
25. N. J. Gazette, Jan. 28. A later house built near the site of this action is unpatriotically called "Tarleton."
26. Laurens 111, J. Laurens to H. Laurens, Jan. 23.
27. HSP ms. coll., Wallace Papers, William Bradford Jr. to Joshua M. Wallace.
28. Laurens 111, J. Laurens to H. Laurens, Jan. 23.
29. N. J. Gazette, Jan. 28.
30. J. F. Reed ms. coll., General Orders, Jan. 20, also Fitz. X 321.
31. Drinker Journal 82.
32. Baurmeister Letters (Jan. 20) 46.
33. J. F. Reed ms. coll., General Orders, Jan. 20, also Fitz. X 321.
34. Laurens 114, J. Laurens to H. Laurens, Jan. 28.
35. Fitz. X 428, Washington to H. Laurens, Feb. 8-14.

36. Clarkson and his assistants quartered at Widow Cloyd's house on the present Charleston-Devault Road six miles west of camp.
37. Fitz. X 362-403 passim.
38. Paine Writings I 132-56 passim.

CHAPTER V

1. Fitz. X 412-3, Washington to John Jameson, Feb. 1.
2. Henkels (Morris Sale) 95-6, R. Peters to R. Morris, Feb. 3.
3. Henkels (Morris Sale) 166-7, Tilghman to R. Morris, Feb. 2.
4. Journals of Congress XI 419-453. See also The Treaties of 1778 and Allied Documents, G. Chinard ed., 1928.
5. Ibid.
6. N. Y. Gazette, Feb. 23.

CHAPTER VI

1. J. F. Reed ms. coll., General Orders, Feb. 4, also Fitz. X 421.
2. Fitz. X 433, Ibid. Feb. 8.
3. Fitz. X 433-4, Ibid.
4. Fitz. X 436, Ibid.
5. Journals of Congress X 141.
6. Fitz. X 65, Washington to Howe.
7. Laurens 122, J. Laurens to H. Laurens Feb. 9.
8. Fitz. X 445-6, Washington to W. Howe Feb. 10.
9. Hillard, Alexander Miliner's account, 41.
10. Warren-Adams Ltrs., M. Washington to Mercy Warren, March 7.
11. HSP ms. coll., Duponceau Letters.
12. Pa. Mag. XL 181 Duponceau Letters.
13. Ibid.
14. Hunter Diary, Pa. Mag. XVII 81.
15. Fitz. X 454, Washington to Greene Feb. 12.
16. Fitz. X 452-3, Washington to Wharton Feb. 12.
17. W. P., Wayne to Barry, Feb. 23.
18. W. P., Wayne to Washington of Feb. 25 and 26.
19. Fitz. X 513, Washington to H. Lee Feb. 25.
20. Journals of Congress X 114-117.
21. Ibid. 155.
22. Ibid. 184-5.
23. Ibid. 188.
24. Ibid. 198.
25. Ibid. 204-5.
26. Fitz. X 469, Washington to Gov. G. Clinton Feb. 16.
27. J. F. Reed ms. coll., McIntosh to Caswell.
28. Laurens 127-8, J. Laurens to H. Laurens Feb. 17.
29. Baurmeister Letters (Mar. 24) 49.
30. Laurens 128-9, J. Laurens to H. Laurens Feb. 17.

CHAPTER VII

1. Journals of Congress X 50.
2. See Kapp (Steuben) for further details as to rank and family.
3. Papers of Cong. Feb. 14.
4. Pa. Mag. XL 172-8 passim.
5. Ibid. 178.
6. Ibid.
7. J. F. Reed ms. coll., Varnum to Greene, (typescript from John Baer Stoudt Papers).
8. Kapp (Steuben) 1045.
9. Fitz. X 519., Washington to H. Laurens.
10. The author's collection contains a letter from John Laurens to Col. Clement Biddle, Foragemaster-General, noting that Steuben "quarters at the house late General DeKalbs." This notation is the only known reference to the initial quarters of Steuben at Valley Forge.
11. Woodman 71 (see Note 26, Chapter III).
12. Kapp (Steuben) 637-8, Bishop Ashbel Greene's later description of Steuben.

13. Kapp (Steuben) 114 et seq.
14. Kapp (Steuben) 124.
15. Steuben Regulations.
16. Laurens 132, J. Laurens to H. Laurens Feb. 28.
17. Kapp (Steuben) 126, Steuben Papers.
18. Ibid.
19. Kapp (Steuben) 130.
20. Pa. Mag. XL 179, Duponceau Letters.
21. Kapp (Steuben) 126, Steuben Papers.
22. Ibid. 128.
23. Ibid. 140.

CHAPTER VIII

1. Papers of Cong. Feb. 12, XI.
2. Marshall Diary 169.
3. Germain Papers, Germain to W. Howe, Dec. 11.
4. J. F. Reed ms. coll., General Orders, March 1, also Fitz. XL 8-10.
5. Lafayette Memoirs I 35.
6. Son of Dr. Bodo Otto to his wife, original letter lost, quoted in Dr. Bodo Otto by James E. Gibson 1937, pg. 149.
7. Duncan 243, Dr. Rush's observations.
8. Middleton 467, Wayne to R. Peters.
9. J. F. Reed ms. coll., Greene to Col. Hugh Hughes, April 16, (typescript) original in private collection.
10. J. F. Reed ms. coll., Original copies Conciliatory and Enabling Acts, printed by Charles Eyre and William Strahan, London 1778 (disbound).
11. Journals of Congress X 217.
12. Ibid. 221. The Oneidas and Tuscaroras were the only Six Nations tribes who favored the Americans. The other Four Nations, the Mohawks, Onondagas, Senecas and Cayugas were pro-British.
13. Henkels (Morris Sale) 75, Duer to R. Morris Mar. 6.
14. Fitz. XI 33, Washington to Board of War Mar. 6.
15. Fitz. XI 45-8 passim, Washington to Wharton Mar. 7.
16. Galloway 29.
17. J. F. Reed ms. coll., Varnum to Mrs. William (Catherine Ray) Greene Mar. 7.
18. J. F. Reed ms. coll., Sergeant Andrew Kemp letter to his mother (typescript) June 13, 1778.
19. Germain Papers, W. Howe to Germain Mar. 20, see also Fitz. XI 44 (note).
20. Fitz. XI 57-8, Washington to Sullivan Mar. 10.
21. Ibid. 59, Washington to Lafayette Mar. 10.
22. Baurmeister Letters (Mar. 24) 48.
23. Niles 463.

CHAPTER IX

1. J. F. Reed ms. coll., McIntosh to Caswell, Mar. 20.
2. Waterman's grave was marked by his comrades with head and foot stones, the headstone bearing the legend "J W 1778". The original headstone is now in the Valley Forge State Park Museum. A tall obelisk on the Grand Parade now marks the site of the grave.
3. Persifor Frazer to Mrs. Frazer, quoted in Valley Forge by H. E. Wildes 1938, pg. 189, 90.
4. Fitz. XI 108, Washington to brigade commanders Mar. 19.
5. J. F. Reed ms. coll., General Orders, March 19, also Fitz. XI 107.
6. Fitz. XI 114, Washington to Lacey Mar. 20.
7. J. F. Reed ms. coll., Broadside.
8. Drinker Journal 84.
9. Roberts would be caught and hanged by the Americans the following summer.
10. Drinker Journal 93-4.
11. Fitz. XI 223-4, Washington to Wharton Apr. 6.
12. Journals of Congress X 238.
13. Baurmeister Letters (May 10) 57.
14. Pa. Mag. XXXIV 70-1, Letters of Robert Proud.
15. Duncan 234, Dr. Tilton's report.
16. Ibid.
17. Steuben Regulations.
18. J. F. Reed ms. coll., General Orders, March 24, also Fitz. XI 141.

19. Fitz. XI 138, Washington to H. Laurens Mar. 24.
20. Marshall Diary 173.
21. Fitz. XI 145, Washington to Heath Mar. 25.
22. J. F. Reed ms. coll., General Orders, March 27, also Fitz. XI 161.
23. Ibid.
24. HSP ms. coll., Wayne Papers IV 115, Wayne to Wharton Mar. 27.
25. Ibid. IV 116, Wharton to Wayne Apr. 2.
26. Fitz. XI 157, Washington to Armstrong Mar. 27.
27. J. F. Reed ms. coll., Minutes of courts-martial by Lacey's Militia "near Doylestown," April 7-12, original MS. in author's collection.
28. Fitz. XI 158-9, Washington to Armstrong Mar. 27.
29. Middleton 469, Rev. James Morris of Conn.
30. Papers of Cong. Mar. 3.
31. Baurmeister Letters (Mar. 24) 50.
32. Fitz. XI 173, Washington to W. Howe Mar. 29.
33. W. P., W. Howe to Washington, (fragment); Pa. Packet Mar. 27.
34. W. P., Am. Pris. Exch. Commrs. Apr. 4.
35. Fitz. XI 213-4, Washington to W. Howe Apr. 4.
36. Penn. Packet, March 28.
37. Fitz. XI 278, Washington to Patrick Henry Apr. 19.
38. HSP ms. coll., Wayne Papers IV 118, Wayne to Bayard Mar. 28.
39. Ibid. V 19, Bayard to Wayne Apr. 23.
40. HSP ms. coll., Potts Papers IV 38, Cutting to Dr. Jonathan Potts Apr. 16.
41. J. F. Reed ms. coll., Shippen to Potts, May 7.
42. HSP ms. coll., Potts Papers IV 57, Blaine to Potts May 2.
43. Middleton 476, Craik to Potts.
44. J. F. Reed ms. coll., General Orders, April 3, also Fitz. XI 201-2.
45. Ibid. April 2, also Fitz. XI 199-200.
46. Fitz. XI 214, Washington to W. Howe Apr. 4.
47. Boudinot Journal 78.

CHAPTER X

1. Fitz. XI 236-40 passim, Washington to H. Laurens Apr. 10.
2. Fitz. XI 276, Ibid. Apr. 18.
3. Baurmeister Letters (May 10) 58.
4. Ibid. (Apr. 18) 54.
5. J. F. Reed ms. coll., Johnstone to R. Morris Feb. 5.
6. Ewing Journal 34.
7. Fitz. XI 267-8, Washington to Wharton Apr. 17.
8. This so-called "Spy Map" is in the Clinton Papers, Clements Lib. Apparently the map was turned over to Clinton by Howe at the former's assumption of command in Philadelphia. A note on the verso of the map attributes it to Parker.
9. Laurens 159, J. Laurens to H. Laurens Apr. 18.
10. Fitz. XI 275-6, Washington to H. Laurens Apr. 18.
11. Fitz. XI 287-90 passim, Washington to Congressman John Bannister Apr. 21.
12. Journals of Congress X 381.
13. HSD ms. coll., Duponceau Diary.
14. Fitz. XI 285, Washington to Congressman John Bannister of Va.
15. Ibid. 290.
16. J. F. Reed ms. coll., General Orders, April 12, also Fitz. XI 252.
17. Fitz. XI 324, Washington to Smallwood Apr. 30.
18. V. F. ms. coll., Col. Alex. Scammell to his brother, original MS. missing from files; pub. in Washington Memorial Chapel (Valley Forge) Chronicle VII 216 (1915).

CHAPTER XI

1. Montrésor Journal 488.
2. Ibid.
3. Montgomery Co. Sketches II 84 (1900), Lacey to Armstrong May 7.
4. Fitz. XI 345, Washington to Lacey May 3.
5. Tammany was a long-deceased friendly Delaware Indian chief who was humorously canonized by the Revolutionary soldiers as the patron saint of America. In 1805 the name Tammany Hall was first employed to designate the Democratic Party organization in New York.
6. Ewing Journal 44.
7. Graydon Memoirs 313-4.

8. Ewing Journal 44.
9. Fitz. XI 332, Washington to H. Laurens May 1.
10. S. C. Hist. Mag. VIII 124, Lafayette to H. Laurens.
11. Journals of Congress XI 457, 458, 468.
12. Fitz. XI 354, General Orders, May 5.
13. Penn. Packet, May 10.
14. Fitz. XI 355, General Orders, May 5.
15. Penn. Packet, May 10.
16. McMichael Diary, Pa. Mag. XVI 159.
17. Penn. Packet, May 10.
18. Ibid.
19. Fitz. XI 356, General Orders, May 6.
20. Fitz. XI 453, Washington to R. Morris May 25.

CHAPTER XII

1. Fitz. XI 351, Washington to Greene, May 5.
2. Ibid.
3. Birch-Henkels Sale 683 (1892) 93, S. Ward to Mrs. Ward, May 5.
4. Fitz. XI 378-9, Washington to Gov. Livingston, May 12.
5. Now the Meadowbrook Golf Clubhouse at Phoenixville, Pa.
6. Fitz. XI 363-6 passim., Washington at council of war, May 8.
7. W. P., Council of War Decision May 9. (See also Fitz. XI 366 note.)
8. HSP ms. coll., Potts Papers IV 63, Dr. James Craik to Dr. Jonathan Potts, May 15.
9. Middleton 482, Dr. James Craik to Dr. Jonathan Potts, May 10.
10. Neisser Diary 436.
11. HSP ms. coll., Wallace Papers I 58, William Bradford, Jr. to his sister Rachael, May 14.
12. Fitz. XI 361, General Orders, 7 May.
13. Records of the War Department, National Archives. When the three packages of printed Oaths sent to camp by Congress were exhausted, oaths were issued in manuscript.
14. Clinton Papars, "Mr. Lee's Plan," printed in The Treason of Major General Charles Lee, G. H. Moore, 1860.
15. Boudinot Journal 79, Montrésor Journal 484.
16. Ibid. 80.
17. Fitz. XI 410, Washington to Lafayette, May 17.
18. Drinker Journal 102.
19. W. P., Moylan to Washington.
20. J. F. Reed ms. coll., Lafayette to Théveneau de Francy, May 14.
21. HSP ms. coll., Wallace Papers I 58, William Bradford, Jr. to his sister Rachel, May 14.
22. Fitz. XI 387, General Orders, May 14.
23. Gentleman's Mag. Aug. 1778, André to a friend in England, May 23.
24. Baurmeister Journal 65.
25. Drinker Journal 103.
26. An "old major of artillery" who witnessed the event. Quoted in The Life and Career of Major John André, Winthrop Sargent 1861, p. 181.

CHAPTER XIII

1. Fitz. XI 418-20, Washington to Lafayette.
2. Fitz. XI 420 note, Laurens to Moylan, May 19.
3. Pontgibaud 53-4.
4. Some authorities state that Clinton had assumed command, but Howe states on page 49 of his Narrative that he did not turn over command until May 24. (The Narrative of Lieut. Gen. Sir William Howe . . . London 1780.)
5. Pontgibaud 53, 54.
6. Martin Journal 121.
7. Drinker Journal 104.
8. Martin Journal 122.
9. Pontgibaud 55.

CHAPTER XIV

1. Gentleman's Mag. Aug. 1778, André to a friend in England, May 23.
2. Ibid.

3. Montrésor Journal 493.
4. Sang XV (not in Fitz.), Washington to H. Lee, May 25.
5. Laurens 175-6, J. Laurens to H. Laurens, May 27.
6. Montrésor Journal 494.
7. Fitz. XI 486, General Orders, May 29.
8. Fitz. XI 487, Ibid. May 30.
9. Fitz. XI 489-90, Washington to C. Lee, May 30.
10. Fitz. XI 496, Washington to H. Clinton, May 31.
11. Fitz. XII 4-7, General Orders, June 1.
12. Fitz. XII 9, Washington to H. Laurens, June 9.
13. J. F. Reed ms. coll., Lt. James Bradford to Capt. Thomas Wooster, June 7.
14. Ibid.
15. Ibid.
16. Montrésor Journal 496.
17. Baurmeister Journal (June 15) 66.
18. Fitz. XII 18, Washington to H. Laurens, June 4.
19. Clinton Papers, Peace Commissioners to Germain, June 15.

CHAPTER XV

1. Carlisle diary-letter April 24-June 17, quoted in The American Revolution by Sir George Trevelyan NY 1909 Part IV 362, first printed 1899.
2. J. F. Reed ms. coll., Eden to unnamed correspondent in England, June 18.
3. Fitz. XII 29, Washington to Gen. Philemon Dickinson, June 7.
4. Fitz. XII 39, Washington to H. Clinton, June 9.
5. Reed, Jos. 8-13 passim. Johnstone to Reed April 11.
6. Ibid. 13-16 passim. Reed to Johnstone June 14.
7. Reed, Jos. 46, Mrs. Elizabeth Ferguson's letter "To the Public."
8. Laurens 184, J. Laurens to H. Laurens, June 11.
9. Fitz. XII 46 note, H. Laurens to Washington, June 14.
10. Rivington Papers 5-6, Laurens to Peace Commission, June 17.

CHAPTER XVI

1. J. F. Reed ms. coll., Lt. James Bradford to Capt. Thomas Wooster, June 7.
2. Fitz. XII 30-4, Ordered by Congress May 27, pub. in General Orders, June 7.
3. Fitz. XII 35-6, Washington to Greene, June 8.
4. Wild Journal 108.
5. Martin Journal 122.
6. Laurens 182, J. Laurens to H. Laurens, June 9.
7. Ibid. 191-2, June 16.
8. Lafayette Memoirs I 175, Lafayette to his wife.
9. Fitz. XII 64, Washington to H. Laurens, June 15.
10. Fitz. XII 75-8 passim., Washington at council of war, June 17.
11. J. F. Reed ms. coll., Samuel Massey Journal.
12. Josiah Bartlett letter, July 13, 1778, quoted in The American Revolution by Sir George Trevelyan New York 1909 Part IV 352 note, first printed 1889.
13. Fitz. XII 80, Washington to H. Laurens, June 18.
14. The divisions were brigaded as follows:

Lee's: Poor's, Varnum's and Huntington's Brigades (see General Orders, June 18, Fitz. XII 91.)

Wayne's: 1st and 2nd Pennsylvania and "late Conway's" Brigades (see Washington to Waync, June 18, Fitz. XII 86.)

Lafayette's: Woodford's, Scott's and North Carolina (recently McIntosh's) Brigades (see General Orders, June 18, Fitz. XII 90.)

DeKalb's: Glover's, Paterson's and Learned's Brigades (see ibid.)

Stirling's: Weedon's Muhlenberg's, 1st Maryland (Smallwood's) and 2nd Maryland Brigades (see ibid.)

Artillery: Knox.

15. The army crossed the Delaware at the following places: Lee's, Lafayette's and Stirling's Divisions at Coryell's Ferry (now New Hope, Pa.); Wayne's Division, which had been scheduled to be commanded by Mifflin, at Sherrard's Ferry; DeKalb's Division at Easton. See Order of March, June 17, Washington Papers, National Archives, pub. in Fitz. XII 74.